TIME TO TEACH
TIME TO LEARN

TIME TO TEACH

TIME TO LEARN

Changing the Pace of School

Chip Wood

Northeast Foundation for Children, Inc.
85 Avenue A, Suite 204, PO Box 718
Turners Falls, MA 01376-0718
www.responsiveclassroom.org
800-360-6332

Library of Congress Cataloging-in-Publication Data

Wood, Chip
    Time to teach, time to learn : changing the pace of school / by Chip Wood
      p. cm.
    Includes bibliographical references (p.) and index.
    1. Teachers—Time management. 2. Students—Time management.
    I. Title.
LB2838.8.W66 1999
371.102—dc21   99-22171
                                             CIP

ISBN 1-892989-01-8 (pbk.)

Editing by Allen Woods
Cover and interior design by Woodward Design
Photographs by Peter Wrenn, Cherry Wyman, William Elwell, Sarah Holbrook
Cover photo: David Muir/Masterfile
Printed in the United States of America
08 07 06 05 04   10 9 8 7 6 5 4 3

To the schoolchildren of the twenty-first century
Especially Isaiah Robert Heaton

The children know us
before we know
the children know us
preoccupied, as we are,
with knowing what the children need—
knee-deep in knowledge,
afraid of what we think
they do not know;
unsure of what we do.

Contents

Preface

TIME TO TEACH, TIME TO LEARN is about improving education by refocusing time on relationships—relationships among teachers and parents and students and great ideas. In these pages I draw attention to the absolutely inappropriate pace of teaching and learning which daily decreases the quality of education and the very quality of life for millions of children and adults who "spend" years of their lives in the place we call school. Although this book does not contain all the answers concerning the enormous time pressures we are facing, it does offer many practical suggestions that will change the use of time at the school and classroom level. I wrote this book because I believe time can be our friend, rather than our nemesis.

However, as long as we see time in school as currency, our friend is likely to stay hidden. We will continue to "spend" it (wisely, of course), "save" it, "account" for it, be "economical" with it, and deal in intellectual "capital." As you read, you will note that I have mostly chosen to avoid these money words. I believe that this is more than an issue of semantics. The pace of school is constructed on an industrial model of speed and efficiency, and our language both reflects and reinforces this model. Test results measure production and comparative scores carry as much weight and anxiety as the Dow Jones Average. Such an industrial model of school will not work in the information age; instead, better communication skills and meaningful relationships hold the key to academic and civil excellence.

There are three sections in this book: Foundations, Observations, and Transformations. They respectively mark the importance of theory and research, direct experience, and practical application. In the

Observation chapters, I have documented how students and teachers experience the time of a single school day. The actual teachers, students and schools depicted are a composite of countless observations in numerous settings, but they are not imaginary. Names used in these chapters are fictional.

I hope that you will not just read this book, but that it will draw you into conversation and dialogue and deeper relationships with others who care as much as you do about children, teaching, and learning.

Robert (Chip) Wood
Greenfield, Massachusetts
July 1999

Introduction

We need to stop hurrying children. Our school days require time. Time to wonder, time to pause, time to look closely, time to share, time to pay attention to what is most important. In school we must give children the time they need to learn. To hurry through the day, to hurry through classes, grades and a timetable of achievements, is contrary to the nature of children and will do irreparable damage to their minds and souls.[1]

IN 1985, WHEN I WROTE THESE WORDS, I was just beginning to fully understand school. I had already decided to devote myself to education for life and had fifteen years experience. But school was still full of mystery.

I understood children well. I had been working with children since high school, first as a Sunday school teacher, camp counselor, and babysitter. During college, my wife and I lived and worked as house-parents in a home for dependent children. Our family began with twelve rambunctious teenage boys. Summers we directed camp beside a meandering Midwestern prairie stream. Those who have held such jobs know they demand attention and commitment twenty-four hours a day. Like teaching.

My first job out of college was as a combination first-second grade teacher. I adored everything about working with the children: teaching reading, math, and spelling; playing on the playground; sharing silly songs and Pooh poetry. But school confused me. The institution kept getting in the way of my work with the children.

I went to graduate school in social work and became a community organizer, working in the field of civil rights before being drawn back to education through the inspiration of a friend.

Jon Ball had a vision that schools could be different. He introduced me to Dewey and to daring. He saw school as a community first, an institution second. He taught me, by his example, to hang on to playfulness when considering how to change school, and to draw adults into mental play the same way you would children into a game of tag. When I chose to postpone doctoral work, he encouraged me to apply for a job as a teaching principal of a small, rural, public elementary school and he coached me through those early years. He also taught me the power of skillful listening. There really is nothing in life quite like a great teacher.

I took that teaching principal's job and dropped summer camp into the middle of a public school. We had school sings and school contests. We ate family style in the cafeteria and everybody had jobs. We sang for people's birthdays at lunch and gathered every morning in a circle of teachers and staff five minutes before the buses arrived to check in, see how we were doing, and look to the day ahead. I made lots of mistakes, but I knew we were on the right track.

I tested my superintendent's patience, questioning everything from inventory to attendance forms, challenging curriculum and testing requirements. To his credit, he gave me some rope but also kept me from hanging myself, though I came close on several occasions. I learned a deep respect for the veteran teachers on staff who knew how to elicit academic skills and the critical personal skill of persistence from their students.

I learned from Betty Mayberry, for example, how to use the seemingly dry and difficult skill of dictation to light a fire under both the reluctant and the inspired student. I used that same technique every year thereafter in my classrooms, whether I was teaching first grade or eighth. For nearly a decade I shared the gathering of such vibrant and useful teaching methods with a dedicated group of teachers.

Gradually, the institution called school began to be different for me, my colleagues, the children, and parents. It took some getting used to, this idea of school as community, but it grew on you. It was infectious and fun and the test scores didn't suffer. I began to wonder out loud with colleagues in other schools and teacher education programs if what we were engaged in could have broader application.

In 1981, some of us joined together to found Northeast Foundation for Children and Greenfield Center School in Greenfield, Massachusetts where I have been ever since. For our first five years I taught full-time and helped administer our new community/institution. Each year I worked a little more with teachers in other schools, something I now do full time.

As we collected more and more ideas about teaching and learning through our own laboratory school as well as through our work in the field, a more elaborate structure of school as a learning community emerged. These ideas were first introduced to the teaching public in 1985 in our co-authored book, *A Notebook for Teachers: Making Changes in the Elementary Curriculum*[2], and later and more widely through Ruth Charney's book, *Teaching Children to Care: Management in The Responsive Classroom.*[3]

Our work is, in fact, now known as *The Responsive Classroom®,* an approach to professional development in education utilized by thousands of teachers and hundreds of schools nationwide. Its central idea is the need for balanced integration of social and academic learning throughout the school day and throughout the school curriculum. *The Responsive Classroom* has now become a respected contributor to the national debate on education reform.

Yet, despite our voice and that of many other national reform organizations, the bulk of educational policy continues to move toward a more stringent, mechanical, narrow, and punitive approach to schooling. Today it is called the standards movement. In its name, schools now cram more into every minute of every school hour of every school day, believing that less time to wonder and more "time on task" will make for better students. What this indicates, however, is that policy makers mistake better test scores—better student *performance*—for better students. These are two different things.

If the focus were really on better students, children would have time in school to consider and reflect on what they were learning and time to care about and contribute to each other and their school. They would have time to ponder where their lives were headed. School would be a learning community, not a fact factory with only enough time to worry about the next test or homework assignment.

In all these years, we have not stopped hurrying children. We have not given them adequate time or space or opportunities for learning. Again and again, we have returned to the assembly-line model of production and alienation, even though extensive research has shown that different models of learning communities are more productive and effective.

If we are to stop hurrying children we must pay attention to what's been proven, and to what's most important—the children themselves, their hopes and dreams, and everyday difficulties. If we are to stop hurrying children, we must stop "busying" teachers. Today, teachers are clearly even more preoccupied than their students. Every new content curriculum a teacher is required to implement these days comes with specific daily time requirements. By simply adding up all the time requirements from the various content areas, it's clear that you would need to stretch the day into the early evening! "Being stretched" does not begin to describe how teachers feel today. Teachers are under extraordinary pressure from principals who, in turn, are hurried by superintendents who are pushed by school boards. It is a vicious and self-perpetuating cycle. All of us are pressured by standards we hurried into because we rushed the children so much they failed to meet our expectations as measured by tests for which we failed to adequately prepare them.

I know it is possible to stop this cycle if, together, our voices grow clearer and more insistent on behalf of the true needs of children in school. In this book, I advocate changing how we structure and use time in school to improve the quality of education. Time, of course, is the major resource at our disposal, and the most significant variable in any reform initiative. But "time on task" is not the answer. Instead, we need to explore both the quantity and quality of educational time, both the way we structure and schedule time and how we use that time. We can teach most effectively and give all students the kind of time it takes to learn and achieve to the best of their abilities if we slow down and listen more.

Thomas Merton, the great spiritual teacher, wrote:

> The rush and pressure of modern life are a form, perhaps the most common form, of innate violence. To allow oneself to be carried away by a multitude of conflicting concerns, to surrender to too many demands, to commit oneself to too many projects, to want to help everyone in everything is to succumb to violence. More than that, it is cooperation with violence. The frenzy of the activist neutralizes his work for peace. It destroys his inner capacity for peace. It destroys the fruitfulness of his own work because it kills the root of inner wisdom which makes work fruitful.[4]

Merton was not talking about teachers or children, but I am.

Section One

F O U N D A T I O N S

NEWSPAPERS, MAGAZINES, AND TELEVISION are always filled with stories about American education: how it is failing our children, our society, and the business world which can't find enough capable workers; and about how tougher standards and more testing are needed to hold students and teachers "accountable."

At the same time, teachers' rooms are filled with talk about how politicians, school boards, and policy makers are failing to support education with money, reasonable policies, and long-range planning.

I believe that changing how we structure and use time in our schools and individual classrooms holds the key to positively changing the lives of students and teachers and, ultimately, to preserving our democracy.

This section looks at some current issues in the educational debate as well as the extensive research and knowledge we have about how children learn and grow. Chapter 1 looks at current issues and directions in education and how they affect our children and teachers. Chapter 2 begins to review the extensive body of research and knowledge which should be used as a foundation for educational reform. It looks at principles important in structuring time in schools. Chapter 3 continues this review by focusing on principles important in how we use time in schools and classrooms.

A mentor of mine, Jackie Haines, tells the story of the kindergarten teacher who was always after her children to hurry up. "Hurry up, it's time for art." "Hurry up, it's time for reading." But she realized something was wrong when she heard herself say, "Hurry up, it's time to rest."

Chapter One

Time to Learn

As a teacher and observer, I have heard the voices of children who are begging for more time to learn, explore, and grow.

"We don't have time to finish anything. The teacher always says we'll finish it later, but we hardly ever do."

"If math was longer, I might get it better."

"I wish we had time for our teacher to read to us every day."

"When do we just get to be with you, Mrs. Chambers?"

As a teacher of teachers, I have heard the frustrated voices of dedicated teachers as they grow more and more concerned.

"There just isn't enough time."

"The day is so rushed, we're always going somewhere."

"The kids beg me to keep going. They beg to finish stuff. I feel like such a time tyrant, but we have to cover so much curriculum."

"I have my class maybe an hour of the day when everybody's here at once. Somebody's always going out for something."

This book is about giving these students time to learn and their teachers time to teach.

SLOW

SCHOOL ZONE

15 MPH

WHEN FLASHING

I passed by the sign thousands of times on my drives to school without noticing the irony that today sends chills up and down my spine.

It seems so obvious. The flashing caution lights warn us as children arrive and leave. This morning, as I slow to 15 mph, I imagine the sign speaking to me as the winter sun glances off the windshield:

> Good morning, there! Glad to have your attention. I work hard at sending my message, so it's nice when someone listens.
>
> Yes, you are entering the SCHOOL ZONE. This is an area where children are in danger because they have not learned all the necessary rules and behaviors to keep themselves safe. They don't always use caution, attention, and self-control as they leave and enter buses, cross the street, walk on the sidewalk, skip, laugh, run, and do all the things children do. In this 'zone,' adults must be responsible for the children. They must go SLOW and keep their attention focused so that any child who forgets and darts out in front of their vehicle is still safe. *Children may move quickly but they don't always think carefully. So the adults have to think quickly and carefully and drive slowly.*

After I park my car and make my way to my office, the analogy becomes clearer. It makes so much sense to go slow in the school zone. It is so obvious when it comes to physical safety, but not when it comes to mental, emotional, and spiritual safety. Why?

After the buses have left and the yellow caution light goes out on the sign on the street, the caution light is turned off inside the school as well. The day begins in a rush and continues from there. We mark children tardy. Children are hurried to and fro. Even in the youngest classes, children in most schools will see several teachers each day and special events are crammed into the schedule, often at a moment's notice. The day is chopped up into small pieces of time with little connection or continuity. There always seems to be more curriculum to cover, more tests to take, but never any time added to the day. Children and teachers are left gasping for air.

The Greek root for the word "school" is *scoleri,* which is literally translated as "leisure!" Consider how far we've moved from our educational roots. Teachers who know they should "Go Slow," who want to dedicate themselves and their classrooms to a pace which encourages investigation, contemplation, completion, and community, must struggle with social and educational influences which force them in the opposite direction.

Threats to Quality Education

The headlines below—adapted from actual news stories—are, for me, the real headlines in the current struggle for the heart, soul, and mind of education in our country.

Standards and Testing

> **Mass. 4th-graders take new standardized tests for 15 hrs.**

In the spring, and again in the fall of 1998, Massachusetts fourth-graders spent an average of fifteen hours over the course of two weeks taking new standardized assessments to measure their proficiencies against new state curriculum standards. It is a scene repeated across the nation, as the "accountability approach" continues to grow stronger in the powerful educational establishment which consists of local and state school boards, national policy groups, politicians, and the "trade" media of education. It is a sad fact that teachers, who often have the clearest insights about children and the most direct contact with them, are seldom included in this powerful group. Teachers often spend their professional lives in one or two school systems, following a child's growth for years, while principals, superintendents, politicians, and board members blithely come and go.

One of the clear choices policy makers are making about time in school is to use increasing amounts of it to test what children are learning. The theory is that the tests will show us what children do not know and we can address these areas more efficiently and effectively by, essentially, teaching to the test. However, the more time we spend testing and preparing to test, the less time we have for real teaching.

Considerable time is being used to prep even the youngest of schoolchildren for the kinds of questions and content likely to be on the latest set of assessments. The children may end up actually doing better on the tests and still know less. The tragedy will be that we won't even realize it. Everyone will end up above average and the emperor will have no clothes.

A good example of pressure to teach to the test appeared recently in our local paper. Reporters highlighted the poor performance of high-schoolers on new state exams based on new standards. In another article on the very same day, teachers and administrators at the local high school indicated they were proposing dropping "block scheduling" (longer class periods that allow the exploration of curriculum content in more depth) because they would not be able to adequately cover the breadth of the material that would be on the test. It is a change driven by the need to perform well on the test, taken at the expense of in-depth learning.

Although the hours of testing and preparation are hours stolen from other types of learning, the attraction to testing and accountability is understandable. The state seeks to protect the rights of their citizens to an adequate public education, creates the standards and benchmarks of that education, and then tests children on those standards. In the simplest view, the consequences are clear. Pass the tests and move on with your life. Fail and use more of your lifetime repeating what you have already failed.

Lost in this accountability approach is any sense of balance about the value of what we are testing. Elliott Eisner once remarked that "We measure what we most value."[1] By emphasizing accountability, the highest value is placed on what an individual child can "bubble in" on a test form. What matters most is your individual achievement and rank among your peers, not who you are. Helping a friend learn the answer to a question, teaching someone else how to solve an equation, learning by watching someone else paint a picture—these abilities carry no market value. They are referred to as "fluff" in the educational jargon; they are nice if we have time for them, but clearly not essential.

The tests do measure individual academic progress, but they are purely objective tests; they provide no measure and indicate no value for social or ethical knowledge. We choose not to measure social growth. There is no test for kindness, no assessment for the development of a sense of right and wrong. We are filling our jails with the people who grew up taking the wrong tests.

We often talk about "the best and the brightest." But the brightest, those who excel on standardized tests of academics, are not always the best if viewed from an ethical perspective. High achievers ran the savings and loan industry into their own pockets, poured PCB's into rivers until they became sewers of death, passed weapons technology around the globe in their own self-interest, and destroyed the rain forest.

Barbara Rogoff, who has devoted a lifetime to observing and writing about the social context of learning, maintains that the purpose of learning "is to act effectively."[2] We learn for social reasons, be they moral or immoral, just or corrupt. We learn so we can live the life we believe we were meant to live. If the purpose of learning, instead, becomes primarily passing standardized tests, all our time will be used up in the pursuit of only measurable objectives. Solving a playground dispute, teaching someone how to think through a word problem, debating the meaning of a poem—these abilities cannot be measured, yet we know that we value these skills deeply, that they are intrinsic to growth as human beings.

What will be the outcome if we continue with so much emphasis on standardized tests? Karl Hertz, president of the American Association of School Administrators, wonders:

What if we found that the great measure of American worth, namely our sense of goodness, was lost in the regimen that was demanded to achieve the easily measurable success of an efficiently scored test? Wouldn't it be strange if we got the highest test scores and then found that our employers were less pleased with their employees than they were in 1998? What if they were then saying that the people in their businesses were quite literate, but unimaginative, poor at innovating and unlikely to solve problems?[3]

When standardized tests become an end unto themselves, the value of investigation, creativity, and positive social interaction is diminished, and ultimately will be lost.

No Time to Play

No playgrounds at Atlanta's new elementary schools

The city of Atlanta is constructing new elementary schools without playgrounds—on purpose.[4]

"Many parents still don't get it," said Atlanta Superintendent of Schools, Benjamin O. Canada, in a *New York Times* interview: "They'll ask, 'So when are we getting a new playground?' And I'll say, "There isn't going to be a new playground."

"What's recess?" asked five-year-old Toya Gray, interviewed for the same article.

The city of Atlanta, according to the *Times,* has "eliminated recess in the elementary schools as a waste of time that would be better spent on academics." The policymakers in Atlanta have moved forward with their plan, even though some parents and educators are duly concerned. Olga Jarrett, professor of child development at Georgia State University, asks: "When do kids learn to interact with kids? We have so many latchkey kids who go home and lock the door until their parents get home. Now if they can't mingle with other kids at school or at home, how are they going to resolve conflict with their peers?"[5]

Learning social skills has often been viewed as something separate from learning pure academic content. Children need to be focused on academics. This means they need to be reading a book, solving a math problem, writing an essay, checking an experiment, taking a test. If they do this by themselves, some educators believe it enhances concentration and "time on task." With technology's help, children in the future might not even need to come to school to fulfill their academic requirements. Instruction could be provided on-line, tests completed, retrieved, graded, and returned without human interaction.

The reason to bring children together in one place—a place called school—would lose its relevance. In this extreme view of the future, children would be on their own, plugged in and taking care of themselves.

But parents and teachers know that children don't automatically know how to take care of themselves, let alone each other. In a computerized future, how will they learn self-control, the ability to make informed choices, the proper degree of assertion in public discourse or on the freeway, if a caring community of adults and peers don't teach them? How will they learn cooperation, empathy, responsibility, and any number of other critical social skills that are as essential to their very survival as reading, writing, and computing?

In our professional development work with teachers known as *The Responsive Classroom* we teach that it is only through practice that such skills can be learned. Just as we expect the budding pianist to practice daily, just as we sit our children down to practice the spelling list for the week on Thursday night before the Friday test, we must give children many regular opportunities to practice their social skills before they have to use them in life-and-death situations. School is the one place in contemporary American society where these skills can be practiced on a daily basis. Without significant practice, children can no more learn social skills or develop ethical character than they can learn to spell or learn how to play the piano.

Instant Information

Computer use tied to higher standard-ized test scores, reduced social skills

In promoting increased computer usage in public schools in an article in *Time* magazine in 1998, Vice President Al Gore cited a U.S. Education Department report which stated that students in classes that use computers outperform their peers on standardized tests of basic skills by an average of 30 percent.[6] It's clear that if we repeatedly put children on the machines with programs that ask the questions similar to those on the test, we can raise the test scores.

The Vice President also noted that kids on the Internet are reported to be more creative in their project work and show a greater capacity to communicate effectively about "complex problems." This study and the Vice President's support emphasized increased computer usage to enhance learning and raise test scores.

But David Gelerbter, professor of computer science at Yale, suggested in the same article that children are already exposed to too much information too rapidly and that their attention span is decreasing as a result. Mary Pipher makes a similar point in her 1996 book, *The Shelter of Each Other,* when she says, "There's too much information and not enough meaning, too much happening and not enough time to process it."[7]

A $1.5 million, two-year, first-of-its-kind study of Internet use conducted by researchers at Carnegie Mellon University found cyberspace not all it is dreamed to be—a place for increased social interaction, communication, and connections. "We were surprised to find that what is a social technology has such anti-social consequences," says Robert Kraut, a professor of social psychology and human computer interaction at Carnegie Mellon in a press release. "Even though people in the study heavily used electronic mail and other communication services on the Internet, the research found that spending time on the Internet was associated with later declines in talking among family members, reductions in the number of friends and acquaintances they kept up with, and increases in depression and loneliness." The research clearly surprised the project sponsors and funders—Apple Computer, Hewlett Packard, Intel, Panasonic, AT&T, and other communication firms.[8]

If we connect this study to the research on reading which shows that more time spent in family conversation enhances interest and performance in reading among school-age children, we can predict a dangerous trend.[9] As more children spend more time on the Internet in school, they will almost certainly spend more time on the Internet at home. They will tend to become more disconnected from family conversation and the time spent in social interaction at home and in school will continue to decrease. Both academic and social skills will suffer as a result.

There is an important place for new technology in education, but it cannot replace the social process of teaching and learning. Receiving more information more quickly does not guarantee an increase in knowledge or the application of that knowledge in positive social or academic contexts.

Attentional Disorders and "Temporal Trauma"

Huge increase in students classified with attentional disorders

In 1995 there were two million children estimated to show behavioral symptoms labeled ADD or ADHD.[10] This represented about five percent of the school-age population, according to Russell A. Barkley in his ground-breaking book *Taking Charge of ADHD.*[11] Most of these children were boys and most children who were formally diagnosed were being treated with a stimulant drug, Ritalin. Recent figures show that 80 to 90 percent of Ritalin produced is used in the United States, and that the number of children diagnosed with ADD who are being treated with Ritalin rose fivefold between 1989 and 1998. If the numbers continue to increase at the same rate, 15 percent (eight million) of all children in our country will be on Ritalin by early in the next decade! [12]

There have always been children whose attention spans and activity levels don't fit traditional classrooms. When I started teaching thirty years ago these children were termed "hyperactive," and over the years behavioral modification programs were developed to address their needs for more immediate responses and their trouble in delaying or controlling impulsive behavior. Although these programs took significant energy and time to implement, they allowed many children to function more productively in school and at home.

When treatment with Ritalin was first initiated, it was used in conjunction with behavioral programs. Today, in our fast-paced, quick-fix culture, many children whose behavior indicates some trouble with attention and impulse-control are simply prescribed Ritalin without any thought of changing the expectations or schedules of their environment. We wish, hope, and expect a drug to fix what's wrong without looking at other factors which affect the problem.

In *Ritalin Nation: Rapid-Fire Culture and the Transformation of Human Consciousness,* psychologist Richard DeGrandpre argues that ADHD has more to do with changes in time expectations in our society than better diagnosis of a physiological problem. He and Dr. Barkley strongly support changes in time expectations for these children. Based on the work of Dr. Jacob Bronowski, Barkley states that children with ADHD "show a more limited sense of the past and, as a result, a more limited sense of the future."[13]

I see children who exhibit ADHD behaviors as suffering from temporal trauma. Sadly, they are serving as "canaries" in the cage of time, especially in our schools, where their failure to thrive should tell us something about their environment.

School schedules speed up year after year, putting more and more pressure on children to manage a world filled with more transitions, extended curricula, less predictability, and less time to accomplish more. It's tough on all children, but for these "canaries" who have a heightened sensitivity to time pressures, it's impossible. Our society and schools are faced with two possibilities. One is medicating more and more children in an effort to decrease their sensitivity to our ever-faster, less-regulated pace of life and education. Another is making changes in the structure and pace of school life to reduce temporal trauma for all of our children.

Less Time with Parents

Parents spending less time interacting with children

Not since the Great Depression have parents been so absent from children's lives. Fear for children's safety and the inability to be with children before and after school has compelled parents to find surrogate caretakers or care programs. Children come to school for breakfast and go home as late as six P.M. following after-school programs. They average 90 minutes more a week at school than they did in 1981 according to a University of Michigan report.[14]

Their free time *after* going to school has diminished as well, from 40 percent in 1981 to 25 percent today, according to the researchers. Children's time is programmed in formal activities supervised by coaches and instructors. Gone is the spontaneous neighborhood association, free play, and fantasy play in sandlots or open fields. In structured programs, all the rules are predetermined. Much of children's fantasy world is presented to them in video games, computer simulations and cartoons. Children end up in one-way conversations with video screens, the screens doing the talking.

We know that whatever time parents do have with their children is precious and essential to their development and learning. Several studies of reading achievement have documented the importance of parents' reading to children at home. Recent studies are also noting that parents' conversation with children contributes to the development of reading skills.[15]

Sunday school, youth programs, and religious instruction at churches and synagogues have always provided a time for children to interact with adults, strengthen their speaking and listening and reading abilities, learn ethical and moral views, and practice important social skills.

It's clear that these interactions between children and parents and other caring adults need to happen for children to develop conscience and right behavior. For Marianne Jennings, professor of legal and ethical studies in the College of Business at Arizona State University, the kitchen table was the center of home life, where adults and children came together every night:

> I cut out my wedding dress at the same place where I memorized my spelling words. It was in the same place that I ate Archway cookies each day after school, and it was there that I prepared for my SAT.
>
> My husband-to-be was grilled mercilessly in the same spot. Much of what I have learned and hold dear is inextricably intertwined with the kitchen table.
>
> This four feet by six feet scratched and worn piece of furniture was a small physical part of my home. Yet as I look back on what we did there, I realize that it was the key to the life I now have.
>
> Each night during my youth, it was the kitchen table where I was held accountable for the day's events—'When is the next report card? Did you clean up the mess in the

basement? Did you practice your piano today?'

If you wanted dinner, you had to accept the accompanying interrogation, which would have violated my Miranda rights if I had done something more than attempt to bathe the neighbor's parakeet. There was no escaping the nightly confrontation with accountability.

But that kitchen table was not just a source of fear. It was my security blanket. No matter how rough the day's tauntings had been, and no matter how discouraged I was over long division, the kitchen table and its adult caretakers were there every night for comfort and support....

As I struggle each night to get dinner on my kitchen table and round up my children from the four corners of our neighborhood, I wonder why I don't just send them to their rooms with a chicken pot pie and Wheel of Fortune.

I don't because I am giving them the gift of the kitchen table. In all of the treatises on parenting, in all of the psychological studies on child development, and in all of the data on self-esteem, this humble key to raising children is overlooked.

Last year, my daughter said she could find only one other student in her homeroom who had dinner each night at the kitchen table with her family. They're both honor students. The other kids, my daughter explained, make something in the microwave and head to their rooms to watch TV.

They have no company, no questions, Wheel of Fortune, and the grades to show for it. How sad that not all children's lives are touched by the miracle of childhood. There's something about a kitchen table.[16]

Now, not everyone remembers his or her kitchen table so fondly. Some tables were full of argument or silence, some frequently missing a dad or mom, but many teachers and parents are as touched by this commentary as I am. The importance of parental guidance and friendly communication strikes a resonant chord. At the supper table in my house growing up, we played a spelling game my father called "ghost" which provided intellectual challenge and excitement.

I'm sure I'm a better speller today because of that game. I think I am a better father for it, too.

Today the kitchen table may be in the car on the way through McDonalds on the way to the soccer game, or it may be nonexistent. But the conversation and modeling, wherever and whenever it can happen, is just as important, and perhaps even more important.

Today, more than ever, it is school which is called upon to provide a constant and predictable environment where children interact with adults. Good schools must offer the intellectual, social, ethical, and moral guidance essential for a healthy life and a healthy society.

A Violent Society

Parents, children, and teachers fear violence in schools

In recent years, a rash of murders has struck the schools of America. For teachers, children, and parents across the country, fear has stalked into new territory.

For me, these shootings are the shattering of a sanctuary, as if the killings happen in church or temple, although I never doubted these unspeakable acts could happen at school. I have seen too much anger, exclusion, isolation, meanness, and hostility in schools in the last three decades not to think it was possible. Human cruelty, if left unchecked, knows no boundaries.

Violence is real in our schools. Statistics tell one side of the story. According to a 1993 study cited by Johnson and Johnson in their book, *Reducing School Violence,* "ten percent of teachers and nearly one-fourth of students in public schools say that they have been the victim of a violent act in school."[17] Although murder is certainly the rare exception, and attacks and assaults are disturbing and noticeable, emotional mayhem is commonplace.

In many classrooms, students don't feel safe enough to share an opinion, risk a guess, formulate a hypothesis, speak individually to the teacher, befriend an unpopular classmate, or cross racial or gender lines when choosing classmates for academic project partners. Ridicule, peer pressure, teasing, bullying, exclusion, and ostracism are familiar experiences for many students.

The seeds planted by widespread domestic violence begin to sprout in school in about third grade as well. When boys and girls begin to segregate along gender lines, the existence and growth of these violent influences become clear. Boys begin their taunting, crude dirty jokes, pinching, touching, punching or worse. The response by teachers and schools communicates our values clearly. Is the teacher too busy to notice? Is the attitude simply that "boys will be boys"? Will the teacher intervene and provide social and moral guidance or stick to purely "academic" subjects because there's no time for social instruction? Does the teacher have the training to handle social issues and the support of the school in confronting them?

There are many violence prevention programs in our schools today. They teach the skills of mediation and conflict resolution to students in elementary, middle, and high schools across the country. But these programs can provide only part of the answer. Teachers must also be given enough professional training to be able to spot trouble before it starts and time to engage in proactive strategies that model non-violent action as a way of life. Teachers who don't have enough time to even address basic academic requirements are reluctant to invest time on strategies which prevent violence.

Beyond Triage in Our Schools

Few people would argue that U.S. education is not in need of change. Children and teachers are caught in an educational system that often does not meet the needs of either the children or the teachers. Children spend less time with parents and other caring adults and have significantly less "free time" for constructive, educational play.

At school, recess and other social activities are minimized in an attempt to increase "time on task" in solitary study or whole-class lessons. Lengthy standardized tests are implemented across the country, and teachers, schools, and systems are compared unfairly. Teachers must not only teach to the test, but also cover increasing amounts of curriculum in school days constantly shortened and fractured with special activities and daily requirements.

But the presence of anxiety, frustration, and often desperation in our classrooms and on our playgrounds does not change our mission as teachers. Rather, it makes that mission more critical. Our action is needed more than our handwringing and blame casting; outrage is more productive than depression and sadness.

By presenting these problems, I do not for a minute discount the extraordinary effort and commitment of the vast majority of our teachers and administrators. They work tirelessly to overcome the obstacles and meet the challenges placed before them each day, each week, each year. Along with their sweat and tears, they provide love which, like blood, is in short supply.

Love can cross barriers and heal emotional wounds. In school, the strongest grown-ups give large doses of love daily, meted out in small increments. They have their million gallon pins from the love bank. Many of the children need daily transfusions. They come to school emotionally anemic or worse. The adults give and give, but somehow it is never quite enough. A few children get stronger, but many do not.

Schools have always seemed to me to be havens for love and learning—the love of learning and the learning of love. Our best is called for as grown-ups, and when we give our best, the children flower. When our shadow side appears, the children wither. It is as simple and complicated as that.

But love, like good intentions, is not enough by itself. Teachers need the knowledge and skills to make their classrooms challenging, exciting, and secure. They need schedules and administrative expectations which fit their children's social and academic needs. And they need an educational system dedicated, from top to bottom, nationally and locally, to giving teachers time to teach and children time to learn.

Changing Time in the Classroom and School

In education, we are often caught in circles of "blame-and-patch" that produce a lot of change, but few long-term results. I know teachers are tired, very tired, of going from one new approach to the next and I suspect most administrators are too. When we don't give any changes the test of time before we move on to more changes, we end up wasting precious time and energy.

There are no quick fixes. When new programs are mandated and piled on top of each other in suffocating layers (which is particularly common in urban schools), they serve as an entropic force, literally winding the clock of learning backwards. More requirements are added, and nothing is subtracted. Most of these "blame and patch" reforms come from "the research," from outside the classroom and school, imposed by state and federal policymakers who would have a very difficult time spending five-and-a-half hours a day with a room full of twenty-five children.

I believe deeply that our schools can be better, our classrooms more purposeful, more disciplined, more generative. We can make the schoolhouse a joyful community of learning, a workplace of deep intellectual exploration and broad creative energy, a trustworthy place for social and emotional support.

To bring about the type of long-term changes which will make this true—which will give children time to learn and teachers time to teach—we must follow a logical and reasonable process. First, we must understand how children grow in their experience of time and in their acquisition of knowledge. By examining well-accepted educational research and theory and adding the accumulated wisdom and energy of thousands of teachers who have dedicated their professional lives to the daily struggles of the classroom, we can change the future by learning from the past.

Once we understand what children need, we can see logical and necessary changes in two areas at once, like two sides of a coin. We see the changes needed at the institutional and administrative level on one side. On the other, we see the changes we can make in our own classrooms within the time we are given each day, regardless of what happens school-wide.

For a quick reference, the following charts provide a list of the changes which will be suggested and explored in the rest of the book. Each is founded on the theory and research presented in Chapters 2 and 3 and is supported by the observations in Chapters 4–6 and the experience of countless teachers.

Guidelines for Changes at the Political Level

- Lengthen the academic year and/or keep schools open longer each day.
- Support high quality instruction by increasing teacher salaries.
- Establish and enforce professional standards for teachers.
- Reduce school size.
- Reduce class size to under twenty.
- Increase the quality of instructional time by eliminating formal tracking.
- Support teaching social skills as an integrated part of the content curricula.
- Support schools as "learning communities" at the school board and "bond issue" level.

Guidelines for Changes
at the Administrative Level

- Narrow the scope of the curriculum and lengthen time blocks.

- Reduce the number of "specials" that pull children out of self-contained classrooms and send those special area teachers into the classroom.

- Construct realistic daily schedules and adapt them to the needs and abilities of children at different grade levels.

- Adjust the school day to allow for mid-day exercise, nutrition and rest—in that order.

- Allow more time for teachers, staff, administration, and parents to interact with each other.

- Care for the physical and social environment of the school.

- Support the balanced integration of social and academic learning.

Guidelines for Changing
Time Structures in the Classroom

- Balance teaching approaches to allow time for individual students, small instructional groups, and whole-class lessons.

- Encourage the social context for learning through large and small learning groups and partner exercises.

- Reduce the number of transitions you have control over.

- Surprise your students with occasional breaks from the normal routine.

- Teach social and academic skills together through established techniques.

- Adapt daily schedules to the needs and abilities of children at your grade level.

- Adjust the middle of your day to allow for a time of rest and quiet in your classroom.

Guidelines for Changing Time Use in the Classroom

- Change the pace of teaching to improve the pace of learning.

- Narrow the number of lessons you teach in any given content area.

- Allow enough time for transitions and closure of lessons.

- Learn about the special needs of children who show behaviors that may classify them as ADHD/ADD and adjust your expectations and responses to them.

- Make school routines valued parts of academic, social, and community learning.

- Open your room to parents and colleagues.

Chapter Two
Time, Growth, and Learning

WATCHING CHILDREN GROW AND LEARN is one of the gifts of teaching. Every morning the classroom is like a birthday present, a surprise package waiting to be unwrapped. Each morning new, never before how it is today.

The knowledge gained by watching children grow and learn is also one of the gifts good teachers bring to the children each morning. The observant teacher is a scientist who notices the patterns of development, the nuances of change, the similarities and differences children exhibit in their learning and behavior each day. As a scientist, she also knows how to recognize and measure growth over time and how to shift her approaches in the classroom. She watches and measures the physical, social, and cognitive growth of her children and then adjusts her room, her schedule, and her curriculum accordingly.

Teaching requires a scientific understanding of children and the use of a scientific process in the classroom for understanding children and changing methods and strategies effectively. It requires the eyes, ears, hands, heart, and mind of an artist as well. Teaching is, of course, one of the most important jobs on the planet.

The better we know our children individually, the more we know about them culturally, and the deeper we understand the patterns of their development, the better able we are to make appropriate and meaningful changes to the institutions and practices of education.

One important factor in children's growth and development which gets little current attention in teacher training, professional development, and educational reform is the enormously powerful and entirely malleable resource we call time. How time is structured in school and how we choose to utilize it are key influences in the school lives of children and teachers.

The principles in this chapter relate directly and profoundly to how we structure time in school. Understanding them allows us to analyze our current time structures and envision changes which will improve teaching and learning. Each is discussed in depth in the following pages. In the next chapter, a group of principles central to the best use of time in school is explored.

Principles of Time in School Settings

- The structure and use of time and space in schools have a direct and significant effect on how, how much, and what children learn.

- Children's understanding and conceptions of time develop slowly and do not fully mirror adult understanding until the ages of 10–12.

- Children's natural daily rhythms are affected by biological influences and are not easily modified without consequence.

- Children of different ages respond to demands on their time differently.

- Some children experience time differently from their peers. This is especially true of children labeled ADHD.

The use of time and space affects learning

Imagine an average-sized elementary classroom and then imagine it filled with fifty students. Cramming this many students into a small space would severely limit the educational activities that take place there. There would be no room for a reading corner or science area, and any transition requiring movement within the room would be extremely time-consuming and hard to manage.

While this example is purposefully extreme, it's clear that the use and availability of space affects children's learning. It's the same with time. If a class were required to finish a one-hour standardized test in half that time, the chances of success would be greatly reduced. If a teacher in social studies were required to cover the federal government in a week of forty-minute periods, what level of understanding could be expected? If an art class were restricted to a half-hour a week, what level of concentration and completion would be likely?

The National Commission on Time and Learning provided a report to the Congress of the United States in May 1994 with eight recommendations that were designed to "put time at the top of the nation's reform agenda." (Today, time issues struggle to even make the agenda!) Their first recommendation was "Reinvent schools around learning, not time."[1] This recognized the central role our use of time plays in learning and how important it is to organize a school day into time periods which meet the learning needs of children, rather than the scheduling needs of adults.

Children's understanding of time develops slowly

"Are we there yet?"

"How much longer?"

The familiar refrain of children in the back seat indicates more than their joy in nagging the adults to pass the time on a long trip. Their anxious questions have to do with their sense of time. The developmental growth of children includes an increasing awareness and understanding of time occurring on both sensory and cognitive levels.

Children live in real time—a natural world of time which knows only the present moment—long before they can tell time. In his magnificent poem, *Fern Hill,* the great Welsh poet, Dylan Thomas, captured the sense of the present moment experienced by the young child awash in the natural world.[2]

> *. . . And nothing I cared, at my sky blue trades, that time allows*
> *In all his tuneful turning so few and such morning songs*
> *Before the children green and golden*
> *Follow him out of grace.*

Lying on his back in an open field, watching the clouds go by, the young child is oblivious to the passage of time. Such a morning is an island of "song" unrelated in time to any other island of experience. Think of the moments you have seen preschoolers absorbed in a puddle or blowing a dandelion. Think back to moments as a child when you were lost in time at the edge of the ocean building sandcastles or playing with imaginary friends. But the grace of these present moments recedes as they become bracketed, contextualized, by past and future.

Children's first experience of time is in a social context: in the arms of their mothers. Their understanding of time expands through their relationships with family and others around them as they grow. By two, they are increasingly aware of time constraints and show their disdain for them with the emphatic "NO," so characteristic of the so-called "terrible two's."

Dawdling is a way to try to control time, as is fantasy play. "Hurry" is an unpleasant concept to toddlers because it has little concrete meaning in their overwhelming connection to the present moment.

Later, in school, we teach children to pay attention to time cognitively by teaching them about hours and minutes, usually between kindergarten and second grade. But learning by rote that ten o'clock comes sixty minutes after nine o'clock does not necessarily provide the six- or seven-year-old with the knowledge of time she needs to navigate her world successfully.

Children's early understanding of time

Piaget was first to recognize the complexity of time concepts in the developing mind of the child and wrote an entire book about it in 1927. In *The Child's Conception of Time,* he broke new ground by making clear that children do not perceive time the same way adults do and by helping us understand that their early conceptions of time explain certain behaviors.[3]

Piaget states that one characteristic of young children's "primitive thought" is that it treats as absolute the particular perspective it happens to be dwelling within, and that it subsequently fails to connect these perspectives into a pattern of past, present, and future. For Piaget, children's sense of time is an example of egocentrism, placing current states of consciousness at the center of everything, and of irreversibility, because moment succeeds moment without leading to a general pattern. These two concepts are characteristic of the "sensory" and "preoperational" stages of development. These ideas are a foundation for much of what Piaget helped us understand about children's developing thoughts and reactions to everything from mathematics to morality.[4]

As children grow beyond these stages of development, they begin to develop an understanding of present, past, and future—of what is called "diachronic thinking." Jacques Montangero studied psychology with Piaget at the University of Geneva and is currently a professor there. For much of the last twenty years, he has continued to explore how children's approaches to time change as they grow. "Diachronic thinking" refers to children's developing ability to show their understanding of transformations over time, such as the growth of living things and changes in the weather. Children utilizing a diachronic approach in their thinking exhibit "a type of attitude or tendency of thought which consists of the spontaneous comparison of a current situation with its past and future states."[5]

This "tendency of thought," of course, develops over time. At five years, children can re-order a set of pictures about a familiar story that they are given out of order and even predict what a next picture might show, but they do not yet have a keen sense of how long the story might take or how much longer it will take to get to grandma's.

By eight or nine years of age, children have a better sense of duration and comparative durations because they are now able to "conserve" concepts, holding more than one idea in their head at the same time. They can conceive of reforestation without human intervention, and struggle with classic math problems such as "If a train leaves the station on track one at 8:00 traveling at 40 mph and another train leaves at 8:30 on track two at 80 mph, what time will each train arrive at the same destination forty miles away?"

At eleven or twelve years of age a cognitive leap is seen in children's diachronic thinking and approaches to problem solving. This coincides with growth in other cognitive processes (such as more abstract reasoning, even about concrete problems) but we do not know exactly why. All this change seems to be the cumulative growth of cognition.

Children can now see changes over time as successive states within an evolutionary process—such as growth of trees, thawing of ice, the evolution of knowledge—all processes studied by Montangero and his colleagues.[6] Children can construct more complicated understandings of time, such as recognizing that the differences between two verbal descriptions, produced by different children but read by an experimenter, have to do with the age of the speakers.

"This new perspective allows children to enrich their evocations and explanations by the use of concepts such as cycles, evolutions, transmission from one generation to the next, etc. to which they previously had *only recognitive access.*" [emphasis added][7] Although younger children may recognize the words which indicate changes over an extended time (such as "evolution" or "reforestation"), they cannot easily grasp the concepts which the words denote.

The rush to "early knowledge"

This understanding of how children's concepts of the passage of time develop draws into question the age expectations of "pushed down" content curricula such as that of E. D. Hirsch and "Core Knowledge" advocates.[8] Hirsch and others argue that specific, sequenced content knowledge about the history of the world, science, and scientific concepts can be acquired by children at early ages. *What Your Second-Grader Needs To Know,* for instance, tells parents to teach their children about ancient Babylonia, Persia, Greece, India, and China as well as about the solar system, elementary physics and chemistry.[9] The concept is that by learning facts about these subjects, children will have the knowledge they need to succeed in school. Knowledge is viewed as the core of learning. Meaning, understanding, taking different perspectives, and the relationship of facts one to another are not overly emphasized by the "Core Knowledge" approach.

When teachers question children in those kinds of subject areas, the children often show enormous difficulty grasping historical perspective and understanding the duration of events which is necessary for a full understanding of complex relationships. Their diachronic thinking has generally not advanced to the degree necessary to grasp these concepts in the larger context of time. Parents of children studying ancient Egypt in the first grade, at a school where I was making a presentation, remarked with humorous understanding that their children were convinced that the Sphinx came right after the dinosaurs or perhaps was one of them.

Exposure to complex ideas is acceptable at young ages; the expectation that they will understand them like adults is not. This is particularly true in the study of history and cultures around the world, a cornerstone of Core Curriculum and many early-grade social studies texts. Many text books for public school make assumptions about children's understanding of time that are simply off target because of a lack of knowledge about child development. I remember sitting in several first grades in a school where children were studying the rain forest and learning about deforestation and the food chain. I was struck by how they were learning words that sounded impressive, such as "canopy" and "floor," but did not understand the concepts or complex cycles being taught. That would have required diachronic thinking at a higher level than they could manage. They had only "recognitive access" to the material being presented.[10]

Montangero and colleagues were able to verify that children move from a quantitative understanding of changes over time to a qualitative one, a difference that allows understanding of not just *what* happened, but *when* and *why*. The idea of true "cultural literacy" as presented by Hirsch and others requires diachronic thinking, not just core knowledge of words and concepts.[11] Both are important to maximize children's education. But the best use of time in school is to have the content of the curriculum match the child's development and ability to struggle with age-appropriate concepts that help make meaning out of the content.

There is much to admire in Hirsch's promotion of sequential content curriculum and many schools are in need of the discipline of such an approach. If the content sequence is matched to slightly older grades, it can be well-utilized as an empirically rich scope and sequence continuum.

The brilliant education writer Susan Ohanian notes that, in the name of tougher and tougher content standards, we are prematurely exposing children to content which makes them want no part of it by the time they are old enough to actually understand it.[12] She describes how children can now read *Moby Dick* as a picture book and are bound to study it these days in high school, when, in fact, most of us will admit that we struggled mightily with Ahab and the white whale as college students.

Understanding children's diachronic thinking

Early in their school lives, children are presented content and constrained in a school schedule that presupposes they think diachronically about past, present, and future. Currently, schools presuppose that children can think qualitatively about concepts (such as refor-estation and historical change) as well as their own time decisions relating to assignments, homework, revisions, and quality of work.

Many kindergarten teachers teach the schedule every morning. By previewing the fragmented bits of the upcoming school day, they hope to help their five- and six-year-olds to better respond to time frames that make little sense to them. First-graders are expected to remember their entire daily routine, which often includes moving from room to room throughout the day for art, music, physical edu-cation, library, computer lab—not to mention lunch and recess—on a timetable that resembles a typical high school day. We expect third-graders, at a stage when they are just beginning to grasp time durations, to keep planning books in which they keep track of homework, daily assignments, spelling words, and more, mimicking the "Week-At-A-Glance" planners of their parents and teachers.

We are clearly asking too much. We are going too fast. We need to remember that children do not experience or understand time in the same way adults do. How they understand and experience time should not only guide curriculum content, it should also guide how we organize the school day and the methods we use to teach.

It is our job as teachers, administrators, and educational policy-makers to think carefully about how we expect children to negotiate the time of school itself. We need to assess the proper duration of periods at different ages and the right amounts of outdoor time and quiet time. We need to decide how much time testing learning deserves in children's educational experience at different ages. We need to consider what are reasonable times for eating and drinking and going to the bathroom, the proper balance of time for singing and playing as well as reading and writing, and how much time chil-dren need for silence.

The development of diachronic thinking explains much of what we need to know about children's sense of time from a cognitive perspective. From a sensory and biological perspective there is another important consideration.

Circadian rhythms

We think of humans as having five senses: sight, hearing, smell, taste, and touch. Our sense of time may be the true sixth sense. Part of this sense has to do with what are known as "circadian rhythms," recurring cycles of approximately twenty-four hours. These rhythms are part of our internal biological selves and are the subject of extensive research in areas such as sleep patterns and disorders, jet lag, and even the common adolescent tendency to stay up late and have difficulty waking up early. It's clear that circadian rhythms are a dominant environmental influence, producing conditioned behavior even at the cellular level.

Circadian rhythms govern children's earliest understandings of time (which are related to the absence and presence of light), their sleep patterns, and the predictable dip in energy after lunch (felt by teachers as well) which the rest of the world responds to with siesta. Teachers note a slight dis-ease in their students when our worldly clocks jump ahead or back in relation to daylight savings time. Students must adjust their "pacemakers" to the curve ball thrown by our tinkering with time.

All these patterns, as well as changes in children's behavior related to the phases of the moon, and weather patterns, remind us that we are biological creatures, part of the universe of time, and subject to its regulation. Some children clearly are more affected by these rhythms than are other children. Some, for example, are deeply affected by light deprivation and suffer from Seasonal Affective Disorder which has an impact on mood, attention, and performance in school.

We know our circadian rhythms affect our sleep/wake patterns, but less is known about the daytime effects of these rhythms on performance. But it's clear that this basic biological relationship to time is a strong force in governing behavior:

> These rhythms are so strong that they are capable of making us commit gross errors, even as adults, *when we are deprived of the means of measuring time.* [emphasis added][13]

"Breathing out" and "Breathing in"

Teacher, by Sylvia Ashton-Warner, was first published in 1963 and has long been my favorite book in education. It combines a personal memoir with a clear, fresh look at teaching elementary children through an approach which emphasizes children's innate drive to learn and the guidance of adults who would focus and facilitate that natural process.[14] It also presented teaching nonviolent behavior to children as an essential and over-riding goal which might save the world from the destruction of armed conflicts.

As a white, native New Zealander who taught classes of predominantly Maori children, Ashton-Warner entered the classroom as an observer who needed to first understand the children before shaping her strategies. When another teacher mentioned the challenges of dealing with the enormous energy of the children in the classroom, Ashton-Warner agreed that this energy is most like "a volcano in continuous eruption." She decided, however, to manage it differently from the other teacher, who believed it necessary to get "your foot on their neck." Ashton-Warner's approach was to "stand back, something like a chairman, and let it teach itself." Rather than trying to dampen and control this natural enthusiasm, she chose to harness and guide it. She listed her daily schedule with the title "Daily Rhythm" which consisted of alternating sections described as a time to "Breathe Out" and "Breathe In."[15] Her unerring sense was that children needed a variety of activities during a day.

To be effective learners and workers, children (and adults) in every culture need to experience this natural rhythm which is an extension of our body's central, life-giving process of breathing. As educators, we must understand this process and be sensitive to children's needs. They can only breathe in new information for so long before they must breathe out and release the tension through some change of focus and attention, whether it is in accepted or disapproved activity.

This sense of children's natural learning rhythms is important in overall school scheduling (length of periods, times for lunch and recess, etc.) as well as daily and weekly lesson plans and the artful and intuitive moments when teachers sense their children's needs and make a change "on the fly." In Ashton-Warner's words, it makes no sense to try to cap the "volcano" of youthful enthusiasm and communication, but rather to "harness" it since "I can't control it."[16] School schedules and teaching strategies need to fit children's natural rhythms rather than trying (and failing) to force them into an artificially adult world which mimics our fast-paced, hard-driving business culture.

Different ages respond differently

There's an old story in developmental education that says the way to test who's ready for second grade at the end of the first grade year is by saying to the children, "Put your work down. We'll finish it when we come back from gym." All the six-year-olds will drop their papers and be in line while the seven-year-olds will whine and ask if they can't just finish the problem they're working on.

Children at different ages respond to time differently. Along with their growth in diachronic thinking, developmental rhythms and cycles of growth affect their reactions. Growth spurts in the body and the brain are part of normal development as children grow. In my book, *Yardsticks: Children in the Classroom Ages 4–14,* I document many of the different time-driven behaviors children normally exhibit at different ages.[17] For instance, eight-year-olds seem to need an enormous amount of time to run, move, and exercise as they experience physical growth spurts around this age. Sitting still with focused attention for long periods is difficult for both boys and girls. Brain research shows that continuous, focused attention (even for adults) is virtually impossible for more than ten minutes.[18] For eight-year-olds, it's clearly less than that.

But this developmental need can be harnessed positively, like Ashton-Warner's "volcano" of enthusiasm, if the teacher changes time in the classroom to respond to the rapid-fire energy of her children. By shortening assignments, engaging in many movement activities, short academic drills, and song and rhythm activities, third grade can be a place of happiness and much learning. However, if a teacher does not recognize children's needs at this age for short time spans and frequent change, there will be no end to discipline problems. Other factors such as personality, culture, and cultural expectations certainly affect how children respond to time structures as well, but the language of the body makes clear demands on growing children.

The most obvious way the body responds differently to time needs during the school day is in relationship to the bodily functions of eating, drinking, and elimination. Bathroom "accidents" in the early grades, for instance, are more avoidable when teachers understand how frequently some of their children really need "to go." Fortunately, most teachers and schools have ended the practice of lining children up to go to the bathroom at appointed times (except in antiquated buildings where bathrooms are in the basement and safety is an issue). Frequent snacks for all children, and especially adolescents, change their ability to focus. "Can I get a drink?" is generally not a diversionary tactic, but a real need. Allowing time for drinks or asking children to bring water bottles can change the number of interruptions for this clear biological need.

Some children experience time differently from peers

There is a strong body of research which shows that some children who exhibit behaviors which classify them as ADHD experience time differently from others. These children cannot judge the duration of time as well as other children, which may make a one-minute wait in line at school seem painfully long and unmanageable. They also struggle with controlling or delaying impulsive actions. This makes solving complex problems nearly impossible since everyone's first, natural impulse is to give up in frustration when difficulties are encountered.

Although ADHD is described in behavioral terms (i.e., children who exhibit certain behaviors are diagnosed as suffering from the disorder), research has not established a definitive cause or physiological tests. Most research currently focuses on a physiological, neurochemical cause. But others are looking at ADHD in a different way.

Richard DeGrandpre is one of several writers who see the huge increase in ADHD diagnoses and the number of children medicated with Ritalin more as a result of our fast-paced society and inappropriate time expectations than as a better understanding of a physiological problem. In his book, *Ritalin Nation: Rapid-Fire Culture and the Transformation of Human Consciousness,* he states that most children today labeled ADHD are casualties of sensory addictions created by a culture of neglect in a hurried society.

> Because our sense of time is determined by the pace and structure of life, our sense of time has become compressed, creating an aversion to situations of low intensity. First come sensory adaptations, followed immediately by rising sensory expectations.[19]

In other words, while we constantly complain about not having enough time, we are actually always looking for ways to do things faster and cannot easily tolerate slowing down. For example, mandating "time on task" in school doesn't necessarily improve learning on any level. But it makes us feel that we aren't wasting time, even if we are less productive. We are attracted to fast-paced, constantly changing activities and experiences which simulate a music video, a video game, or a TV commercial with bright, multiple images bombarding us each second.

Although he doesn't discount the possibility of physiological causes for ADHD behavior, DeGrandpre sees a need for changes in our culture and in our treatment of children who struggle with time expectations:

> It may indeed be that a small percentage of children are either born with or develop an early tendency toward the restlessness that many see as the classic sign of ADD. This early trajectory may even yield a child who is completely out of control. The real tragedy lies, however, in the very real possibility that had a child lived a slower, more structured life, he or she might have just as easily become a vital

member of society. Only history will tell us the long-term consequences of letting this uniqueness be twisted into something so unwanted that we end up eliminating it with a powerful, mind-altering drug.[20]

Appropriate Time Expectations

It's clear that children's diachronic sense of time develops gradually. Their understanding of past, present, and future slowly expands until they can fully understand the duration of events and the interdependent nature of their sequence. However, today's school schedules face children with greater expectations in shorter time periods and at an unpredictable pace. Schools continue to pack more and more activity into the same amount of time. The day is more halting, more chopped up into bits, little bite-sized, microwaved portions, with more transitions and often-shifting expectations.

In such a discontinuous setting, children are less able to use their developing skills to measure time, causing increases in errors of learning and in behavioral judgment. As covered in the previous section on circadian rhythms, research has shown that these types of "gross errors" are noticeable in adults who are "deprived of the means of measuring time." Think how much more susceptible developing children are who have not yet fully developed a means of measuring time, whose thinking is still focused in the present moment.

Young children experience time in successive moments of the present and some children who exhibit ADHD behavior seem to be stuck in the present, even at much older ages. Yet we increasingly expect them to make decisions and take actions which rely on past experience and consider future consequences.

Drawing on the work of Dr. Jacob Bronowski, author of *The Ascent of Man,* Russell Barkley carefully documents the extreme difficulty ADHD children have holding onto past and future to help them in their experience of the present. This, he believes, is due, among other things, to their inability to wait, to delay an impulse, an ability Bronowski identifies as central to the "ascent of man."[21]

What Piaget and Montangero have taught us about the development of children's diachronic sense is consistent with Barkley's beliefs as well. "Normal" children struggle developmentally with a sense of past and future, even up until the age of eleven. If a child is prone to ADHD (that is, existing mainly in the present time with little connection to past and future), imagine the struggle required to make decisions which add past and future considerations.

Writing a fictional account of a world where there was no future time, Alan Lightman noted in his brilliant, small book, *Einstein's Dreams,* "A person who cannot imagine the future is a person who cannot contemplate the results of his actions....(These people) leap out of bed in the morning, unconcerned that each action leads into nothingness, unconcerned that they cannot plan their lives."[22] A common adage says, "there's no time like the present." For these children, there may be no time but the present.

Children who experience "temporal trauma"

I believe that just as light affects circadian rhythms, the way we choose to distribute time to children affects their experience of that time and their behavior. The intricate micro-rhythms that control overall circadian rhythms are, we must remember, rhythms. Scientists do not tell us that these "pacemakers" fire irregularly or adjust quickly to sudden shifts in external time demands.

As mentioned earlier, some children suffer from Seasonal Affective Disorder which is influenced by the presence and absence of sufficient amounts of natural light. If less light can change mood and performance, so can less time, rushed time, condensed time, and frantic time. Children may suffer from temporal affective disorder in response to the presence and absence of sufficient time to meet expectations. Inappropriate time expectations or requirements can force some children into adaptive behavior that is not helpful to them, the teacher, or other students.

Many children experience temporal trauma on a regular basis, to varying degrees. For those most severely affected and who exhibit behaviors which clearly classify them as ADHD, drug therapy can positively change their world. But adjusting time environments along with or instead of drug intervention for these children could make a more substantial and longer-lasting difference. When school activity is engaging, stimulating, and matching their natural rhythms and developmental needs, these children are more apt to be focused and appropriate. When school activity is lethargic, mindlessly repetitive or frequently changed without warning, then these children become more restless.

A more complete discussion of how schools and teachers can better serve children with attentional disorders is presented in Chapter 9. We can significantly change the numbing life experience of many children who are now labeled with attentional disorders if we seriously address how we structure and use time throughout the school day. By changing the pace of the school day and making our expectations appropriate, we improve learning for all children.

Chapter Three
Using Time Wisely

OUR EXPERIENCE OF TIME IS UNIQUE and the passage of time is relative. It flies like a bird when we are having fun and crawls like a snail when we want to be doing something else. Children of different ages experience time differently and respond to time limits and expectations with varying degrees of success. Individual children may experience time differently from their peers, and some children live only in the present with none of the tempering influences provided by past memory and future expectations.

We've seen that the structure of time in school strongly affects the quality and quantity of children's learning. How that time is actually used in schools has an equal effect. Although the principles that follow are well established in educational research, many school practices disregard these findings. In order to improve the educational structures and practices which will change the pace of school, we must understand key principles of learning related to time.

Principles of Learning Related to Time

- Children show greater achievement academically when taught in class sizes of twenty or less, especially in primary grades.

- Children attain the greatest cognitive and social growth through social interaction; i.e., their intellectual, social, emotional, and physical growth depends on the social environment of the classroom and the conversation of play, collaborative projects, constructive conflicts, and problem solving.

- All children's cognitive growth is enhanced in classes with a mix of academic abilities when time is devoted to well-managed, differentiated instruction.

- Children need time for in-depth learning and regular completion of tasks to feel the pleasure of accomplishment and to fully develop the capacity for sustained work over time. Persistence is a skill which children develop when given the time to endure.

Classes of twenty or less help children

Between 1950 and 1985, hundreds of studies on class size were completed. Most focused on academic achievement rather than social achievement which has been shown to be more important in life success measured in terms of income, job and marriage stability, crime rates, and other indices.[1]

The Educational Research Service reported on 100 major studies of class size in a 1986 research brief.[2] Their summary and report on a meta-analysis of the research by Glass and Smith found two significant trends:

(1) ERS found that within the mid-range of 25–34 pupils, class size seemed to have little if any decisive impact on the academic achievement of most pupils in most subjects *above the primary grades*. [emphasis added]

(2) Glass and Smith found that within the wide range of 20–40 pupils, class size made little difference in pupil achievement (only six percentile points). *The major benefits from reduced class size were obtained as size was reduced below 20 pupils*. [again, emphasis added][3]

However, this pioneering research on class size did not move researchers or policy makers to a consensus on what should be done, although there was general agreement that at the primary level, class size under twenty would be beneficial.

In 1990, a study now considered one of the "great experiments in education in U.S. history" was completed.4 Project STAR (Student/Teacher Achievement Ratio), a study of the educational effects of class size in Tennessee, reported significant and irrefutable evidence that class size matters.5 Conducted by E. Word and eight colleagues between 1985 and 1990, Project STAR received high praise for design as well as results.

> The most important aspect of the Tennessee studies on class size flow from the fact that a large, sustained, randomized, controlled experiment was carried out and that it provided substantial and definitive findings.6

The findings were impressive. The study of over 7,000 students found that a small class size (between 13–17) in K–3 increases achievement, not only during the primary years, but also in later grades for children who were in smaller classes early, even when class size is large in the upper grades. The study also showed that smaller classes with one teacher provided better results than larger classes with one teacher and classroom aides. Academic gains were reported for all types of students in all types of districts: rich, poor, rural, urban, ethnically diverse, or homogeneous—as long as class size was small.

Despite the quality of the research and the overwhelming evidence, Tennessee proceeded cautiously, translating research into action in only seventeen districts with the lowest per capita income, reducing the size of only about four percent of classes. The limiting factor was cost.

California now has a law providing incentives to districts that reduce class size in the primary grades to eighteen or under. They are having trouble finding both dollars and teachers to keep up with the demand. It is unclear how far proposals for nationwide class size reduction will get in a Congress usually more interested in tax cuts and military spending than in funding education.

It's nice that we now have solid research to back up what every classroom teacher has known for years: smaller class size changes what is possible in a classroom and ultimately changes the quality of the educational experience for the students.

The research proves that academic achievement will go up. And so much more can happen for children and teachers. I believe smaller class sizes can profoundly change relationships in a classroom and improve communication between teachers and parents. Class size deeply affects the teacher's ability to know and reach each of the students for whom she is responsible.

Think of an average elementary class of twenty-five students and then remove five to seven children. Think about how that change affects nearly everything else in the classroom, especially in relationship to time. The time needed for all types of class management is reduced, from lining up for the fire drill to handing out papers. There is more time to hear everyone's idea about a math problem or an answer to a reading question. There is a much better chance of getting around to each student when they are writing in their journals. It is much easier to observe behavior while children work on projects. There is more time for everything—conferencing with each child about their spelling or their science folder, conversing with children to enhance vocabulary development, more time for each child to work on the two computers in the room each week.

Think about special-area teachers and the children they teach in elementary school. The physical education, art and music teachers see hundreds of children each week. They barely know the children's names, let alone their learning styles or individual needs. With less than twenty in each class, think how this would change. In every forty-five minute period, the specialist would have that much more time to help children with their individual needs. They would be able to manage classes more easily, spending more time on their specialty.

One United States Department of Education study of teachers' use of time in three countries (U.S., Germany, and Japan) made the connection between time and class size, and reported class size as being a paramount concern in the minds of teachers in all three countries. Average class size in Japan is 34, in the U.S. and Germany about 24 (across all grade levels). Teachers in all three countries reported more stress as class size rose. "In the United States," the report concluded, "reducing class size is important because, no matter what the reform strategy, class size is always first on teachers minds."7

Growth through social interaction

From the time the school bus pulls away from the corner stop or children trundle out their doors for the walk to school, they are immersed in a complex and fascinating social curriculum. This social soup is as nutritional for their growth and development as the academic curriculum they are fed each school day.

In fact, both curricula are deeply entwined, inseparable cognitive structures. Because the teachers on the way to school are peers, the learning is not always what we wish it would be. The bus—that yellow, mobile classroom—carries lessons about cooperation and friendliness, but also, too often, about exclusion and cruelty. So do the regular classroom, the hallways, the bathrooms, the lunchroom and the playground. All are places for learning.

Each moment of every school day is a moment of learning. When children are in a reading group they are also in a social group. They are learning to read and they are learning citizenship; they are learning what it means to comprehend a sentence and what it means to listen to someone else's idea about what a sentence means. When children are engaged with a lab partner in a science experiment, they are learning about the scientific method and they are learning cooperative strategies for working with colleagues on the job at hand. When children are solving equations in a math lesson, they are exploring their own solutions and comparing them to the work of their classmates. When children compete in a relay race in physical education, they are learning about their own physical abilities and they are learning what it means to be part of a team.

This all seems so obvious and so natural. And it is. The extraordinary and unnecessary problem lies in the fact that the academic curriculum has been established as the primary business of school, the social curriculum secondary and less important, when in actuality they are inseparable.

Teachers who attend to social problem solving or social skill building are often made to feel they are wasting valuable academic time. Principals feel compelled to adjust school schedules to eliminate homeroom and study halls; to reduce lunch and recess time to provide more state-mandated "time on learning." The pressure to "get through" or "cover" the curriculum is a major part of the faculty culture in every school. Covering the curriculum presumes that content is more important than character, though no one would ever say they believed that.

For some reason, the standards movement does not overtly champion social standards alongside the academic. The truth is that many of the serious problems facing education today would be addressed if we raised academic and social standards at the same time and together.

Picture two children on a see-saw, on the opposite ends of one of those long wooden planks with handles (that have mostly disappeared from school playgrounds for safety reasons). Perhaps you can remember the feeling of playing on the see-saw with a friend as a child yourself. The joy of being on the see-saw was in taking turns going up and down, in balancing enough to make the up and down possible and sometimes in balancing so well that you could float suspended deliciously in mid-air because you were so evenly paired. Sometimes, in an act of mischief or meanness, you or your partner might jump off the teeter-totter, sending the other crashing to the ground.

The secret of the see-saw, of course, was in the two of you: interdependent in your action, whether supporting or teasing, challenging or resting. This is the metaphor for what we need in our schools—a balance, a symbiosis between academic and social learning.

How children learn

The connection between academic and social learning is deeply rooted in educational and psychological theory, but not reflected in much educational practice. The classic developmentalists (Piaget,

Montessori, Erikson, and others) all saw aspects of social and cognitive growth as interwoven, intertwined. But it was the brilliant Russian psychologist, Lev Vygotsky, writing in the 1920s, who first brought the social context of teaching and learning into the mainstream of Western thought.

He challenged Piaget's theory that learning was mostly an internal and individual struggle between assimilation and accommodation of new experience; he proposed instead that learning appears twice, first on the social level between children and second inside the learner. "This applies equally to all voluntary attention," Vygotsky wrote in 1927 in *Mind in Society,* "to logical memory, and to the formation of concepts. *All the higher mental functions originate as actual relations between people.*" [emphasis added][8]

This simple, yet breathtaking construct was essentially unknown in the educational and psychological circles of the Western world until the 1960s and not fully appreciated until the late 1970s. Since that time, scores of major writers and researchers in the fields of developmental psychology, linguistics, and education have applied Vygotsky's ideas concerning the social foundations of thought and language to their work.[9]

Several of Vygotsky's key ideas have major implications for the classroom and many of them have been used intuitively by great classroom teachers for generations.

One of Vygotsky's concepts is that learning is the "social negotiation of meaning in practical activity."[10] Children constantly seek to understand their world, to know the meaning of things. This cannot be a solitary activity because of its nature. It requires comparison and contrast. It requires other's ideas to test your own. It requires social interaction. Conversation alone will not produce all the answers. Ideas need to be tested and explored, hence "practical activity." In the midst of the practical activity of the science experiment, the social studies project, the block corner in kindergarten, much social negotiation is evident. Out of this social negotiation in practical activity comes new learning.

Learning is aided by social negotiation with more capable peers and adults in what Vygotsky referred to as the "zone of proximal development": that place where the child's ideas meet the ideas of a more capable peer or adult. I think of this zone as the stretching place—the mental place for cognitive tension, struggle, disequilibrium and growth; the place where mistake-making leads to meaning-making. Guided participation or guided discovery with teachers—whether more competent peers in the classroom, parents, or professional educators—can enhance breakthroughs to new levels of cognitive growth and understanding.[11] The social context of teaching and learning is a venue for the greatest cognitive growth, for academic and social excellence.

Classrooms where social discourse and active learning (experimentation, project work, field research, performance assessment and the like) are valued have historically applied Vygotsky's basic concepts about social interaction whether they knew them or not. These include John Dewey's ideas as applied in schools at the turn of the century; Bank Street College of Education and many so-called progressive schools in New York City; the National Science Foundation-sponsored Elementary Science Study (ESS) of the 1960s; and the work of the High Scope Foundation in Michigan (which based its work on Piaget initially). More recently, the work of the Developmental Studies Center in California and our own approach at Northeast Foundation for Children have used Vygotsky's concepts as guiding principles.

Social learning in other cultures

The importance and value of the social context of teaching and learning is not unique to, and certainly not paramount in, Western thought. In Africa, however, its value is primary. The social context of teaching and learning can be defined in a word: "Ubuntu." It is a way of being. According to Mzamo P. Mangaliso of the University of Massachusetts, "A central part of *ubuntu* is the interdependence of humans in a social context. The driving norms are on reciprocity, the suppression of self-interest, and the primacy of symbiosis. Hence it is often said *umntu ngumntu ngabanye* [a person is a person through others], a statement which conveys the notion that a person becomes a person only at the point when others recognize or become aware of him/her."[12] Descartes gave us "Cogito Ergo Sum." *I think, therefore I am.* African wisdom would propose "Notus Sum, Ergo Sum." *I am known, therefore I am!*

Learning, then, has a social purpose and exists in a social milieu. In Africa, Mangaliso notes, this milieu is deeply influenced by a different sense of time and clearly different ideas about the meaning of learning and living. "Unlike in the Western context, where time is a strategic commodity to be frugally used, in the African context it is treated as the healer, with a lot being allowed to pass before closure to the issue at hand is arrived at. . . . In the African setting … the highest modality is attached to the group's well being, efficiency maximization takes a lower priority to, say, societal harmony."[13]

In Japan, the social context of teaching and learning is a required and respected part of the national curriculum in primary schools before the educational style is changed to one highly driven by standardized tests in secondary schools. Primary teachers spend a fourth of their teaching day with their students during such times as lunch, clean-up, and mid-day breaks. A U.S. time study of Japanese schools states, "While this study uses the term 'non-instructional' to mean time not devoted to academics, Japanese teachers view all of their time with students as instructional. The lunch and clean-up drills are important times for instilling social and cultural values in children."[14] In America, duty-free lunch and recess is normative and, "a standard pattern in many U.S. schools is that teachers spend no non-instructional time with students."[15]

The Japanese approach in primary schools is embodied in the concept of *hansei* or group reflection. Teachers spend what most American educators would consider excessive amounts of time discussing with children and having children discuss with each other how their study, work together, learning, etc. is progressing. The social aspect is seen as essential for all learning.

In her important book about Japanese education, *Educating Hearts and Minds,* Catherine C. Lewis explains how "personal and collective reflection, by students and by teachers, is a central practice in Japanese elementary schools. More often than not the school day, the week, the semester, the school year end with reflection. What did we learn? What did we do well and poorly? What should we do differently next time?"[16]

Reflection is valued. Time for reflection is assumed to be not only available in the schedule, but mandatory! Lewis notes, "The aim of reflection went well beyond social skills, to the very values children brought to group life and the strength of children's bonds to one another. As one teacher said, 'Children's whole way of looking at one another changed' as they reflected on help and kindness offered by classmates. As children reflected on whether they had cleaned up spilled water without recrimination and whether they'd done their 'utmost' on group projects or chores, they were building an appreciation of certain values of group life: kindness, responsibility, doing one's best. Too, they were learning—through their own thinking and the comments of others in the group—how well they approximated these ideals."[17]

Thinking about the social context of teaching and learning in American and Japanese schools, Lewis makes a most telling point. "Both Japanese and American children," she notes, "work in groups. So the question is not *whether* children will work in groups of some kind but *what values* will govern children's work with one another. In their small groups, are children encouraged to treat each other with fairness and respect or simply pressed to 'get the job done' as expeditiously as possible? Is the power of the small group used to humiliate dissenters or to provide a forum where all children can be heard?"[18] These questions should be just as important to American teachers as they utilize cooperative learning strategies in their classrooms.

In her years of study in Japan, Lewis observed that, "schools that meet children's needs—for belonging, autonomy, meaningful contribution—are likely to be rewarded with children who care about school."[19] When time is used to teach social skills as well as academic skills, children care about school. When children care about school, they become better educated. They spend more time learning because learning is something they care about.

Caring about school is not only important for the education of the individual, however, it is a critical and practical experience for caring about your town, your city, your state, your country—for maintaining a democracy. Generations of researchers and writers, from John Dewey to Sheldon Berman, Nel Noddings, and Deborah Meier have shown that the social context of teaching and learning is essential to individual learning *and* the well being of our nation.[20]

Classes with mixed academic abilities enhance growth

The generally acknowledged goal of tracking, or "regrouping" as it is sometimes called, is to allow children with greater academic abilities to achieve at higher levels through classes geared to their abilities and for those of lower academic levels to be presented with less challenging material that better fits their ability to learn.

Tracking separates students by academic ability in our schools, particularly in math and science. It also has the unintended effect of often separating students by race and socio-economic status. Not only does tracking send the wrong message about our democracy, it also doesn't work. It doesn't produce the academic results it purports to accomplish. Reports by the U.S. National Research Center regarding the Third International Mathematics and Science Study (TIMSS) in 1988 made it crystal clear that the practice of tracking is detrimental to U.S. student achievement in math and science. U.S. twelfth-graders rank well below students in 19 other countries in mathematics and 15 other countries in science yet *are above the average in the amount of time spent on these subjects!*

What's wrong? These reports conclude that two practices carry the primary responsibility for the poor showing of U.S. students: (1) the practice of tracking and (2) the practice of covering the curriculum "a mile wide and an inch deep."

The U.S. is (also) selective about who takes what courses, especially in mathematics. We do this even before high school and are essentially unique among TIMSS countries in doing so. As early as middle school, we offer different content to different groups of students. We presumably do this to improve our educational 'efficiency' and increase learning for all students or, at least, for the students in our most demanding courses. It doesn't work. 'Facing the Consequences' [the name of the first report] used TIMSS results to examine these practices in some detail and found that they did little to help most students learn mathematics. The report also found that this practice contributed to exaggerated achievement differences among U.S. students (presumably in different tracks). The new twelfth grade results make it clear that tracking also fails to provide satisfactory achievement for either average or advanced students.[21]

For tracking to be replaced by a more effective model of education, a new social and academic framework needs to emerge in its place, a new framework with new time frames. Such frameworks can be found in classrooms today where the full integration of social and academic learning is the first priority of the teacher. In these classrooms, teachers instruct children on the process of working independently and in small groups so that the teacher can maximize her instructional delivery in small groups and know that students are utilizing their independent time well. In this framework, teachers have more time to reach high- and low-achieving students, and the value of social interaction for cognitive growth is maximized. Curriculum tends to be more integrative between content areas and fewer subjects are studied, but in much greater depth, as recommended by the U.S. report. In schools where the social context of teaching and learning is understood and valued, character education is as important as content education.

Although these classrooms are found in schools in many different parts of the country, they currently represent the exception rather than the rule. If we are to become more competitive with other national education systems, we must improve the skills and approaches of more teachers to be able to teach in greater depth about fewer things in a non-tracked, democratic, and caring environment. In educational language, this is referred to as "differentiated instruction." Such an approach requires highly skilled and well-trained teachers. Our children deserve no less. All of our children.

It is also clear that tracking or regrouping wastes an enormous amount of time in school. Transitions to re-groups double the number of beginnings and endings of lessons, double the time needed for clean-up and moving from room to room, taking out and putting away, collecting papers and assignments, pencils and book bags. Children are shuffled like so many cards in a deck and abruptly moved from place to place. "Time on task" is greatly extended by using differentiated instruction in self-contained classrooms. It is a definitive way to slow time and improve learning in school.

Children need time for in-depth learning

The same report that details the failure of tracking also finds U.S. curriculum requirements inappropriate:

> That report suggests that tracking is not the only problem with the U.S. approach to mathematics and science education. U.S. science and mathematics curricula cover many topics but without devoting much time to any one topic. This makes it unsurprising that there appeared to be only very small differences in what had been learned by U.S. fourth-graders compared to third-graders or by eighth-graders compared to seventh-graders. This was true for all mathematics and science topics examined. Schmidt said, 'We have characterized U.S. science and mathematics curricula as 'a mile wide and an inch deep.' We can hardly be surprised to find the achievement gains in all those topics only an 'inch deep' as well.[22]

This issue is at the heart of the life-and-death struggle going on in America's classrooms over "standards." In an effort to raise test scores, more time is being devoted to discrete bits of learning. Block scheduling allows students to explore, question, try out ideas, master skills, connect content across subject areas, discover historical and scientific themes, and represent their learning through reports, projects, and presentations as well as tests. To meet the standards, this type of learning is being erased.

Many schools are now "teaching to the test." But even those students with the best memory for test information will not be able to apply that memory without the full experience of the scientific, mathematic, and writing processes. More time devoted to particular, isolated bits of information means less time for the continuity of in-depth projects, research, observation, repetition, reflection, revision, and creativity—all of the attributes students need to apply their learning in the real world.

Teachers, parents, and employers complain that no one can stick to anything anymore. The common attitude is that if you can't get it right the first time, throw it away, buy another, or have someone else do it for you. Doing it over, trying again, finding another way, changing your approach, editing, doing another final draft, pondering over complicated word problems in math which offer more than one answer and many dead-ends—these activities require persistence. Persistence can be applied on a timed test, but it cannot be learned there. In today's education, there is no place and no time to learn persistence. Persistence is a skill which children develop when given the time to endure.

Picture for a minute a class of children, say fifth-graders, all ability levels, some with ADHD behaviors, some with learning disabilities, spread out around the classroom, deep in concentration reading the books they have chosen themselves for a unit on biography. The room is quiet; perhaps there is music playing. Some children are taking notes, others are sketching from time to time. There are no interruptions. This was the picture of my own classroom on its best days for many years. While the children worked, I would confer with individual students about their projects or about their math or their homework or their sick grandmother. I did not always ask them directly about their reading, or give a test on the book when they were finished. Sometimes I worried about this. Were they learning? Would they do well on the standardized tests? As Susan Ohanian says,

> Leaving a child alone to savor a book, to get from it what he or she will and then holding your tongue when the child closes the book requires a tremendous act of faith—faith in children and faith in books. Sad to say, school systems are not designed to accommodate acts of faith. They demand records: competency checklists, scope and sequence charts, national tests.[23]

The joy of learning motivates students to keep learning. The joy of learning comes from hard work done well, shared thoughtfully, acknowledged appreciatively. We must make time for such learning in our classrooms and schools.

Conclusion

Time is a central element in human existence, and our consciousness of time is instilled in us on biological, cognitive, and societal levels. Children develop a sense of time in much the same ways as other cognitive processes, with a significant change at the age of eleven or twelve, during the same period when more abstract reasoning develops. Children's responses to time expectations change as they grow and often change within a school year. Children with attentional disorders aren't able to handle the same time requirements as their peers and the explosion in the numbers of these children may be related to the increased pace and expectations of today's schools and society in general.

It is also clear that smaller class sizes result in greater academic achievement and in a richer, more satisfying teaching environment because of the increased time available for all types of group and individual activities and contact.

Educational theory accepts the inseparable connection between teaching academic and social skills and the central role of the social context for both social and academic learning, but these concepts are not commonly supported at an administrative level or put into practice in today's classrooms.

How children experience time and how they understand it and respond to it play an important role in their learning. How schools and teachers organize children's days and their work should fit children's needs and their abilities to manage and comprehend time. By keeping these basic principles in mind, we can see the impact of school schedules and teaching methods on the children and classrooms in the following chapters.

Section Two

O B S E R V A T I O N S

OBSERVATION IS ONE OF THE WAYS that children build knowledge.

Observation is also a key to scientific research. Daily observation is an invaluable component of good teaching.

In this section, I invite you to come to school to observe and reflect. You can experience time as students know it through the course of a typical school day by following Phoebe through an entire seventh grade day at Longfellow Middle School (Chapter 4) and Mark through a first grade day at Briarwood Elementary (Chapter 5). For many educators, this will be a first. During my years as a teacher and principal, I worked with students for thousands of days without ever taking the time to follow one through an entire school day. This is probably the case for 99 percent of teachers and administrators.

When you stop to think about it, this is rather remarkable. Entire careers are spent designing and implementing daily educational schedules for students that haven't been field-tested by any of the adults. Instead, we rely on the memory of our own institutional experiences as students, the cultural history of the school in which we are employed and, occasionally, on the writings of university researchers who may or may not have done the direct, thorough observational research required.

For Chapter 6, I experienced first grade by following Mrs. Chambers, a dedicated and delightful professional, through the entire school day. This was a unique experience for me as well, entirely different from a principal's typical drop-in observation or formal forty-minute teacher evaluation.

These full days of observation were eye-opening for me. I saw things that surprised me and heard things that both delighted and disturbed me. I came away from my visits with fresh insights about what it is like to be a student and a teacher in school today. I encourage everyone connected to education—parents, teachers, administrators, school board members, researchers, and reformers— to find the time for the same experience. There is an enormous amount to be learned from experiencing school as students and teachers do.

In each of these chapters, my commentary on the issues, struggles, and triumphs which are a daily part of the educational process are indicated by a different type-face. I also provide a basic analysis of how time was structured and used during the day.

Chapter Four

Floating on the Surface
in Seventh Grade

What happens to a dream deferred?

Does it dry up
like a raisin in the sun?
Or fester like a sore—
And then run?
Does it stink like rotten meat?
Or crust and sugar over—
like a syrupy sweet?

Maybe it just sags
like a heavy load.

Or does it explode?

Langston Hughes[1]

THERE IS AN INSIDE AND AN OUTSIDE to being in seventh grade. The outside bubbles along with multiple energies. There is the sweet energy that takes in everything at once, sucking in the news from everywhere simultaneously: what four friends tell you at the lockers, what your Walkman is telling you at the same time, the bell sounding, the physical pleasure and displeasure of jostling bodies in the hall.

There is the heavy energy of boredom: the unbearable waiting for this class to be over, the squinch-eyed energy it takes to concentrate on what the teacher is telling you will be on the test tomorrow. There is the kinetic energy of interest: attention to the detail of what everyone else is wearing, which song is "phat" this week as compared to last week, what it really might have meant for the women with Lewis and Clark to survive in a world you can only imagine.

And then there is the inside: the place of doubt and wonder, of beauty and ugliness. Here the energy can be slow and peaceful, lethargic and lonely, or spinning out of control.

Teachers and parents see the outside. Young adolescents make sure of this with their trendy clothes, hairstyle, body decorations, and unpredictable behavior. Or they show us the good child, the star, the high achiever, the cheerful dancer. Sometimes we see the contempt of what I call the "distancing dance" of the adolescent years.[2] The hair-flipping, eye-rolling, big-sigh attitude that says, "Oh, Dad!" or "You're not going to wear that today, are you Mom?" or "Whatever, Mr. Apps. I did the assignment!"

Inside is a different story, hidden from view. It is a precious and fragile thing, a developing person in the springtime of life, needing temporary protection by an outside layer, like the thin eggshell covering the nascent birds in the nest in the hemlock tree outside my bedroom window.

The danger is that sometimes something is wrong on the inside and there is no way for the teacher or parent to know, blinded as they are by the flashes of color on the outside and the apparent sounds of wellness from inside. In a cartoon image, a mother bird presses a stethoscope to her eggshells. The ability and willingness of grownups to listen for the inside voice, to see the signs of the emerging person, can be the most important thing about seventh grade. These teenagers clearly need us while they show us how much they need each other.

When I spend a full day with Phoebe in the seventh grade, the most striking thing she tells me is how much she wants to be a sixth grade teacher. This comes up because the teachers on her team (the Ocean team) are working together to integrate a unit on careers in several different subject areas. In homeroom, it's her assignment to write in her journal about the career that most interests her and she is also researching the career in social studies.

She clearly adored and respected her sixth grade teacher last year. "She was the best ever," Phoebe tells me. "She did lots of neat stuff with us like projects. She would always talk with you."

Phoebe's choice of careers speaks to me during the day in many ways. Her experience last year lies in sharp contrast to the day I am with her. Today, she is taught by many teachers in many different classrooms. They care about their work, are engaged in innovative middle school efforts, and enjoy their students. Phoebe, a well-behaved, academically competent seventh-grader, is motivated to learn, conscientious about her work, but clearly disengaged from her teachers, though she reaches out to them.

Something isn't working in the way she or her teachers would like. Some of it is adolescence, but some of it is the difference in the structure of Phoebe's education this year compared to last. It revolves around the issue of time. Phoebe does not talk about wanting to be just any teacher. She wants to be a sixth grade teacher. She pines for the community of learners she remembers so well from last year. She adapts to the changes in schooling imposed on her, but it is not easy and there is sadness and wistfulness in her ways.

The School and the Schedule

Longfellow is a 7–12 regional school that brings students from several small towns together for their secondary education under one roof. Heavily financed by the state, the school is organized into a middle school, grades 7–8, and a high school, grades 9–12. The middle school is divided into three teams—each with approximately 100 students, four core subject teachers and a special needs teacher. The teachers work together to plan some integrated themes for study during the year.

The teachers at Longfellow Middle School are working hard to exemplify a middle school model. They have created a project period each day where students can choose from a number of mini-courses offered by the faculty. They have designed the courses based on their own interests as well as those of the students. Today, a special girls' program will take up project time and a special activity is planned for the boys to cover the period.

Phoebe moves through the day with the same core group of students, a part of her homeroom group. All of her classes except math are heterogeneous, with a wide-range of abilities evident. Phoebe's daily schedule changes some each day, but basically looks like this:

7:45	Homeroom
8:00	Transition
8:05	Special (Today: Physical Education)
8:45	Transition
8:50	Special (Today: Art)
9:30	Transition
9:35	Language Arts
10:15	Transition
10:20	Social Studies
11:00	Transition
11:05	Homeroom (Theme projects)
11:45	Transition
11:50	Lunch
12:15	Transition
12:20	Activity Period (Today: Special girls' assembly)
12:55	Transition
1:00	Science
1:40	Transition
1:45	Math
2:20	Getting ready for dismissal
2:30	Dismissal

7:45–8:00

On a sunny and warm Tuesday morning in April, I sit down with Phoebe in her homeroom. The principal has told the teachers I will be shadowing Phoebe today. I had asked if I could meet with Phoebe's parents and Phoebe to explain my book project before homeroom, but her parents told the principal that wasn't necessary and it was fine with them for me to be with Phoebe for the day.

> *It may just have been inconvenient for Phoebe's parents to meet on the day I visited, but it is typical that parent involvement at middle school is significantly less than at the elementary level. Some of that is the distancing dance of teenagers who don't want their parents at school. Some of it is parents needing help from the school to know ways to be appropriately and significantly involved in their children's education. A parents' night about middle school expectations at the beginning of the year, a letter home on a regular basis, or a welcoming phone call from a teacher often helps.*

In any case, Phoebe seems to know what is going on when I introduce myself and sit down at an empty seat at her table of six in homeroom. Phoebe is twelve. She will turn thirteen early this summer. She wears one of the badges of adolescence: a full set of braces. Her build is slight and her reddish hair is in a ponytail. She talks with her hands when she is excited.

The homeroom teacher, Mrs. Collins, is collecting money for a museum field trip they are taking at the end of the week. While she is talking, so are the kids at Phoebe's table.

"So, you like playing 'flinch'?" Manny challenges Phoebe from across the table, perhaps for my benefit.

After I tell Phoebe that she should be thinking through the day about the pseudonym she would like me to use for her, Brian quips, "Name yourself Rachel." Her friend Rachel smiles at the end of the table.

"Or maybe Butch," shoots out Manny with a barbed look and mean tone. She takes the name Phoebe.

"How many of you have two journal entries so far?" asks Mrs. Collins.

> *Homeroom serves as an entry point and social check-in, a place for attendance, lunch tally, announcements, and academic catch-ups such as journal entries.*

"What's a journal entry?" Stacey, a girl at their table, wants to know, asking no one in particular. Phoebe has her project log open on the table. Mrs. Collins asks a student to turn on "Channel One," the commercial, in-school media baby-sitter in thousands of middle school homerooms across the country.

> *Schools receive free classroom television monitors in exchange for an agreement to broadcast the "news" each morning to students. The news is full of interesting topics at the middle school level and two to three minutes of commercials. In most of the middle school classrooms where I have seen Channel One, it benignly serves as background noise as students do what students typically do in homeroom, rather than serving to tune them into the academic purpose in the day ahead.*

This morning, homeroom is pretty quiet. Some students, including Phoebe, are watching the monitor. Others are writing in their journals. The show on Channel One is about imported automobiles. Mrs. Collins asks how many of the student's parents have cars that were made in another country.

"I have no clue," Phoebe says under her breath. She intones the last two words slowly and distinctly.

"We don't have no Jap car," snarls Max. No one at the table responds to the racial slur. The teacher didn't hear it.

Mrs. Collins gets the monitor turned off and announces that the girls have a special program in the auditorium at 12:20 today. The boys will go to Mr. Christopher's room. Question marks appear on the foreheads of boys and girls alike.

8:00–8:05

There is no time for questions about the day's change in schedule.

The school's electronic tone chimes. Students scurry in all directions in the halls. I follow Phoebe and one other girl down two flights of stairs. It is time for gym class. The girls tell me to meet them outside on the playing fields and disappear into the girls' locker room.

8:10–8:45

It is a beautiful day for April, warm enough for shorts and T-shirts which soon appear on the gangly bodies emerging from the locker rooms. Laughing and pushing their way to the edge of the grass, this group reacquaints itself in the time it takes to get to the place where their physical education teacher waits for them.

> *This is not Phoebe's homeroom class. She knows all the kids in each class, but she doesn't travel with the same group all day.*
>
> *Today this group will work on lacrosse fundamentals for the next half-hour, though it's a forty-minute period. The locker room and travel time takes up the other ten minutes. Their teacher, Mr. Merrill, is the girls' softball coach. Some of these seventh-graders are trying out for the middle school team. This is a relatively small 7–12 school and middle schoolers will be watched carefully for varsity potential.*
>
> *As the period gets under way, Phoebe teams up with some-one she seems to know well to practice the lacrosse moves Mr. Merrill is teaching. He makes each move into a game . . . "three misses and you're out" . . . "the first team with ten catches, wins."*

Phoebe and her partner are trying, but the plastic lacrosse sticks, the sun in their eyes, and the new skills all conspire to make for a frustrating go of it. On the outside, this doesn't bother the girls at all. They laugh and cavort, keep count and forget, pick up the ball with their hands instead of the cradle, apologize constantly to each other for bad throws and missed catches.

"The sun is killing my eyes," says Phoebe.

"I'm sorry, I can't throw. Is that eight or nine?" her partner answers.

Calm on the outside, what are they feeling on the inside?

Mr. Merrill is encouraging, and business-like in his approach to the class. He changes drills often, keeping most of the kids engaged. Of the twenty kids in the class only a small group of four boys seem intent on avoiding as much physical exercise or cooperation as possible. Mr. Merrill basically ignores them and concentrates on the kids giving the drills a try.

> *The class is skill oriented, appropriately challenging, well-run, and efficient. The other kids ignore the non-participants as well, and it doesn't matter that they are invisible because there is no sense of community, only cliques connecting playfully at various points during class.*
>
> *The middle school schedule and organization of the day conspires against any sense of group identity during this time. Adolescence is the time when children search out a sense of identity and a sense of belonging. The structure and use of time in middle schools either promotes and fosters this deep need or corrodes it.*

8:40–8:50

At the end of a half-hour, Mr. Merrill has a few kids collect the equipment, their signal to head for the locker rooms. On the way back, Phoebe leapfrogs two waist-high, concrete road barriers. "Do you guys know what we're doing for art?" she asks, catching up with two other girls.

"Clay," says one of them.

"A play?" asks Phoebe incredulously.

"Clay!" chorus the two girls.

"Oh, I thought LA (language arts) or something," says' Phoebe sheepishly, as the girls disappear into the locker room.

> *"What are we doing for …?" Or "what are we doing in …?"*
> *is a familiar question in school. If we examine it closely we see*
> *some of the assumptions students make almost subconsciously*
> *about learning. They will be participants—"doing" some-*
> *thing—but passive recipients of the activity that will be*
> *determined by their teachers. The planning is left to the adults.*
>
> *Yet teachers complain that some of the things students have*
> *the most trouble with are planning their assignments, budgeting*
> *their time, completing their projects. A balance of teacher-directed*
> *instruction and student-initiated learning is critical to the devel-*
> *opment of capable students. "What am I doing in art today?"*
> *or "What do we need to be doing on our science project today?"*
> *are the kinds of questions that help students gain meaning from*
> *their schoolwork.*
>
> *Too often, "What are we doing in math?" can eventually*
> *lead to "What am I doing in school?"*

8:50–9:30

> *There are five minutes for transition between classes and Mr.*
> *Merrill allowed five minutes at the end of class for transition into*
> *the locker room, but still . . .*

It's a race from the girls' locker room to the art room in the far reaches of the third floor for next period. Phoebe and three classmates enter breathless.

"Girls, you're a *little* late, how come?"

"We were in gym," they reply in unison.

"Please get your portfolios," instructs the art teacher.

> *No one is to blame for the tone at the beginning of this class for*
> *Phoebe and friends. They did not spend excessive time getting*
> *to where they needed to be. The physical education teacher gave*

them five minutes to get changed, the school gave them five min-
utes to make it to where they were going, and still they were late.
    We might be quick to blame the girls, as is the art teacher,
but these are conscientious students with no need or desire to
break the rules or delay to avoid art. The system just doesn't
work the same for everyone all the time. Students in classes close
by the art room got there in plenty of time. For Phoebe and
friends, that was impossible.

Phoebe gets her portfolio from a stack on a back table and begins
to check through it. She is quietly blowing small bubble gum bubbles through her braces. She checks the watch on her left arm.

The art teacher is just returning from a long illness and she
entreats the class to help her with their self-control and cooperation.
She gives several precise instructions about the use and abuse of clay.
She then explains their assignment: to construct a container from
clay, using their imaginations.

"Did we draw figures in here?" she asks.

The "in here" is short hand for "I can't remember if I taught
this to this particular class or not." It is part of the middle school
lexicon. The art teacher will see hundreds of children and hun-
dreds of clay containers over the course of the next few weeks. It
is the way most schools organize the time of the gifted teachers
of art, music, and physical education in their midst. Every child
will get the same exposure to clay containers. This translates into
mass production and limited time for instruction, guidance, con-
versation, nuance.
    The structure traps the art teacher and the students. It is
a rare middle school which has a radically different schedule,
smaller teams, art studios with longer blocks of time, modified
curriculum standards, and a dedication to the construction of
meaning in teaching and learning. Changes in both institutional
schedules and organization and in teaching techniques can

*allow deeper explorations of creativity as well as a deeper con-
nection to the school and the educational process.*

*The construction of clay containers strikes me as a fitting
metaphor for the struggles of middle school education. The art
teacher wants creative clay containers utilizing her students' rich
imaginations. The time allotted guarantees that the containers
produced can only be creative in a limited way, can push the
boundaries only so far. Most containers will bear a striking
resemblance to each other, some modeled after the teacher's, some
modeled after a friend's. A few will be brilliantly unique; some
will crumble and never be finished.*

Mrs. Baldwin, the art teacher, spends the first ten minutes of class
on clay instructions. They will have two or three periods to finish
their clay containers.

*How many adult artists would put down a pot in the middle of
the creative process because that's the best way to create it? It makes
more sense to block schedule classes which involve the work and
persistence required for a creative process. It's one way to model
the skill of perseverance that is generally acknowledged as lacking in students, particularly in adolescence. And think of the
valuable time wasted in getting out the clay and putting it away
each period, as well as the inevitable disasters of dried out bags,
mislabeled or unlabeled work when students next return to art.*

Phoebe has a question. "Are the different color clays different
textures? Is one easier to use than the other, Ms. Baldwin?"

"Good question. The biggest difference is the amount of water,"
Ms. Baldwin responds, with a partial answer.

Phoebe is sitting at a table with two of her friends from gym. One
of them, Amy, was her partner for lacrosse. I notice that Phoebe now
has her hair down, no longer in a ponytail. She must have fixed it in
the locker room after gym. Phoebe is taking her time getting her clay.

Is she still wanting an answer to the other half of her question?

"Just take a big piece," Amy says to Phoebe, who is now across the room digging her clay out of the container. Phoebe returns and sizes up her ball of clay next to Amy's.

"Leave yourself five minutes," says Mrs. Baldwin, "We'll be working for several weeks with this clay," she remarks as if to justify the fact that only twenty-five minutes of the forty minute period are actually spent with the clay today. "Don't forget about how to put things away," she continues. "If your name isn't easily visible on your plastic bag, then I'll put your clay back in the bucket. I will grade you on set up and clean up. I think I've said everything I need to. Your project should look like something you would buy. At this stage of your development in seventh grade, this is what I expect."

"Phoebe, you two, you're not working on your tray, O.K.?" Mrs. Baldwin instructs with one of those questions meant as a command. Phoebe continues to work on the tabletop. Her ball of clay is becoming a cylinder. Mrs. Baldwin has moved on to someone else in the class who needs her attention. Phoebe gets some sculpting tools and cleans them off. Amy asks her, "How did you make it round?"

Phoebe answers, "Manuel got suspended. George got kicked out. I don't care, George is a royal pain in the behind."

"Jason, you're sad!" she exclaims, engaging the attention of a boy across the table without missing a beat, while all the time working carefully and methodically on her clay cylinder on the table top.

Suddenly, she glances across the table at Jason's clay cylinder. "That's a good idea, maybe I'll copy you," she says grinning. Mrs. Baldwin looks over her shoulder at Phoebe's work but doesn't say anything. Phoebe turns to helping Amy with her cylinder-shaping, then returns to her own work.

The artists are digging into their work, teaching each other, stretching each other's thinking as they stretch and mold the clay.

Suddenly, Mrs. Baldwin's voice says, "Look at the clock. You have three or four minutes to work before it will be time to clean up."

> *This time reminder immediately disengages some students from their learning, while others keep working. No two children respond to the requirements of an imposed time schedule quite the same way, though we act in school as though they should.*

Some kids start cleaning up right away. Phoebe has hollowed out about half of her cylinder. She turns it gently in her left hand and scoops some more clay out with the tool in her right. Then she cleans up the scraps, walks over and tosses them into the bucket. She continues around the room to the teacher's desk to get some masking tape to properly label the plastic bag that will hold her cylinder for consecutive weeks. Surreptitiously, she takes a peek at her art grades in the grade book lying open on the teacher's desk. Then she retrieves a wet paper towel, wraps her clay, puts it in her plastic bag complete with name label.

"Where's the stuff? What stuff are we supposed to put this with? Mrs. B., we're supposed to put it here, right?"

"No, Phoebe, over there."

Phoebe puts two plastic bags, hers and Amy's, on the proper shelf and goes to wash her hands. She is the last one finished in the class.

"Remember," says Mrs. Baldwin, "I dismiss by tables."

Phoebe sits down quickly. Her table is dismissed as soon as she is sitting.

9:30–9:35

The hall is crowded. Phoebe gets something out of her locker and grabs a couple of friends heading down the hall. "Are we going to LA (language arts)?" she asks rhetorically.

> *Some students are talking at their lockers; some are grabbing a bite to eat from backpacks. Others are copying down assignments*

or writing notes in notebooks as they scrunch down in front of their lockers. Five minutes of time they control. Thank goodness the school provides this time to breathe and think.

9:35–10:15

Phoebe arrives at language arts just before the tone chimes the start of the next period and sits with her friends in one section of desks in the big horseshoe configuration the teacher uses in this class.

Mrs. Schaefer is explaining their science writing project, another teaming effort by the teachers. Language arts class is writing reports about their weather project in science. Mrs. Schaefer goes over the assignment. Her voice is calm and reasoned, like all of the voices of all the teachers Phoebe has encountered thus far today. Phoebe has her assignment book out and is dutifully recording the assignment from the board. She is to have three questions written to ask the guest meteorologist from the local TV station who is coming in next week. While she is writing with her right hand, Phoebe has her left hand up to answer a question Mrs. Schaefer has asked the class. Other students are called on and Phoebe eventually drops her hand.

> *Watching Phoebe's arm get tired, her other arm eventually reaching over to prop up the raised hand, and finally watching the arm come down, I am reminded of a visit I made to another middle school some years ago where I shadowed an eighth grade boy through his morning classes in a large, urban school. The classes were larger than Phoebe's, but the schedule was similar. The student I shadowed was clearly seen as a leader in eighth grade. He had his hand up in each of four classes I sat in with him. He spoke one sentence during that time.*
>
> *Phoebe's classes are not huge, averaging slightly over twenty students, but participation for her is not much better than it was for the urban eighth-grader. The limited time given to each content area necessarily limits the possibilities for participation by even the most vocal and engaged students. It also limits the*

engagement of the teacher, making her more of a time manager than a Socratic mentor.

For the marginal student, short instructional periods often provide easy places to hide from participation. There's not even enough time for the teacher to notice silence or complacency because she is busy getting through the material, covering the curriculum and remembering if she has already taught a particular concept "in here."

The teacher enlists a student to pass out the books. They are reading *Les Miserables*. Phoebe, without raising her hand asks, "Do we *have* to ask him our questions?" still referring to the meteorologist.

"No," says Mrs. Schaefer, "but we encourage you, you know that, Phoebe."

Everyone now has a part. Phoebe is Madame Magloire. "I remember in this class we were in the middle of the fight scene," Mrs. Schaefer reminds herself as much as anyone else. Several other of her classes, of course, are reading the same play. Phoebe, whose part in the play is a small one, volunteers to read the introduction. She reads quickly, her leg swinging, both feet moving.

Les Miserables swings around the classroom from one student to the other as they read their parts. A student is serving as director, reminding others when they forget their turn or are off track. Mrs. Schaefer shows respect for the students' engagement with the words and the plot, stopping only infrequently to ask a focusing question. The kids seem pleased by the lively pace of the repartee. Mrs. Schaefer stops the action at a suspenseful moment. The students gather their belongings. The period has passed quickly.

Time flies when you're having fun. Mrs. Schaeffer engaged most of the students during this fast-paced, lively lesson. Most of them kept their eyes and minds on the script, so as not to be caught unprepared with their lines. The technique worked within the allotted time, but there was no room for reflection, for stopping to discuss a salient moment, a character's feeling, an analogy. The teacher is doing the best she can in the time she has.

Compare this experience to what the lucky few who are cast in the spring school play will remember. They will have hours of repetition, reading for understanding, thinking about how a tone of voice might change the meaning of a line. Think of their memory of the passion of a teacher for a particular playwright, a particular moral theme, a point of view. Think of the depth of learning and the depth of a relationship created over time. Why should this experience be relegated to only a few?

10:20—11:00

The next period is the same length as language arts but it seems to take twice as long. In this class the teacher does most of the talking.

Phoebe walks in with Amy and Rachel. I'm beginning to see that they are inseparable. They sit at the window side of the class, away from the door. The desks are also arranged in a horseshoe with the teacher's desk in the traditional placement at the front of the class. Phoebe engages Mrs. Barcum in a conversation as the class waits for the other half of the class to arrive from physical education. They are late, just as Phoebe and her friends were after first period.

Phoebe's conversation starts about tennis, clearly important and engaging to Mrs. Barcum. Then it moves on to a discussion about a student who drank too much over the weekend and was taken by ambulance to the hospital.

Mrs. Barcum is someone Phoebe feels comfortable talking to. She is friendly, involved in the lives of her students, knows what they like, what they do outside of class. Once class begins, however, she takes on a different persona. When she "gets down to business," she is one step removed from her casual, friendly engagement.

She reviews the War of 1812, the Monroe Doctrine, the Louisiana Purchase, Lewis and Clark. She asks questions. Few students risk responses. There are some furtive glances across the room.

> *Is it uncool to answer? I remember that this class combined students from different sections. There is some social dynamic I can't quite pick up and I can't decide whether it's among the students or between Mrs. Barcum and her students.*
>
> *In either case, the social context of learning in this particular class is thwarting the desired academic engagement. In similar situations, I have seen students hesitate because they think there is a particular answer the teacher is looking for. In others, students wait because they know the teacher is going to give the answer anyway.*

Mrs. Barcum answers a number of her own questions, before a student asks one of her.

"Why did Napoleon sell it?" a boy ventures, referring to the Louisiana Purchase. Mrs. Barcum answers something about Napoleon losing interest in the New World.

> *Unfortunately, her students are losing interest in the New World, too.*

Phoebe is putting on lip balm, her notebook closed. No one has pencil and paper out or a book open. Some have their heads down on their notebooks. Some are engaged in side conversations.

"Would you please stop talking while I interrupt," Mrs. Barcum says, smiling at a group in the back left corner of the room. Phoebe starts a game with her pen cap. Rachel opens and closes her notebook. They both yawn and start playing with each other's notebooks, then each other's fingers. Mrs. Barcum is now reading excerpts from Lewis and Clark journals and does not notice. They stop and put their heads down on their notebooks. On the other side of the class, Susan, a tall gangly girl with a nose ring asks a question with some passion.

"But what about the women, did they come back with Lewis and Clark?"

"Anybody want to respond to Susan? Excuse me!" Mrs. Barcum exclaims, trying to get attention. Jackets slide on, bodies slide to the edge of chairs. The electronic tone chimes. "Don't leave yet, you don't have your homework," says Mrs. Barcum.

"Oh, I'm so hungry," moans Phoebe.

> *Susan's question is dismissed by Mrs. Barcum's response to her question with another question, rather than acknowledging the depth of her inquiry. The class is dismissed without their homework. Phoebe temporarily dismisses her hunger and heads for homeroom.*

11:05–11:45

Back in homeroom, Manny takes up where he left off.

"So, Phoebe, like playing 'flinch'?" his voice rises while he punches the air in front of her face.

> *The epidemic of domestic violence in our society spreads from abusive homes to institutions of benign neglect. Mean boys often grow into abusive husbands and fathers. No one is stopping Manny. Unfortunately, Phoebe has adopted the cultural norm that silence is safer than confrontation.*

Mrs. Collins asks the class to get out their career booklets and simultaneously moves two boys from Phoebe's table to separate tables away from each other. Susan, of Lewis and Clark fame, takes one of the seats vacated by one of the boys. "Wazup?" she asks Phoebe.

"I'm so hungry!" moans Phoebe.

> *Lunch is next period, forty minutes away. Phoebe has not had a snack, a drink of water, or gone to the girls' room, except for her time in the locker room before and after phys. ed.*

Now there are career projects. Mrs. Collins explains report requirements. "I was wondering if I could meet with Ms. Tobin because I'm doing teaching," Phoebe asks Mrs. Collins who is moving across the room to talk to another student. There is no response. She may not have heard Phoebe. Phoebe thumbs through her career booklet. She intends to interview her teacher from last year, the one she wants to be like, the one who was "the best ever." She thumbs through the book some more. "Are we supposed to be working?" she says to the air. She opens her career booklet to a specific page, picks up her pencil and begins filling out her career project research notes. "Are we just working on this?" she says to herself, checking in again.

Her hunger is getting the best of her.

She gets up and throws away a piece of paper, comes back to the table, thumbs through her book again and eventually begins to write a letter. Just as she gets settled in to this task, a boy across the table starts in.

"This project stinks!"

"I know, " says Phoebe, "I have so much to do. And they give you this science project to do!"

"I know, they give it all at *once!*" says the boy through clenched teeth.

"And I have *softball,*" mirrors Phoebe through her braces, getting into it, *"every day during vacation!"*

> *In some way, Phoebe seems to be getting a kind of perverse pleasure in complaining about all the things she has to do. She enjoys commiserating with her tablemate about them. It seems to me she may be simply responding to the over-arching message of the adults around her and around most teenagers today: staying busy, even when it stresses you out, gives meaning to your life!*
>
> *As Richard DeGrandpre notes in* Ritalin Nation, *"It's*

not just that we and our children are more hurried; we also feel more hurried. This feeling should be taken as a warning that we have fallen into attitudes and habits toward living that are not in fact leading to the promised land, for neither ourselves nor our children." [3]

Giving children more homework than they can handle is one of those habits. It is not Phoebe's fault that she has so much homework, softball, and more other things to do than are reasonable for a twelve-year-old adolescent. The fault is that the adults see this as normal and appropriate.

"I'm just going to go for a B on this," says the boy.

"I've got to work on this letter to the guidance counselor," responds Phoebe as if thinking about what a B would mean to her. "If you interview someone you'll get credit for it," she suggests to the boy across the table and settles into the task in front of her. More than half the period is over.

Mrs. Collins comes by and suggests to Phoebe that she show me a project she recently completed on the hurricane of 1938 that devastated her hometown. She gets up and gets a large poster board display down from the top of some cabinets where it is stored. She seems proud as she shows me her work. "I chose this because my grandfather lived through it and is always telling me about it," she says quietly. "He had pictures and stories." Phoebe's report is neatly mounted and displayed with factual captions. After she returns her display to the top of the cabinet, she returns to her table with some new energy. She gives some ideas to her tablemate—the one working for a B.

As Mrs. Collins is her teacher and as her grandfather has been her teacher, so Phoebe knows how to be one for the B Boy. Barbara Rogoff notes that "The structure of problems that humans attempt to solve, the knowledge base that provides resources, and the strategies for solutions that are considered more or less effective or sophisticated are situated in a social matrix of purposes and values."[4] *This is why children need to learn in schools that value and maximize productive social interaction.*

The B Boy is trying to create a careers project on the FBI. He doesn't seem to know where to start, but Phoebe does. "You could draw a magnifying glass and have clues around it and stuff like that," she suggests, her voice rising at the end.

After a few moments, the teacher in Phoebe makes another suggestion: maybe he could interview someone on the Police Department.

The boy shrugs and doodles with his pencil in his careers packet. Phoebe finishes her letter. It is to Ms. Tobin, the middle school's guidance counselor, not to last year's teacher. She tears the letter out of her notebook, retrieves a pair of scissors and trims the margin confetti, all the while following Mrs. Collins around the room. Mrs. Collins checks her letter and gives her a hall pass to deliver the letter to Ms. Tobin. The letter to the guidance counselor is designed to get her school time to interview her last year's teacher for the project.

I wonder why she won't just pick up the phone at home and call last year's teacher? Or ask permission to use the phone in school to call the elementary school at lunchtime? Or write her a letter directly? My hunch is that Phoebe has made a connection with Ms. Tobin close to the one she had with last year's teacher. She may see her as an ally.

Phoebe also clearly knows all the rules of middle school three-quarters of the way through her seventh grade year, the written ones and the unwritten ones. The hall pass to Ms. Tobin is an acceptable ticket of independence and responsibility, acceptable to both teachers and peers. I wonder when in her schedule Phoebe will see Ms. Tobin. It won't happen today.

Phoebe's shifts from attention to inattention to involvement with her tablemate during this period illustrate the energy tugs and pulls at the end of a long morning. Phoebe's attention wanes when she is trying to concentrate by herself but picks up when urged to share about her project or when helping her table-mate think about his project, or when provided with a change of scenery through the delivery of her note to Ms. Tobin. Social engagement is valuable currency for learning.

11:45–12:15

Lunch. Lines lead quickly to trays of hot food. Phoebe had signed up for soup and sandwich in homeroom, but takes a full hot lunch. It doesn't seem to matter and when I ask, that's just what she tells me. Phoebe and friends—Amy and Rachel—are joined at one end of a long lunch table by a fourth girl I hadn't noticed in any of the morning classes. Phyllis is a petite bundle of energy; witty, fun, and trying desperately to shoehorn her way into the threesome that travels together most of the day.

"They don't even tell you what it's about," she says with exasperation, waving her hands and rolling her eyes. "I mean, 'Girls and Their Voices?' What's that supposed to mean?" The four of them wonder aloud about the special assembly happening just for the girls after lunch.

At the next table an aluminum missile is launched, its trajectory arching in a direct path over three tables across the cafeteria. I had heard a teacher previously remind boys at this table that they would lose their cafeteria privileges for a week if caught throwing things. The teacher is now at the other end of the cafeteria where the missile has landed, but he has his back turned to the launch site.

The girls seem unaware or unconcerned about the boy action at the next table. "Who do you really not like—for a girl?" Phyllis starts a new line of conversation.

"Well, Phyl," Amy starts, rolling her eyes and flipping her shoulder length blonde hair, "there's you ... just kidding," she says in the same breath.

The constant shifting of seventh grade—outside/inside, inside/outside.

I ask if they always sit at this particular table at lunch. "Yeah, usually," Phoebe answers, "all the Eastside kids sit down there," she says, pointing to the other end of the cafeteria.

Although kids from different towns and neighborhoods are mixed on their teams, they often self-segregate in the cafeteria as middle schoolers, by town and sex. It is rare for a middle school to see the cafeteria as a classroom, but lunch can be taught as intentionally as careers. For example, during this unit on careers, there could be "business dining tables" set up for those who would like to invite a business person from the community for a lunch-time interview. At the beginning of the school year, rotating lunch table assignments for the first few weeks might allow some students to get to know each other who might not otherwise.

By high school, sex and town have disappeared as clear markers for where you sit, but other measures emerge—jocks, geeks, druggies, hippies, wanna-be's. Right now, in seventh grade, it's a bit simpler, but it's all beginning.

"You have new sneakers," Amy says to Phyl; not "radical" or "phat" new sneakers, just matter-of-fact "new" sneakers. The remark does not go unnoticed. Phoebe starts putting new rubber bands on her braces and glares at Amy. Phyllis is looking down at her sneakers.

"How much longer do you have to wear yours?" Phyl says to Phoebe, changing the subject to braces, "Mine are supposed to come off next month." Phoebe doesn't answer, but picks up her tray and heads to the trash line, Phyllis, Amy, and Rachel trailing behind.

"Another year of braces," she says quietly to Phyllis as they dump their trays.

12:20–12:55

The auditorium is about half full, but with 150 seventh and eighth grade girls assigned to the center section, the room is certainly full of energy. Phoebe makes her way right to the front row. She decides, for the foursome still together since lunch, where they will sit. When the hall quiets, Mr. Fielder, the science teacher on the Ocean Team who has invited the guest speaker, introduces Miranda, a tall, self-assured high school senior from a nearby university town. Miranda is writing a book responding to Mary Pipher's best-selling book, *Reviving Ophelia*, which has made such an impact on adolescent girls and their parents in recent years.[5]

She is collecting writings from teenage girls, the many voices of Ophelia. She hopes some of the girls will write their stories and send them to her. She shares some stories about her own experiences growing up, talks a little about Ophelia, who she was, what her drowning means metaphorically. She asks what it's like for the girls here. It takes time for them to get started; the sharing is guarded, sparse, tense. Last year, the school had experimented with same sex classes for a while. She asks about that. Some girls volunteer that it was easier to learn, but others say, you're gonna have to live in the real world. Yeah, but the boys do get more attention from the teachers, say others. A lotta girls spend a lotta time impressing the boys, comment still a few more.

> *In small groups this discussion might have really gone some-where. In a large assembly, it is going nowhere. It reminds me of something Mary Pipher wrote in her book:*
>
> *"Junior highs often ignore what is happening to students as they are herded from one class to another. Between the ages of eleven and fourteen, students' issues are relationship issues, and their problems are personal and social. Academics take a backseat to urgent developmental concerns. Schools could foster groupings organized around talents, interests, and needs, rather than cliques.*

They could offer students the clarity they need—supervised activities in which adolescents work and relax together, conflict-resolution training and classes in which guidelines for chemical use and sexual decisions are discussed. They could take responsibility for helping adolescents structure all the social and emotional turmoil they are experiencing."[6]

Mr. Fielder's heart is in the right place. As a young teacher he is bringing relevant issues to the school. What the school now chooses to do with these issues is the next step. I hope there is follow-up: a writing teacher who encourages the girls to submit their stories to Miranda; a discussion with the boys in one or two homerooms tomorrow; student council taking up the difference between teasing and the type of harassment that Manny is using.

Mary Pipher is right. The school can take responsibility and create meaningful ways for students to appropriately address and explore the key issues of the middle school years: issues of identity, sexuality, life choices. The careers unit is a start. Through literature, writing, science, and social studies, but most importantly, through well-facilitated discussion, the content curriculum can be made respectful, relational, and relevant for the young adolescent.

1:00–1:40

Outside science, Phoebe and friends are confronted by a group of boys piling into the doorway. "What did you guys talk about?" one of them asks with genuine interest.

"Adolescence," they chorus in unison, rolling their eyes.

Mr. Fielder does not mention the assembly the girls just came from even though he was the teacher who arranged it. Now it's time for science. So much for follow-up, at least right now.

The class will be going to the library today to do some research on their weather projects. He asks the class to get into their "production groups." Each group is responsible for a video production of a weather show highlighting local weather conditions. He reviews production requirements with them. Phoebe checks herself out in a cracked mirror hanging by the sink as she waits in line to go downstairs. The class finally gets to the library about 1:25 after some detailed instructions about what should happen once they get there, the instructions about the weather videos, and some lengthy lining up time.

> *In the end, most of the period is taken up with transitions of one kind or another: into the science room, into production groups, into line and down to the library, finding a spot for individual production groups in the library, scoping the library for appropriate resources, lining up, dismissal to the next class.*

"I've got a table for us," says Phyllis, who is on the production team with Amy, Rachel, and Phoebe, an inseparable trio.

Phoebe goes to retrieve an encyclopedia, whacking a boy waiting beside the reference shelf. It's unclear what the whack was in retaliation for, if anything.

"You guys are too slow," the boy says in an effort to defend himself.

"I'm not too slow," she says, sucking her teeth.

"Of course she isn't!" says Amy, jokingly coming to her defense.

"Let me check in with this team," says Mr. Fielder, who is roaming the expansive library, "What's your report, Phoebe?"

"Snow and snowflakes," Amy answers.

"What are you looking up?" he asks, noticing they have the "T" encyclopedia.

"Whoops," whispers Phoebe and heads off looking for the "SN," back by the shelf with the distracting boy waiting to be whacked again. Returning quickly, with one eye on Mr. Fielder, she speaks to Rachel as if picking up in the middle of a conversation that might have happened the last time they were in science. "Or maybe we could have the camera already set up . . . I'd probably drop it if

I held it," she concludes, quickly changing the subject.

"Well, Phyl, I hope it doesn't *rain*," she intones, as if the rain could be so impudent as to spoil her opening softball game. She drags Phyllis over to the encyclopedias again, then returns to the group's table.

"Should we get together and work on this?" Phyllis asks hopefully.

"No, we have the car wash on Saturday," Phoebe explains.

"When I call, *you always turn me down*," Phyllis says forcefully. Turning to Amy she asks, "Amy do *you* get turned down, too?"

"No comment," Amy answers tactfully.

"It's just my Mom, she always says be nice so I say, like 'I'm so tired'," Phoebe responds truthfully.

"So from now on I can ask, 'Is that a valid excuse?'" Phyllis wants to know.

Phoebe doesn't say and instead turns her attention to the encyclopedia and their project outline. The rest of the girls follow suit. Phyllis makes up the newspaper weather report out loud and then goes to check with Mr. Fielder to see if they are on the right track. The boy on the team is nowhere to be seen.

"If you keep saying that to me, Phyl, I'll strangle you," Phoebe threatens, trying to get Phyllis to back off from her desire to get the group together to work on the project outside of school.

"No you wouldn't; only I can strangle you."

"That's right! You smacked me! I couldn't believe you did that!" exclaims Phoebe in mock astonishment.

"It's not like I did you bodily injury," Phyllis retorts.

"Do you think it's going to rain?" Phoebe asks, back in the softball mode.

A school library can be a valuable resource, a place to model and teach effective research practices, but today, for Phoebe's team, it is a site for action research about friendship and social negotiation. This is not an unusual picture in any middle school. To keep young adolescents focused on the business of academics requires much more than reform rhetoric and strict state standards. It requires teamwork and planning by the adults, the same kind of teamwork Mr. Fielder is trying to engender in his students.

Yet there aren't any signs of it in the library today. Everyone is separate—the librarian is working at her desk, some high school seniors are working at a nearby table, and another teacher is searching the shelves for a book. Team teaching can be the most powerful expression of "teaming" in middle school. The high schoolers in the same building with middle school students might be enlisted in peer or cross-grade tutoring as both community service and a powerful learning experience.

1:45–2:30

Last period. Math. Phyllis is sitting next to Phoebe and there are two other girls at their table. It's Mrs. Collins again, their homeroom teacher whom they've seen twice previously today. Now she is the math teacher. Her students are studying the results of a survey they took to determine what career might be right for them.

The career theme is potentially deeply engaging for students at this age. It allows them to think, write, research, and report on a subject that is not too distant on the horizon or in history, yet it can be related to both. Their young adult sense of diachronic time makes looking at careers in the past, present, and future a meaningful exploration. I hope the school will be full of adults from a variety of careers in the weeks to come and that Phoebe will visit her sixth grade teacher soon.

"That stuff always happens to me!" exclaims Phoebe glumly. "I wanted to be a teacher and on the test it says I'm going to be a farmer. I like *frogs* and I have some at home," she jokes.

"I live on a farm," says one of the other girls at the table.

"Remember when we made fences for the play," Phyllis interjects, ignoring the other girl's comment.

"Yeah, in fourth grade!" Phoebe responds. "Doesn't your earring hurt?" she says turning to face the girl who told her she lived on a farm. "What happened to your face?"

"I got hit in softball with a line drive," she tells Phoebe.

"Did it hurt?" Phoebe asks, perhaps now thinking a little differently about her own upcoming softball game. She pops a piece of gum into her mouth and takes some rubber bands off her braces. The conversation suddenly turns, without an apparent connection, to the subject of chanting monks and how chanting can change the shape of the roof of your mouth.

I wonder if the preoccupation with braces may have inspired what seems a non-sequitur.

"Mrs. Collins, do you have any more copies of the survey?" Phoebe wants to know. She wants a second chance at being labeled a future teacher rather than a frog farmer. Mrs. Collins helps her look over the survey and tells her she could take it again tomorrow.

The kids now have a math sheet to do. It is 2:20. Ten minutes to go. Phoebe yawns and pushes Phyllis. "Get your butt out of my face," she laughs. "Have you ever had Mr. Mastrioni? He has a really small nose and he says, 'Now *listen,* people . . .,'" and she laughs again.

Mrs. Collins is asking the class about negative numbers. Phoebe and Phyllis are punching each other on the arm. Phoebe is digging in her backpack.

"Phyllis, what do you think?" asks Mrs. Collins, redirecting the punching match.

"What was the question?" Phyllis says, raising her eyes to Mrs. Collins without raising her head while trying to get in the last punch on Phoebe.

"Is zero a positive or a negative?" Mrs. Collins repeats.

The tone chimes dismissal. Saved by the tone. It's 2:30 and soft-ball is next.

> *Every teacher today has taught right up to the last minute of class. Perhaps this is considered "time on task" or "covering the curriculum," but there is little sense of closure in any class and no opportunity taken for review or reflection. I miss the questions I value most: What worked? What could we do better tomorrow? What do you need to focus on in the library tomorrow? Who's going out for softball? Did Mrs. Barcum give homework today?*

Phoebe heads for the hall, opens her locker and takes out her glove.

As I finish my day in seventh grade, I thank Phoebe for letting me follow her around all day and acknowledge that it couldn't have been easy. "Sure," she says, "it was OK."

I catch up to Mr. Fielder in the hallway. He is heading to a grad-uate class at the university and apologizes for rushing out. He expresses interest in my observations.

> *What will I tell him? He and some of the other teachers and the principal of Longfellow are interested in continuing to add mid-dle school reform approaches to the structure and schedule of their school. I know Mr. Fielder, the principal, and the other teach-ers want the best for these kids and that they want their school to work the best way possible. I hope my reflections will be help-ful in their discussions and planning for the future.*

The Structure and Use of Time

The total middle school day was six hours and forty-five minutes long. If we use the definition of core academics of the National Commission on Time and Learning (which includes art) the day for Phoebe and other students on her team at Longfellow looked like this:

CORE ACADEMICS *(art, language arts, social studies,* *theme projects: careers, science, math)*	240 minutes = 4 hrs.
SPECIALS *(physical education, girls' assembly)*	80 minutes = 1 hr. 20 mins.
TRANSITIONS	45 minutes
LUNCH	25 minutes
HOMEROOM	15 minutes

As you can see, time on core academics was well shy of the Commission's recommended 5.5 hours. During the four hours of core academic time, a good deal of that time was also spent in getting started at the beginning of the period and finishing up at the end of the period.

With this type of schedule, the time needed for transitions during the day equals more than a whole additional academic period. However, in this school, students really do need five minutes of time to move from class to class. (Many other schools provide almost no time for transitions, leaving students frantic.) It is a common dilemma posed by this type of schedule in many schools.

For teachers, the day was hectic, even though core subject teachers (other than art) at Longfellow have 80 minutes of common planning time with their teams (when students are scheduled for consecutive "specials"). This is much more time than teachers have at the elementary level and it represents one-fifth of the teaching hours during the day. It is important for teachers to have this time, but it must be used carefully and productively to improve individual classes and the entire school environment.

Phoebe moves through the day with the same core group of students, but only part of her whole homeroom group. All of her classes except math were heterogeneous, with a wide-range of abilities evident. This is another dilemma, since heterogeneous grouping is preferable for academic growth of all students but is fully dependent on well-managed, differentiated instruction within reasonable time frames. That type of environment wasn't generally what Phoebe experienced.

Assessing the Day

Clearly, time is more than a trivial problem for teachers. Shortage of time warps the course of innovation. It draws teachers away from their students. And it drains the energy of teachers themselves.

Andy Hargreaves, *Racing with the Clock*[7]

As I review Phoebe's day, I am struck by its superficiality. Shortage of time results in superficial teaching and learning. It prevents the development of meaningful teacher-student relationships. It minimizes investigation and exploration, and limits academic content to the shallow surface of knowledge and understanding. There is a significant shortage of time at Longfellow.

I watched Phoebe move through her day as if she was in a river being carried along by a strong current. The middle school day is hectic. She doesn't resist, but pushes obstacles out of her way (changing the subject of a conversation, checking in on assignments), and checks with other students for navigational cues ("Is LA next?" "What are we doing in art?"). She floated on the surface of a deep river of learning, unaware of the beauty, intricacy, and mystery below. Her social engagement was keen and sharp, her academic involvement nonchalant. As an outside observer, I saw time passing, but little learning taking place.

It's particularly hard for teachers in middle schools configured like Longfellow to see this because they are not immersed in the moving river with the children, although they are certainly affected by the speed of the current. They are at stationary docks, receiving different students each period, some of them twice, or in the case of Mrs. Collins, three times over. The children arrive and the teachers dispense assignments, measure progress toward project deadlines, send them downstream, and receive another batch.

They meet as faculty teams to review the progress of hundreds of students, develop new projects, coordinate due dates, and flag kids having difficulties, like barge masters scheduling the flow of river traffic. Due dates come and go; school marking periods punctuate the year like the seasons. Students complete their course of study by navigating the fast-flowing river, some more easily than others. Passage is completed downstream to eighth grade, to high school, to the open sea of graduation while the teachers remain stationary.

I hypothesize that Phoebe, on the outside, is mostly thinking about getting through her day, not floundering in the river. I think this means fitting in, having a niche, being comfortable, watching out for all the riffs and eddies and backwaters that come her way during the day: Manny in homeroom twice, getting stuff done on the careers project, the weather project, making sure to sit in the front row in assembly.

It takes considerable adolescent energy just to navigate on this level, to take care of business on the outside. On the inside, however, I wonder about the questions, the cold spots in the river. In a single day, there were constant and conflicting pressures and expressions of adolescent concern. There's a pony tail vs. hair down to her shoulders, braces, a leap over the concrete barriers in the parking lot, her project with her grandfather on the hurricane of 1938, wondering if she will ever really get to talk with her sixth grade teacher for the careers project and how that will happen, her struggle to deal with her friendships with Amy, Rachel, and Phyllis (especially Phyllis, whom she really likes, but is afraid to show it too much for fear of losing Amy or Rachel), wanting to do it all (softball, school, friends, family), to become someone, but who?

I believe that for many seventh-graders like Phoebe, time passes and too much happens, too much without someone really asking her to think harder or deeper. Too much happens without someone listening to her ideas, her questions, what's on her mind; too much happens without knowing why. The day's a blur. The next day it will happen again. That's the best these kids can do. This is the product and legacy of the busyness of school.

In Alan Lightman's *Einstein's Dream,* each chapter recounts a world where time is experienced differently.[8] In a world where time passes and little happens, (which I think is close to Phoebe's day), "a person who holds no ambitions, suffers unknowingly; a person who holds ambitions, suffers knowingly, but very slowly." I worry that school at Longfellow might be that kind of a world for Phoebe, a girl deciding about ambition. I'm sure it is for some students, some who have already given up their ambition, like the boy settling for a B.

What happens to a dream deferred?

Relationships are at the heart of learning. The relationships at Longfellow often appear distant, superficial, and fleeting. Time makes them so. No one wants them to be that way, but they are. Without more time devoted to the building of a learning community where dialogue and understanding, listening and reflection occur on a daily basis, academic accomplishment will also remain on the surface. The school may actually be able to meet state "time on learning" standards by some objective measure, but the quality of that time will finally be measured by both the performance of students on state assessments and by the lives lived by the students in the future.

Chapters 7–9 contain a wide variety of suggestions for changing how we structure time in schools and how we use it. All of these changes are intended to balance social and academic learning, and to provide the opportunities and atmosphere in schools which make students excited about learning and their involvement in a learning community. They are changes which make it possible that a seventh-grader, at a school like Longfellow, might consider her career project and say: "I'd like to be a middle school teacher, on a team just like this one."

One Possibility for Changing Middle Schools

There are many ways to change the structure of time, space, and the allocation of human resources in middle schools. Many prestigious groups and national experts in the middle school arena have clearly detailed how to do this and provided evidence of the advantages, both academic and social, of these changes.9 Despite this clear evidence, most middle schools remain mired in unproductive time structures. Something powerful is keeping time from changing and change from happening.

Here, I would like to add one proposal for institutional change to the national dialogue (along with those in Chs. 7–9). I've believed for thirty years that instead of exclusively moving students to different rooms and areas, moving teachers to the students some of the time would force a significant change in the quality of middle level education.

If core subject teachers moved some of the time, students and teachers would travel together through the day, carried by the current which is controlled by the schedule. Together, students and teachers would need to construct safe and comfortable places to stop and learn together. Teachers would move as often as the students. Students should move through the halls to the special areas like art rooms, gymnasiums and playing fields, science labs and orchestra pits, but the teachers of literature, mathematics, social studies, health, and other special subjects which don't require extensive equipment or materials should move to classrooms that are designed as true "home rooms" based on student's developmental needs for space, music, nutrition, quiet, and settling-in. Students would spend at least half of their school day in a comfortable, continuous spot.

This would alter the passage and quality of time for the educator and the student. It would slow and focus and improve time for the students by reducing transitions and providing a safe and comfortable home base. It would force educators to manage their own time more carefully: both those who moved to the students and those who had students moving to them. It would create a time balance and empathy between students and teachers since each group would experience time in a similar way for part of each day.

It is a change which requires considerable planning at the administrative level and full involvement by teachers dedicated to a middle school which meets students' developmental needs. But like all change that lasts, the result is worth the effort.

Chapter Five

On Your Mark, Get Set . . .
Seven Years Old in First Grade

NOT MANY BOYS are called mischievous these days. We call them athletes or label them ADD, computer wizs or ADHD, achievers or ODD (an acronym for "Oppositional Defiant Disorder"[1]).

Mark is mischievous. He is mischievous in the playful sense: smart, engaging, independent, and speedy. He is usually first in first grade: first finished, first cleaned up, first lined-up (behind the line leader of the day), first to help out someone who needs help. He is thoughtful of others and wondering about the world. He turned seven two months ago, in December.

His teacher, Mrs. Chambers, chose him when I asked for one of her students to follow through the day—someone who did not jump out in her mind right away, but who, as she thought about it, had learned the ways of first grade as she hoped. Yes, that was Mark.

On a previous day, Mark's mother came to school while the class was on its way to the library. I watched Mark spot her in the hall, carrying his new baby brother, only a few weeks old, bundled up and snuggled down in a comfy baby seat. She told me later how much Mark loved the baby, which was obvious when Mark came over from his place behind the line leader, hugged his Mom, kissed his baby brother, and skipped off to the library.

When we sat and talked, Mark's Mom told me he had been a happy baby, just like the one in her arms; that he had experienced loss and sadness in his family in his young life, but was still almost always happy. He was a joy to have around. She said he had been worried when he started first grade because he didn't know how to read and he thought all the other kids could. She had reassured him that lots of kids were learning to read in first grade.

She, her husband, and Mark were delighted that he now was reading everything in sight and zooming ahead in his schoolwork. She would be interested to read what Mark did in school, she said, because when she asked Mark, the answer was usually (you guessed it) "nothing." She had high praise for Mrs. Chambers and all the interesting things the children studied and was pleased that Mark was so excited to go off to school every day.

It was fun and enlightening to talk to Mark's mom before I observed him for a whole day. I had gotten a glimpse of him during two previous visits and his mother's assessment seemed right on. She was clearly proud, but not overly so. She impressed me as a quietly strong, confident person who knew her son well, trusted her son's teacher, felt comfortable in the school, and expected Mark would be a good student academically and socially.

The School and the Schedule

The school that Mark attends, Briarwood, is a sprawling urban school of eight hundred and fifty students in grades K–5. It has a diverse student population, both ethnically and economically. Several children in Mark's first grade class are just learning English. Half the class is on free or reduced lunch. Many are eligible for special education services, but in first grade, few have yet to receive them. The process for referral and assignment of services is slow and often backlogged.

There are twenty-four students in Mrs. Chambers' class this year. She feels fortunate. Last year she had twenty-eight and some years she has had more. The district limit is thirty before a new class is configured or an aide is placed in the classroom.

The research on class size and achievement is known by administrators in this district, but they are struggling with budgets as they try to keep up with mounting enrollment, building maintenance, special needs services, and a bond issue for the construction of a new high school.

Mrs. Chambers has been teaching at Briarwood for ten years. She is a graduate of the nearby state teacher's college and is currently working on her master's degree. She has a total of seventeen years in the classroom and, like many teachers, stayed at home for several years with her own children when they were small. I have known Mrs. Chambers for the past four years through the professional development work I have done in her school and district.

Many Briarwood teachers, as well as other teachers across the district, are utilizing *The Responsive Classroom* approach to teaching and classroom management. Mrs. Chambers has become a locally certified trainer in this approach and now is part of a team offering *Responsive Classroom* courses at the state college as an adjunct faculty member. She is a master teacher, and yet, like most "self-contained" elementary classroom teachers today, she struggles daily with the constraints of time, the demands of the curriculum, and the extraordinary needs of the children she teaches.

Mark's daily schedule is typical of the majority of elementary school students, not only in his community, but nationwide. There is a large block of time for language arts in the morning. The teacher has flexibility for how she fits in math, science, social studies, handwriting, and other curricular requirements. She must fit these around a schedule that daily has one or two "specials," such as art, music, physical education, library, etc. There is a mid-day recess and lunch period. At Briarwood, school starts quite early and children return home or move into after-school programming early in the afternoon. For Mrs. Chambers' class, the day is generally planned as follows:

7:45	Arrival
7:50	Morning meeting
8:20	Language Arts
10:00	Snack
10:20	Special—Art
11:10	Calendar/Math

11:20	Academic Choice
12:00	Lunch
12:30	Recess
1:00	Special—Book buddies
1:30	Closing Meeting
1:45	Dismissal

7:45–7:50

It's Thursday, two days before Valentine's Day, but that's not the first thing on Mark's mind. First, he takes down his chair from its custodian-friendly, upside-down spot on the table where he left it yesterday. He is the first child to hang up his coat in the closet. He comes out, gets a drink, slides on his knees to his backpack slung over his chair, takes out a pencil, zips the backpack closed, zips the backpack open, takes out his homework, walks across the room and puts his homework in the homework bin, and heads for the morning meeting chart, all in the space of two minutes.

> *I'm already exhausted and I'm going to follow Mark for the entire school day. He's just warming up.*

7:50–8:30

He reads the message on the chart, writes his response, and goes to the back of the room to check out the science experiment the class had done with the student teacher yesterday. There are two cups with eggs in them, covered with plastic wrap.

"This one's getting blue! It smells gross!" he says to no one in particular. He returns to the morning meeting rug. It's 7:52. The student teacher, Mrs. Robinson, is running Morning meeting today. She begins with Mrs. Chambers' routine of taking attendance by saying good morning to each child. The student of the day is Amelia and as such she will lead the next part of the meeting. She picks the "name tag greeting" for today, where each child says good morning to another after picking up a nametag from a pile of all the students' names in the center of the circle.

A daily greeting provides each child with an immediate reminder, first thing each morning, that they are a part of a learning community where every person is valued and there are clear expectations for the ways in which they treat each other and take care of each other in the classroom.

Mark gets his nametag from his cubby along with the other children from his table. While he is away from the rug, I notice his name is under Thursday (today) on the Sharing Chart.

"Mark, I want to go first," Tony says as they put their nametags in the stack in the center of the rug.

I think for a moment this must have something to do with the greeting, but then I remember Tony's name is also on the chart for Sharing today. They are negotiating for airtime later in the meeting.

After the greeting has gone around the circle, Mrs. Robinson calls on Mark to share first. So much for negotiation.

Sharing is a time in the meeting for children to tell their "newsy news" from home or about something they have done in school. Often it is about a trip, a visit to a friend or a grandparent, a pet, or an art project they have completed. Children tell their news and then receive some questions and comments from others. Mark is ready.

"A few days ago I dropped my toothbrush in the toilet. I'm ready for questions and comments." He is straight-faced, with only the slightest hint of an upturned lip, even though several children giggle in recognition of the event's possibility in their own home. Around the circle, half the hands go up. This sharing has grabbed their attention. Mark calls on them one at a time.

"Who fished it out?" asks Angel.

"My Dad."

"Did your Dad do something to fish it out?" wonders Wanda.

"No, he just used his hand."

"What color was your toothbrush?" questions Hector.

"Yellow."

"Was it acid yellow or electric yellow?" Corey elaborates. Everyone looks with surprise at Corey. It's quite a question.

"Acid, I think."

"Did you throw it away?" Eduardo wants to know.

"Yes."

"When did you get a new one?" inquires Micki.

"When I was at school, my Mom got it."

Mrs. Robinson puts up two fingers to indicate to Mark that he can have two more questions or comments. When these are finished, the sharing turns to Tony who has brought in his Pinewood Derby racer. There is more interest in the toothbrush than there is in the race car, though Tony and Mark seem to hold equal status with their peers. But overt competition isn't a problem as Mark is one of the children with a question for Tony, and later in the day they choose to work together in blocks.

> *Mark and Tony's sharings took all of four minutes, but during those four minutes the value of the social context of learning is clear. The social skills of listening and respectful questioning and commenting are being constructed and strengthened through the daily routine of sharing in morning meeting. They are what every teacher would like to be used in math, reading, spelling, lunch, and recess as well. This type of consistent modeling and practice in morning meeting establishes expectations and patterns which can serve as a foundation for all interactions at school, both academic and social.*

Because the topics in this daily dialogue are highly interest-
ing, evocative questions are raised. The topics are so interesting,
of course, because they come directly from the children. I have
never seen a "story starter" in a teacher's guide called "The day
I dropped my toothbrush in the toilet."

Mark stays thoroughly engaged through the rest of morning meeting. His hand is up to guess who changed what during the game of "Presto-Change-o." He has ideas when the class works on phonics with the chart at the end of the meeting. Amelia's "secret word" has slowly been filled in to become OLYM_I_S, when Mark volunteers "C", seeing the whole word in his mind.

When morning meeting is over, Mrs. Chambers keeps the kids on the rug to demonstrate an art activity they can do later at the art table to make a Valentine card for their "book buddies" in fifth grade, whom they will be with later today. At the end, Mark has his hand in his mouth.

8:30–9:20

Journal writing is next, prefaced by a little stretching and movement activity for the whole class and the transition back to their tables. Brandy, Amelia, Sean, and Julio are at Mark's table. They all get right to their writing. Mark quickly fills up a page of first grade, skip-line rule paper within two minutes. He knows that when his page is checked by the teacher he can go on to make his Valentine card for his book buddy. His hand goes up. He waits for another two-minute period for Mrs. Chambers with his hand up. Then he has an idea about his writing and makes a revision. He then gets interested in thumbing through his whole journal. Sean notices.

Mrs. Chambers didn't see Mark with his hand up, but in the
social context of the classroom, there are clearly other teachers
paying attention.

"Mark! Page empty right there. You skipped a page. Good thing I reminded you. Let me do something. I'll put a star just so you remember," he says with authority as he draws a crossover star with his pencil on Mark's empty page.

It's a writer's shortcut. Did Sean learn it from the teacher, a parent, a book buddy? It is part of the mysterious social transfer of learning.

Now the star method belongs to Mark who accepts it without comment and puts his hand back up in the air. Two more minutes have transpired. Still no teacher except Sean.

It's hard to guess Sean's motivation for the star. It may have been a genuine attempt to help, but I also remember Mrs. Chambers telling the class that they couldn't have a new journal unless their old one was completely filled up. The new journals are commercially produced, while the ones they are working in are papers stapled together. Mark's journal is now full, except for the page he skipped. Sean is struggling in a half-full paper journal. His motivation could be to move Mark in the right direction toward a new journal or to forestall that possibility until he's caught up to Mark a little more.

Mark has his right hand raised in that slung-over-and-resting-on-the-top-of-the-head posture. He idly traces Sean's star with the pencil in his dominant left hand. Mrs. Chambers is now across the table with Brandy and she is taking a long time.

Mrs. Chambers is paying extra attention to Brandy, a new arrival in class, whose entrance into the group, based on the personality she has already shown, could clearly be volatile. It is time that Mrs. Chambers knows will pay off in the long run because it establishes attitudes and expectations which won't have to be repeated endlessly and fruitlessly later on. It is proactive time, prevention time, time truly saved in the pursuit of understanding and learning for all children in the class.

Still, in these passing moments for Mark, it is a long time to wait. And for Sean and Julio, too. A full seven minutes pass before Mrs. Chambers is kneeling beside Mark's chair.

This is one of the dilemmas of time in the classroom. No matter how energetic and skilled a teacher is, there is only so much time to respond to individual and group questions and needs. It is a problem which can be addressed by reducing class size, requiring greater educational funding to hire more skilled teachers.

As a country, we give only lip service to dealing with this problem, as well as other related critical social needs such as children's health care, quality day care, preschool education, parent education, job training, drug and alcohol prevention, and others. The time, attention, and financial support given to children and families to prevent problems is a national disgrace. It seems we would just as soon spend our money on jailers as on teachers.

Mrs. Chambers is an extremely skilled and dedicated teacher, using many of the best techniques to use time most effectively each day. She knows that right now, extra time with Brandy will make a positive difference, but without additional teaching support or fewer students in the class, this time for Brandy can only be taken from Mark's time, from Julio's and Sean's. There is only so much time.

In this classroom, under Mrs. Chambers' tutelage, the boys managed themselves well while they waited. In other classrooms I have been in, waiting leads to disruption and sometimes bedlam. Even in Mrs. Chambers' room, a certain outcome of regularly waiting too long will be boredom and disinterest in the learning at hand.

"Let's see what happened to you today," Mrs. Chambers says to Mark, as she quickly reads his completed journal page. "I can't wait to get this back when it's finished," she remarks, smiling and putting a check mark in the corner of the page.

She moves over to check Sean's work.

"How do you write baby?" Julio asks.

"B–A–B–Y," Mark chants softly, another teacher in the classroom.

> *The well-managed classroom makes use of all its learners as teachers. The common problems of "cheating" and "copying" in other classrooms are of little concern in these learning situations because Mrs. Chambers is constantly reinforcing the value of helping and cooperation.*

9:20–10:00

Mark puts away his journal and goes to the paper shelf and retrieves some white and red paper to make his Valentine card for his book buddy. Valentine's Day production is beginning to swing into gear. He begins to draw on the white paper. He leaves his table again to get a piece of tape. On the way back he has a conversation with Marisol at her table. When he gets back to his table he tapes a piece of candy to the front of his card. Mrs. Chambers has given one sweet treat to each child for their book buddy.

"I hope they give us candy, " he says, looking wistfully at what he has just taped down. "What could I write inside?" he asks himself out loud. "I know." He writes something down and heads for the door of the classroom, passing Mrs. Chambers and giving the "fist" signal to go to the bathroom. He leaves the room at 9:25 and returns at 9:27. It hardly seems like time to have made it to the bathroom and back.

> *As he re-enters the room, I notice there are still children who have not had their journals checked. Their hands are still up. It's been over ten minutes of waiting for some.*

Mark, however, is deep into his Valentine. He cuts out a paper heart from the red paper using the fold-over method Mrs. Chambers demonstrated at the end of morning meeting. He gets up to get the glue and asks Mrs. Chambers for help opening it while she is help-ing Angel with his journal. She does not respond and he goes back to the table and gets the glue open himself. He gets a "place mat" paper to put down on his table for gluing purposes. He knows to do this automatically; it is one of many things Mrs. Chambers has had them practice earlier in the year through the use of "guided discovery" which establishes expectations and rules and intellectual possibilities for different materials, equipment, and areas of the room.

> *Guided discovery is another proactive strategy of* The Responsive Classroom *that takes a good deal of time during the first six weeks of school. Later, it creates enormous amounts of instructional time because children have learned how to utilize their environment and the things in it with respect, attention, and interest. It is time invested in prevention and positive action, like spending money on teachers rather than jailers.*

Mark cuts out a second small red heart using the fold-over method. He then glues the two hearts upside down and half off the bottom of the right-inside page of the card. He looks pleased with this design and continues to cut out more small hearts and glue them into the pattern.

"Amelia, you can't use that glue," Mark says without looking up or at her. She has a green bottle of white glue. Mark's is white.

"Can too."

"Can not."

"Can too."

"Can not."

"Can not," says Brandy, taking Mark's side.

"See, Brandy believes me," says Mark, not looking up from his growing line of upside-down, half-off hearts.

"Hey, this tape's not working," whines Micki, at the art supply shelf. Mark goes over and gives her a hand and returns to his table. It's 9:35.

"I've got a book buddy now," announces Brandy to her table.

"What's her name?" challenges Micki, passing by on her way back to her table with her piece of tape. The new girl in class is still being tested.

"I'm not telling," says Brandy.

"I guess you forgot," says Mark, matter-of-factly, but in league with his new tablemate. "She's a good writer," he announces to show he is defending Brandy as he goes off to get more red paper. On the way back to the table, he looks over Sean's shoulder. "Hey, how did you make the skeleton, Sean?" he asks. Sean has put glue inside a folded red heart, squished it together and then opened it up. The emerging pattern looks like a skeleton, sort-of. "He made a skeleton out of a heart," Mark says proudly to the table. "Hey, I'm going to try that." He does. "Hey, skeleton body! I'm going to keep this one."

> While this is not exactly what Mrs. Chambers had in mind for the red paper and the glue, this is what teaching and learning in first grade is like. Mark, through Sean, has made a small discovery about symmetry. They are slightly off task, but they are experiencing "the having of wonderful ideas," as the title of a famous essay by Eleanor Duckworth eloquently describes it.[2]
>
> The teacher has to constantly judge the fine line between inventive art, real discovery, and plain perseveration. She needs to stop and redirect senseless or needlessly repetitive and mindless activity. But just as penicillin was discovered in the pursuit of a wholly different end, first grade ought to have time for surprising discoveries. Seven-year-olds need time for experimentation and support for the always unpredictable and sometimes messy process of discovery.

Sean seems to know just how Mrs. Chambers will view this. "I'm going to tell Mrs. Chambers how to do this and then she can do it. Then she can show Terrance," he says confidently, as other children at the table begin to copy his glue-ghost renderings with their red hearts. [Terrance is Mrs. Chambers' grandson the children have heard much about.]

But Sean's latest skeleton catches his eye and he remarks, "That looks like a bird with a long tail and it died."

The social context of learning stretches the imagination of both Sean and Mark. As I glance around the room I see that no one is working on journals anymore. Book buddy Valentines are everywhere. It is 9:50, two hours since school began. Mark is having a good time.

"Look at me!" he says to his table as he peeks through the cut-out silhouette of a heart that now serves as a Valentine mask. "I'm Mr. No Eyes. Grrrr!" He goes back to gluing his upside-down, half-off hearts. "Just one more," he sighs as he cuts quickly and glues the last one that will fit at the bottom right of the page. "Oh, no! It's stuck!" he exclaims, having realized his card is fixed to the place mat underneath where the half-off hearts are now glued. "Don't break," he instructs the hearts as he swiftly lifts each heart off the place mat successfully. Smiling, he goes to show his teacher what he has made.

"I can see you like it, Mark," remarks Mrs. Chambers, glancing up from a table full of red and white.

I cannot help but be drawn back to one of those red and white flurries of my own school days. Do you remember days which seemed to go on forever, the passage of time punctuated by another Valentine and another and another? Here, a little paper-lace doily; there the faded, but soft red of old construction paper against the bright red of the new; making sure how to spell the names of friends; dropping Valentines into the big box in the front of the room; exchanging hand-made cards in the warm and cozy light of the winter afternoon.

In the classroom of the nineties, several decades past these

remembered days, Mrs. Chambers isn't allowed time for endless
Valentine making. She sent home a class list with every child (as
do most teachers in her school) giving the children the option of
addressing their mostly drug-store-produced envelopes at home
and bringing them in for an exchange tomorrow afternoon.

10:00–10:30

As soon as Mark and the rest of his table clean up they can get their
snacks from their backpacks.

Mark is in his own world, made possible by Mrs. Chambers.
He is always in motion and in a hurry, but he is not rushed,
nor will he be. Her skill at so many things assures this. She gives
the children longer periods of time to do their work than is true
in other classrooms using the same school schedule. Transitions
are easy and unrushed. Her voice is low and comforting. She
does not talk over the children.

Mark is also comforted by the social presence of his table and
classmates, but not dependent on them for his gratification. In
fact, much of the conversation Mark had this morning was with
himself—out loud, but with himself. This is typical first grade
vocalization and parallels the seemingly physical need to speak
aloud while reading, even if "sustained silent reading" is asked for.

The physical layout of the classroom is also carefully
matched to the developmental needs of first-graders. There is
enough "stuff" in the room, but not too much. I often see pri-
mary classrooms which barely provide a place to sit and where the
walls and ceilings are jammed with stimulating visual and kinetic
displays with hardly a space in between.

In observing, it is evident, even this early in the school day,
how different Mark's day is from Mrs. Chambers'. I know that
she often feels rushed and exhausted in her thinking, in her abil-
ity to get to all the children, in her need to remember so many
things at the same time. She can barely keep up with the needs

of each child during this language arts block, especially during the almost hour-long journal writing and conferencing time.

By the time snack rolls around, she is full of twenty-four stories, notes on skill needs for twenty-four children, strategies for small groups to address these needs, ideas about whole-class lessons, and the hope that everyone has finished their Valentine card for their book buddy.

Mark, on the other hand, is thinking about one thing— snack.

When his table is given the OK, he dives out of his chair, pivots like a NBA forward, and slips his snack out of his backpack and onto the table from a kneeling position. It's a move I sense he has practiced before. He has some juice and some dry cereal. Sean makes a grab for some cereal. "Don't think about it!" says Mark, smiling and pulling away. "Amelia, did you say you never got to go to the store? Believe me it's boring," he tells her while slipping a few more flakes into his mouth from the plastic bag inside his bright blue lunch box.

Mark has a way of expressing subtle empathy. He is referring to the "store" Mrs. Chambers has set up in the drama area of the classroom and is remembering being there recently. He is also thinking ahead to academic choice this afternoon. The snack probably helped him do that.

It's a shame that "snack" ends for most schoolchildren in kindergarten or first grade. Remember how much time Phoebe was distracted from her work because she had to pay attention to her hunger in the late morning? Few adults go through the day without a mid-morning cup of coffee or afternoon treat. Waiting long periods of time for nutritional refueling inhibits focus and attention.

The snack conversation turns to "getting stitches" for no clear reason. It just starts. Everyone has a story.

Gore and eating often go together in first grade. Such conversation might gross out older children or adults. It seldom seems to bother six- or seven-year-olds.

As children finish their snack, the classroom routine allows them to spend a few minutes on a choice of puzzles, writing, or reading.

This is the way Mrs. Chambers evens everyone out before they plunge into the next lesson. It is a time when children show great autonomy, care for themselves and others, and seem very relaxed. The break and the food have probably helped. The ability to make their own decisions for this brief period of time without any teacher direction is impressive. Again, it is a testament to Mrs. Chambers' ability to organize the day, model and set expectations, and then trust the children.

As Mark is finishing his snack, Daniel comes over to show him he likes the cover of the book Mark made for Angel two days ago. Mark puts his snack away and goes over to Angel. "Want to finish the book?" he asks. He sits down at Angel's table. Almost instantaneously he is up to retrieve the spray bottle from the sink along with a wad of paper towel. He shoves these both in Angel's hand so he can clean up after snack faster and have a few minutes to work on their book project. After Angel wipes the table, he returns the spray bottle and the two of them find a single, empty desk to work on the book they are making.

This is their book project. It has not been assigned, it is not homework, it will not be graded or even turned in. But these two boys have made a pact; signed, sealed and delivered two days ago at the art table. This is a cool thing to be doing they seem to be saying by the way they intensely bend over this self-motivating work. The joy of learning for its own sake is not something that can be taught from a textbook. Mark and his classmates are learning it with the help of a great teacher.

Everyone has finished eating and is busily engaged with a friend on some simple joint adventure with a book or puzzle. It is almost time for art, as Mrs. Chambers reminds them with the sound of the chime and a gentle word.

10:30–11:10

Mrs. Chambers and Mrs. Robinson leave for a well-deserved forty-minute break and planning period as Mrs. Shapiro wheels her art cart into the room. Mark is magically back at his table, leaving no signs of the mutual book project behind.

> *I didn't even see where they put it. Mark is quick. In the flash of a second he anticipates the next thing to happen in class and moves ahead.*

Mrs. Shapiro knows something of Mrs. Chambers' routines. She raises her hand and waits for the children's attention. She asks the child who is first today to pass out the papers. She calls the tables one at a time to get their scissors.

The intercom interrupts with the news that recess will be inside today.

> *I look out the window. The sun is shining. It just must be too wet on the playground. I am surprised that the news evokes some cheers. Most of the children seem not bothered at all that they will be staying inside. The comfort of their own classroom must outweigh the run-around frenzy of the hardtop, at least today. Mark has a smile on his face. Maybe he is thinking about Angel and their book or his book buddy.*

Mark's table is called second to get their scissors and glue. "No one should be playing with scissors or glue," Mrs. Shapiro announces as other tables are called. Mark is already trying out the scissors and twisting the top of the glue, as are all the children at the table. The reminder does not change what Mark is doing. It is as if he didn't hear it. "Does everyone have what they need?" Mrs. Shapiro continues, "Did I say to touch glue or scissors?" she asks.

Out loud, Mark says, "No!" in a friendly and cooperative voice.

Here is one of the mysteries of childhood that developmental psychologists have yet to fully understand: How do children acquire self-control, the inner moral authority to do the right thing and to know what that is without being told by an outside authority?

First Mark had to learn to trust and obey his parents, then his nursery school and kindergarten teachers in place of his parents for a few hours a day. Then he turned over this authority to Mrs. Chambers. We see that he is eager to follow Mrs. Chambers' rules and is usually one step ahead of her routine. Here, in art, we see that he anticipates what he wants to do (use the scissors and the glue), but he is not doing such a good job anticipating what Mrs. Shapiro expects of him.

He is eager to respond when asked a rhetorical question about expectations. It does not appear that he is deliberately defiant and he seems good-natured throughout this exchange. He does not appear to feel chastised by Mrs. Shapiro, he simply seems to be responding to a slightly different routine, perhaps remembering "Oh, yes, this is Mrs. Shapiro. She does things differently than Mrs. Chambers. I have to remember!"

Mrs. Chambers has been struggling with this issue as a teacher because she has a special assignment to leave her classroom one day a week as a consulting teacher for the district. She has a permanent substitute, Ms. Miller, who understands her routines and keeps them as best she can. However, the class does not always behave appropriately for Ms. Miller, Mark included.

For Mark, the transfer of authority from one adult to another seems to be a bother. He is happy to move through the day following his own agenda in his own speedy way without thinking, because someone else he fully trusts is in charge.

It's fun to flash down the waterslide at a summer water park because someone who knows about these things has built the chutes and slides that keep you safe. You scream as you come to the edge on a dangerous corner, but inside you know it's only so dangerous because "they" would never build something really unsafe. We trust the designer, the owner, and operator.

Mark trusts his teacher. He likes having some control over what he does in the classroom and Mrs. Chambers is a skilled teacher who gives the children lots of practice with making choices. But too many choices would feel unsafe. Most of us really wouldn't want to try an "anything goes" water park where the sides might collapse, or have our children in a classroom without carefully constructed teacher controls. Yet, we also want our children to eventually learn self-control.

This encounter with Mrs. Shapiro and the weekly experience with Ms. Miller are probably a good thing for Mark in his development. He is comfortable in following Mrs. Chambers' routine because it is so predictable, he hardly has to think at all to follow the rules.

With Mrs. Shapiro and Ms. Miller he is forced to think about the rules; to have his mind jostled a little; to ask himself "What am I supposed to do? What is the right thing to do? What if I don't?" *To reach back in his moral memory to ask,* "Will Mrs. Chambers find out? Will my mother find out if I do the wrong thing?" *And eventually, as he grows up, to transfer this moral authority fully to himself, to ask* "Is this right for me? For my friends? For my school? My community? The world?" *This developing sense of morality parallels the child's development of diachronic thinking and each helps with more elaborate and complicated thinking about important issues.*

I hope that special teachers like Mrs. Shapiro see themselves as bridge builders in the moral development of the young and that we take the same view. They are not just specialists who see hundreds of children each week and therefore have a harder time with discipline. Mark can be good for Mrs. Chambers, and really for Mrs. Shapiro too, but the struggle to internalize the process of control is one which is not easy or smooth.

Today, Mrs. Shapiro is helping hundreds of children make Valentine baskets—beautiful, big, red paper baskets in the shape of a heart to carry tomorrow's Valentines home. She leads Mrs. Chambers' class patiently through the challenging process of folding, cutting, and gluing properly, step by step, just as she did the class before and will with the class after.

"I did it, Mrs. Shapiro!" shouts Mark, as he holds his first fold-and-glue up for her to see. Then he turns to his tablemates. "Julio, want me to do it? Sean, want me to do it for you?" Mrs. Shapiro comes over to the table and draws a cut-line for Julio. Mark looks on. "Cut what? This?" His mind is racing ahead. He traces a cut-line with his finger, but not with a pencil like Mrs. Shapiro. He cuts across the love-red paper with his right-handed scissors in his left hand. The predictable jagged results do not seem to bother him.

I sympathize as I keep taking notes with my left hand.

"Look, Sean, I'm going to eat you," growls Mark, holding up the jagged edge.

As the children make this rounded-cut for the top of their baskets and unfold them, Mrs. Shapiro comments how the paper looks like a giant Band-Aid. Suddenly, you can see Band-Aid construction replacing Valentine baskets in children's heads.

"Oh no, Sean, I have a real bad cut and I need a Band-Aid!" Mark exclaims in fake agony. He looks at the big red Band-Aid and takes his pencil and begins to draw the air holes for the Band-Aid where they belong. He then looks over at Mrs. Shapiro, looks back at his Band-Aid and furiously erases his air holes. The Band-Aid is transformed back to a Valentine basket in the making.

"Mrs. Shapiro, do I got it? Mrs. Shapiro, do you do the other side?" he says, moving out of his seat towards her, playing catch up. Mrs. Shapiro gives him a wait signal and he returns to his seat. He glues quickly, draws some stars on the bottom of the basket using the Sean cross-over method learned at journal time and starts reciting to himself, out loud, "Dilly dilly piccalilli, tell me something very silly . . ." He picks up his basket and tracks down Mrs. Shapiro at another table to see if he's got it right, comes back, presses hard, opens, re-glues, and presses again.

"Hurry up and stick," *he seems to be saying to his basket.*

He glues past the stop-line, saying out loud to no one in particular, "Cuz the Valentines will fall out," but then thinks better of it and rubs off the extra glue. Mrs. Shapiro comes by and shows him how to wipe off some more with a tissue without comment. Sean helps him hold his basket still. "Thanks for holding it, Sean," he says smiling.

Cooperation and helping have definitely carried over into art!

Now Mrs. Shapiro is showing them how to make the handle. This is a complicated process for first-graders because they have to glue on one side of the strip and then reverse the strip to glue on the inside of the basket.

> *I think it resembles a Piagetian conservation problem. I may be able to see who understands reversibility and who doesn't. Mark doesn't.*

He glues his handle wrong, looks at Julio who has it right and re-glues correctly.

> *The social context of learning provides many teachers for Mark at his table. This time it's Julio, sometimes it's Sean or Brandy.*

Everyone has a skill or a talent or a gift to offer to someone else. In this class, there is no special test to be labeled "gifted and talented." All the children are treated that way.

Mark writes his name on the bottom half of his basket. "THERE!" he announces, adding a symbol under his name. It is the unmistakable Superman S inside a diamond.

"I'm going to collect all of them," instructs Mrs. Shapiro.

"Why! You gonna give them back to us tomorrow?" implores Mark. There is no response from the teacher.

I suspect she's heard this a few times already today. No response may be better than the impatience that might naturally show through in this moment. Mark does not seem to need an answer, either. The sides of the waterslide are holding.

He happily hums as he cleans up, puts the scraps where they belong, returns his scissors and glue, and waits at his table for Mrs. Chambers' return.

11:10–11:20

It's Mrs. Robinson, the student teacher, who returns to the room and declares, "We're going to do calendar next," as Mrs. Shapiro rolls her cart out into the hallway.

"No-o-o-o-o, I don't like calendar," moans Mark making vibrating trombone sounds between his hands. His table is called to the rug next to last. "YeSSS! We're not last!" He punctuates the air with the ever-popular pulled-down pumped-fist motion of athletes clearly learned from big brothers and sisters or from TV. At the rug, Mark slips in and out of conscious attention. First, he is engaged with his hand up to answer a question, then he is wrestling with Jason trying to keep him from raising his hand. He stops and leans on Jason's shoulder. This is reciprocated by a hug from Jason followed by a good pounding on his back.

Brandy, imitating Jason, pushes Mark in the back too. "Stop it, Brandy," he turns, annoyed. It was all right for Jason. How was Brandy to know? This is her tablemate, the one who says nice things to her.

Mrs. Robinson leads them through the familiar "yesterday and tomorrow" drill, exercising their developing sense of diachronic time by asking them to remember the past and predict the future. The "Yesterday" portion teaches Mrs. Robinson some of the humility necessary in teaching. The children remember that yesterday they had music, saw a video of Peter and the Wolf, and had fun at recess.

The large chunks of the familiar are the predictable schema recalled. They do not remember the wonderful science experiment she created for them, that she gave each of them a shiny new penny as they studied money, or that she wrote and copied a penny poem for each of them that they are memorizing. She spent hours of her time focused on these things and they do not recall them. I hope she will come to understand that the time she took to be so prepared really matters, even if the experiences she worked so hard on do not remain in the immediate memories of her students. One of the eternal paradoxes of teaching is that we seldom get to know what it is we have really taught.

11:20—12:00

Mark moves up on his haunches, leans back on his hands, sits up. Mrs. Robinson is sending them off to an academic choice time. Mark chooses blocks. His mind chose well for his body, it seems to me. He'll have a solid half-hour to work on his own choice of activities. Tony has also chosen blocks and he has his Pinewood Derby car in his hand as he moves to the block shelf and building space at the back of the room.

"I'm building a city, you build what you want," Mark says to Tony, heedless of the Pinewood Derby car of which Tony is so proud. "Hey, are you two here?" he snaps at Marisol and Melissa who have also chosen blocks and are busy building a bed on the corner of the block space. "What are you making?" he says in a challenging voice, "Don't waste all the blocks."

"Mark, don't make it so big, the girls have to work here," says Tony. It's the kind of remark I've come to expect from Mark, but Mark is in no mood for cooperation. He shoves the blocks he is building with over on the rug, ignoring the girls. He then leaves Tony and goes to see what's happening on the game table. Tony tries to join him, but as soon as he does, Mark returns to the blocks.

> It seems like something is bothering Mark, that he is annoyed.
> Something about this choice isn't working.

Mark reaches over to the shelf where Tony has put his Pinewood Derby car. He picks it up and examines it. "You used nails?" he questions, pointing to the car's axles. Tony puts the car on the blocks. "This is the start line," announces Mark unilaterally. "This is where it starts. This is where it starts. This is where it starts," he repeats until he has Tony's attention. Then he goes and retrieves more blocks for the racetrack. He reaches over the girl's building to get his blocks instead of going around. "Mrs. Chambers! We're building a race track," he says excitedly, catching a glimpse of his teacher who has just returned to the classroom.

> Was his teacher being out of the room enough to unsettle him?
> Was this another instance of his struggle to do "the right thing"
> even when his teacher wasn't in sight?

"What's going to race there?" she asks, starting to move over to the paint easel where Hector is painting clouds again. He shows her Tony's race car.

"Hey, Mrs. Chamb . . ." He stops. She does not hear him. "I'm just testing," he says to himself. "These things are on the corners so it knows where to turn." It is unclear if he is speaking to Tony. He builds some tunnels with the curved blocks. He asks Tony, "You mean it has to jump from here all the way over here?" Tony gets an airplane off the shelf as if to answer the question with a different machine, but Mark isn't watching Tony as he soars the plane from ramp to ramp. Mark is over getting more blocks.

> *This feels like the parallel play of much younger children. The developmental principle of younger behavior under stress comes to my mind. Is Mark behaving in a younger fashion because this choice time is not working for him, because he's stressed or angry, hungry or restless? Does he need to* breathe out, *as Sylvia Ashton-Warner charted, and this feels like* breathing in *to him?[3]*
>
> *There are times for reading and writing and social studies— for breathing in new skills and new cultures. There are times for singing and dancing—breathing out, exhaling, expressing the joy of being in a group, exercising the body. There are times for breathing in through concentrated attention to number accuracy, precision drawing. There are times for breathing out—outside on the playground each day, breathing fresh air. There are times for breathing in by listening to the teacher read a story or give a spelling test. There are times to breathe out just by resting or day dreaming for a few moments of enforced silence. Each and every child and each and every class needs to follow their natural rhythms, breathing out and breathing in.*

Mark goes to get more blocks and knocks over the bed the girls have been building. "Sorry, it was an accident," his words say, although his actions convey a different message.

"Hey, you can't have all the blocks," Melissa says.

"Well . . ." says Mark, thinking what to say, or maybe just how to get out of this situation. He takes a bunch more blocks in his arms back to the racetrack. He turns and pauses for a moment, looking at the girls' building. He goes and gets more blocks, walking around their bed this time. There is no complaint. Back at the racetrack, he seems to finally settle. He is on his stomach, down in the pits with the car and driver. "The cool car is winning. It won!" He looks at Tony and smiles. They now work together to rebuild the road in another configuration.

> *Mark is clearly in charge. He is able to draw Tony into his play, but Tony could not engage him with the airplane.*

When they are told to clean up, Mark goes directly to the chore at hand. The routine seems to comfort him. Structured time is a help to him. For Tony just the opposite happens. When time is up he seeks more time, a common occurrence in first grade classrooms. He starts ramming his beautiful, handmade, parent-assisted Pinewood Derby car into a wall of solid maple blocks. He does this four times in a row. After the fourth ram, the weights, carefully secured in the rear undercarriage of the car, fall out. He seems genuinely surprised.

"The weights came off . . . Hey, Mark!" he yells.

"I didn't do it!" says Mark, putting his hands up in surrender. He is clear across the block area and he is looking at Mrs. Chambers who is gathering up the children on the rug. Tony goes to Mrs. Chambers and tells her what happened to his car, then puts it in his backpack.

> *I wonder what the reaction will be at Tony's home tonight and why this choice period for Mark was so hard. Was it that Mrs. Chambers was out of the room? One of the things primary students need most is a growing understanding of limits and expectations. If these are neglected or are inadequate at home or in school, or in combination, then children have difficulty acquiring the internal controls they need for self-regulation, including the ability to regulate their own time.*
>
> *Richard DeGrandpre argues that the rapid rise of ADHD behavior in children is partially a result of combining and cumulative negative forces which conspire to keep children from being able to develop the controls they need. Among these he cites*

(1) cultural neglect—more parents working and away from their children for longer periods of time, (2) lack of outdoor play with neighborhood children and in quality after-school care, and (3) an increase in time spent with "speed" technology such as computers, television, and video games.[4]

The children are at the rug reflecting on their use of choice time with Mrs. Chambers. There are five minutes until it's time to go to lunch. Mark is sitting right up front near Mrs. Chambers and Tony is right next to him. Mark has his hand up.

"Me and Tony made a track and he tried his race car on it," he shares.

"How did that work out?" asks Mrs. Chambers.

"Good," is all Mark offers. Melissa and Marisol do not share about their building project.

Later Mrs. Chambers remarks to me how she noticed that Mark was unkind to the girls during the choice time, but let it go during reflection time. She knows it was atypical of Mark, which I sensed too. Now he has himself back on track. Did it have to be at the expense of Tony, Marisol, and Melissa? Will he learn to handle times of frustration without taking it out on others? Somehow, I think he will, especially if he gets consistent social guidance in his classrooms as I know he will at home.

Will Marisol and Melissa learn to speak up for their own space and rights? I hope so.

12:00 noon

Mark is ready for lunch. The walk down the hall is a scuffle of friendship among the boys; pushing, poking, slapping, swinging lunch boxes, but somehow staying enough in control not to be stopped; they're going 68 miles per hour in a 65 zone.

The girls are talking all the way down the hall, some are holding hands. The trip takes about four minutes. The children have assigned tables by class, but can sit where they want at those tables. There is some competition for seats. Since I am sitting next to Mark, there is only room for three more at the table we have chosen in the long line of tables. Daniel and Eduardo and Manny are our tablemates. The lunchroom quiets as the lunch room staff raise their hands. The school has been working on the climate of the lunchroom. The children get quiet quickly and are praised by the staff. Children getting hot lunch are dismissed to their line. Mark has lunch from home in his blue bag, so does Eduardo. "Whatja got, Eduardo?" Mark wants to know.

"Peanut butter and fluff," says Eduardo.

"I got that, too," says Mark, biting in.

Daniel pounds Mark's thank-goodness-empty lunch bag.

The crunched and compressed nrgy *of boys condenses the space between us at the table and the time that lunch takes in the growing din.*

As the noise in the lunchroom increases, the boys' bodies begin to hum. There is no containing them. Conversation gives way to thumb wrestling, shouts punctuating the air around me. Lunches are finished and trays returned to the kitchen. Mark puts his lunch bag in the wagon across the cafeteria, returns to his table and sits quietly. He gets up again and takes Eduardo's bag over for him, comes back and waits for lunch to be over.

It is already OVER as far as the children are concerned but there is still time on the schedule before recess. The waiting becomes creative. Thumb wrestling turns to bench sliding competitions. Mark is under the table grabbing Eduardo's leg. Manny is sitting on Julio. "He just farted in my lap," shouts Julio. The table explodes in falling-out laughter.

The allotted time for first grade lunch is probably just a little too long! If adjusting the schedule is impossible, then adjusting what happens when children are finished eating and just waiting might help. At some schools I have worked with, baskets of cards or coloring sheets, or guessing games help children occupy waiting time.

The chime sounds. It is a five-minute warning. Five more minutes before time to return to the classroom for indoor recess. The sun is shining but there are puddles on the playground. The boys are nearly puddles on the floor when the next chime sounds for lining up.

Mrs. Chambers' class knows just where to be in the long line snaking its way down the long hall back to the classrooms. The sign in the hall says

STAY TO THE RIGHT

WALK QUIETLY

HOLD THE DOOR FOR THE PERSON BEHIND YOU

FOLLOW THE GOLDEN RULE

The children are definitely following the Golden Rule for those in line with them. They have their arms around each other, smiling and talking, bumping and smiling, slowing down and catching up, holding the door for each other, but the first two rules on the sign are another story.

Some rules are coming naturally now in the friendly, practiced spirit of the school while others remain a struggle.

12:30–1:00

It is hard to tell the difference between indoor recess and academic choice. In every corner of the room children are deeply engaged in small groups. There is lively discussion and quiet activity. Some children play in housekeeping. Others surround Mrs. Chambers as she reads a book. Mark and Angel are working on their book as expected. There is music playing quietly. There is contentment in the room.

1:00–1:30

The children are back on the rug. Mrs. Robinson is leading them in a "twenty-questions" kind of guessing game, except this one ends up with 120 questions before it ends, six times around the circle.

> *To my amazement, the children are settled throughout this time of waiting and thinking. I believe indoor recess made this possible—breathing out. They are still, comfortable, happy, and engaged with each other, now breathing in.*

Mrs. Chambers then gets them up and makes a circle around the perimeter of half of the classroom. She re-teaches them a spirited "play party"—a song and a dance they have done before.

Snow, snow, snow,
Where is the snow,
Heard the weatherman today,
Snow, snow, snow.

They sing and dance, dance and clap, change partners and begin again, happily, *breathing out.*

Mark is thoroughly engaged, spinning and smiling; he is happy with every partner, happy with himself.

Mrs. Chambers gathers the children on the rug again. Mrs. Robinson passes out the Valentines they made this morning that they are going to give to their fifth grade book buddies. The excitement in the room mounts as the fifth-graders enter with their own Valentines in hand. They approach their young buddies slowly, smiling, sidling up to them like big, friendly ponies, next to small, excited children at a county fair.

This is not an isolated event at Briarwood or for this first and fifth grade. The value of cross-age tutoring, mentoring, and friendship has been demonstrated over and over again in this school and everyone is sold on the idea. Parents report how often they hear about buddies at home. Teachers of older children report what the experience has meant for some of their less able students. Teachers of younger children tell how much it has helped their students to learn to read and to love reading.

Our schools provide endless possibilities for these types of relationships, some of the most powerful learning connections imaginable. All we have to do is arrange the time and take control through careful planning.

Mark gives his book buddy the half-off-the-page, sensational Valentine. The book buddy reciprocates with his creation and they start off to a back table to read, which is what they remember to do. Mrs. Robinson calls everyone back to the rug as soon as Valentines are exchanged. The candy in the cards the fifth-graders received is being eyed by both buddies. The fifth-graders have brought heart-shaped lollipops for the first-graders. "It's OK to go ahead and eat your candy," Mrs. Chambers says. "Sometimes it's OK to stretch the rules," she says with a wry smile.

1:30–1:45

Finally everyone is back on the rug.

"Raise your hand if you don't like poetry," Mrs. Robinson says to the sugar-eyed children. Mark raises his hand. Mrs. Robinson reads them a really funny Shel Silverstein poem. "Did you like that poem?" she asks when she finishes.

"No," says Mark, with a twinkle in his sugar-eye.

Mrs. Robinson shows them the poet's picture on the back of the book, that bigger-than-life picture. "I have two books like that at home!" exclaims the poetry hater.

After the poetry reading, book buddies are sent off to write some poetry together. Mark and his buddy write:

McDonald's Fries

I like french fries because they are good
and they are the best ever
because they are my favorite food.

They both seem happy with their product, although I'm not sure they recognize their near rhyme.

Mark's book buddy notices Mark's Superman signature symbol on his Valentine card. "What's this?" he asks. One of the other fifth-graders at their table tells him it's a Superman S. Mark beams. All the fifth-graders start drawing Superman S's on their cards, the perfect way to end this day as far as Mark is concerned. Mark's book buddy waves as he leaves the room with his classmates. Mark waves back.

The chime sounds. The children stop. The day is done. "First-graders, it's time to get your hundred-day projects and your back packs and get on line for the buses," instructs Mrs. Chambers.

"Yeah!" says, Mark, heading for the coat closet. Where has the time gone?

The Structure and Use of Time

The total elementary school day was six hours long, forty-five minutes less than Phoebe's middle school day. This makes sense from a developmental perspective which considers younger children's needs for free time and free play (although many of these children will go to structured programs after school).

Using the same definition of core academics from the National Commission on Time and Learning as we did in the previous chapter, the day for Mark and other students in his class at Briarwood looked like this:

CORE ACADEMICS *(art, language arts, social studies,* *academic choice, science, math,* *morning and closing meetings)*	230 minutes = 3 hrs 50 mins.
SPECIALS *(Though art is a special at Briarwood* *it is counted as a core academic by* *NCTL's definition.)*	0 minutes
TRANSITIONS *external (arrival, dismissal, lunch)* *and internal (moving from one* *subject/area to another, clean-up, etc.)*	50 minutes
PHYSICAL NEEDS *(snack, lunch, recess)*	80 minutes

As you can see, time on core academics was well shy of the Commission's recommended 5.5 hours, especially within a 6 hour day! On most days, at least one special (not counted as core academics, such as music or phys. ed.) would subtract another chunk of time from this "core time."

In a self-contained classroom, the need for external transitions is greatly reduced, but it is still necessary and desirable to move within the room, physically and mentally, from one subject to another with music, stretching, and other transition activities.

We will focus more specifically on the teacher's day in the following chapter, but her basic schedule included one 40-minute planning period away from the classroom during art, and one 30-minute lunch period, with the remainder of the day in the classroom without scheduled breaks.

Morning meeting and closing meeting are counted as time on core academics and are perfect examples of how social and academic skills can be taught at the same time. For example, even the greeting first thing in the morning teaches verbal skills and practices memory while setting the tone for a respectful, friendly, and exciting day of learning.

Mark's classroom is clearly heterogeneous, with a wide range of academic abilities evident. Mrs. Chambers provides the well-managed, differentiated instruction which enhances the academic growth of all students by insuring that the social context of education is encouraged and supported.

Assessing the Day

For Mark, time in first grade this blustery February day felt whole, markedly different than the fractured middle school day for Phoebe. From 7:45 in the morning to 1:45 in the afternoon, he was *in* school. We followed him from one activity to the next without a sense of disruption or jarring transitions, except, perhaps, for art and lunch and his own struggle with academic choice. When he left morning meeting to go to language arts no bell rang. He did not need to line up, move through a hallway, go to his locker, receive new instructions, meet a new teacher. He got up, got his journal from his cubby, moved to his table and started writing. Expectations were clear, routines well remembered.

There were actually numerous transitions during the first grade day, accounting for nearly an hour's worth of time. But these were the breathing in/breathing out points thoughtfully inserted into the schedule by Mrs. Chambers along with the necessary transitions controlled by the whole school schedule.

Mark, however, did not experience time the way an analytical time study records it or feel the effects of a time schedule like Phoebe's (although both contain similar amounts of time for instruction and transitions). He was *in* school and he was learning all the time. What made the difference?

Our first inclination is to simply say one child is seven and one is twelve, one child is in first grade and one in seventh. True enough. We know about the developmental differences between Mark and Phoebe and even about the different ways they experience the passage of time as diachronic thinkers. But their "time-on-learning" during their school day was only partially a function of their development. It was more dependent on how time was structured (as determined by the educators who control the clock) and how time was used (as determined by both administrative expectations and individual teachers' choices and skills).

A major difference, in my estimation, is a difference in the level of understanding by educators of the developmental needs of their students and how administrative decisions affect them. At the elementary level, at a school like Briarwood, schedules and classroom time are organized around the developmental needs and abilities of the students, and instructional content is delivered within that structure. At the middle school level, at a school like Longfellow, time is organized around the imposed curriculum: the content subjects needing to be covered and the time required for a teacher to typically deliver that content.

The developmental needs and abilities of young adolescents are largely ignored.[5] Middle school teachers are more prone to comment about the number of students they have to teach and whether they are reaching them than they are about the amount of time they have for teaching content. Phoebe's longing for her sixth grade is, to me, her way of telling us that she has known better times and, certainly, known teachers better in a different setting.

In contrast, Mark's day allowed him to stretch and grow and learn to the full extent of his capabilities. Working with an appropriate schedule and set of expectations, Mrs. Chambers used her skills to *teach*, rather than simply manage. As she did for the entire class, she honored his need for nutrition and exercise. She understood when he could pay attention in a large group, when he needed to be at a table with a smaller group, when he needed to be working with a partner and when he needed to be alone. She kept track of the content skills he needed to acquire and observed his growth in these areas as he wrote in his journal, worked with Tony in the blocks, communicated with the class at morning meeting.

She focused on Mark and his needs, Brandy and her needs, Julio and his needs, Tony and his needs, Marisol and her needs, and provided the academic content appropriate for them within the scope of the first grade curriculum. She worries about whether she is covering the curriculum, getting it all in, meeting new state standards. There isn't enough time for her to do everything she needs and wants to do. But as far as Mark is concerned, there is plenty of time for learning every day.

The skillful organization of time in school requires a deep knowledge of children's development as well as knowledge of academic content and classroom management. Using this knowledge and practicing these skills involves a balancing act, a nimble dance of rhythm and grace, which is a key to quality education. In the next chapter, we see the energy and skill required of teachers every day in school.

Chapter Six

Working to Be
"All There at Once"

A teaching day passes too quickly. Grabbing the teachable moment, grabbing the teachable kid running by, there's no time to spell out theories, the merely academic.

Maxine Hong Kingston,
from her 1986 foreword to Teacher[1]

IN THE PREVIOUS OBSERVATION CHAPTERS, we looked at school through the eyes of students. In this chapter, we experience the day with a master teacher, the one who taught Mark in the previous chapter.

Good teachers know their students intimately, both individually and as a group. Mrs. Chambers says this class is one of the most challenging she's had in her career. "They are such a young class," she worries, "and not just young. They lack so many social skills. It's so hard for them to wait their turn, not to tattle, to share."

Her work with them feels painstakingly slow. "I've got to teach them to care—about each other, their classroom, and their education but I'm concerned we'll never cover all the curriculum we're supposed to. But if I went faster, I wouldn't be sure I was really reaching them."

I remember the pressures from fifteen years in my own classrooms, two of them in first grade. How do I reach twenty-plus children with so many different needs? How do I spend enough time with each one? How do I prepare them for a world of tests and more tests? How do I find time for joy and play and dancing? How do I meet the requirements of each curriculum area? How do I get through it all by June so that the second grade teachers won't be mad at me next year because I didn't get all the way through the primer?

The smells, giggles, and squeals of this first grade are familiar and comfortable. But I know much has changed for teachers. I see the extraordinary needs of the children they teach, how little the children have internalized control over their behavior, how distracted they are. I see the demands put on teachers by their school district policies, the testing pressure, the pace of the day, the unrelenting stress. Teachers are clear. There is never enough time.

Even with all of her experience, considerable skill, and reasonable support from her peers and administrators, Mrs. Chamber feels torn each day as she makes the hundreds of split-second decisions which guide children's education. With only so much time, choosing to follow one road leaves many others not taken. Concentrating on one subject, one child, or one social skill leaves so many others unattended. "Where can I find the time?" she wonders.

In describing his observations of first grade in his now classic study, *A Place Called School,* John Goodlad described the interplay of the physical setting, the materials used and content covered, the students' activities, and the teacher's use of time as "All . . . there at once."[2] Teachers must be aware and attentive on many levels at the same time while retaining a clear vision of the "big picture": children's needs for growth and learning as individuals and as a group. Each day and each moment is framed, and sometimes limited, by the school time schedule, curriculum requirements, class size, and physical environment which may range from distracting to destructive.

This pressure is a constant for every teacher, every day, 180-plus days of each school year. Mrs. Chambers and other teachers struggle to be "all there at once." Sometimes she is successful, and at others, there just isn't enough time.

The School and the Schedule

This is the same school, Briarwood, and the same first grade class as in the previous chapter, but observed on a day earlier in the year when I focused my attention more specifically on the teacher.

It is also a day affected by another holiday, with the winter holiday break only a few days away. One holiday replaces another through the year, each drawing the attention of the children. Particularly in elementary school, holidays have always been a major competitor or a companion for learning. From Halloween in the fall to Easter and Passover in the spring, with all the other cultural holidays in between, religious and secular, children's attention is attracted by school bulletin boards, special assemblies, TV advertising, and myriad other distractions.

Mrs. Chambers' planned schedule has the same basic outlines as in the previous chapter, and uses the same basic structures (such as morning meeting, academic choice, and reflective meetings), although the arrangement and content of the "specials" is different. As it turns out, it is a day when Mrs. Chambers adjusts some of the scheduled times to meet the immediate needs of the class. My commentary is concentrated on time periods where we can focus intently on Mrs. Chambers. This is the planned schedule going into the day:

7:45	Arrival
7:50	Morning Meeting & Transition
8:20	Language Arts
10:00	Santa pictures
10:20	Language Arts
11:00	Snack
11:10	Academic Choice
11:30	Calendar/Math
11:40	Special—Library
12:00	Lunch
12:30	Recess
1:00	Reflecting Meeting
1:15	Academic Choice
1:35	Closing Meeting
1:45	Dismissal

7:40–7:50

Mrs. Chambers hurries to the familiar door of the school she has called her teaching "home" for the last ten years. Before the bell rings and the door swings open, she takes a deep breath. For the next six hours she will need all the breath she can get. She retrieves twenty-four students at the door. It is time for school.

Children and teacher put away their coats, the children behind maple closet doors which pivot on floor and ceiling hinges. They hide messy hang-ups on the inside and serve to hang up children's art on the outside. They occasionally pinch little fingers and they make for great hide-behinds for just-getting-to-school conversation.

Mrs. Chambers hears Bethany and Corey as she looks over the room for the day. "I feel bad for Alyia," Bethany says to Corey in the cramped space of the coat closet.

"Why?" asks Corey.

"She was puking yesterday," grimaces Bethany.

Mrs. Chambers moves to the front of the room where several children are busily reading the message she wrote on a chart stand in the front of the room before leaving yesterday.

GOOD MORN_ _ _, TEACHERS!

TOD _ _ IS _ _ ESD _ _, DE _. 9, 1997.

STEVEN CUSHMAN IS _ _ _ _ _ AND

WANDA MARGOLA IS _ _ _ _ _ _ _ _ _ _.

DO YOU THINK OUR AMARYLLIS IS TALLER

THAN 3 INCHES TODAY?

YES   NO

Most of their names are clustered under the "Yes" column. As Mrs. Chambers sits at her desk, more and more children gather around the chart, and then sit down on the edge of the rug to wait for morning meeting.

7:50–8:45

Mrs. Chambers raises her hand, but says nothing. The room gradually quiets. Some of the children raise their hands too. When it is silent, she speaks.

"It's time to start our morning meeting, boys and girls."

More children make their way to the rug. A small group of boys already there amuse themselves with a guessing game while they wait for the others. I join them cross-legged on the meeting rug.

Mrs. Chambers' hand goes up again. The circle is almost complete. "Marisol, I need you to leave your coat right there and join us on the rug," Mrs. Chambers instructs a late arriver with a smile. "Please make room for Marisol and fix up our circle."

The office intercom blurts out an announcement, the first of many during the day.

> BUS SEVEN IS LATE TODAY. DO NOT MARK
> THE CHILDREN TARDY. THANK YOU.

Mrs. Chambers says good morning to each child as a way of taking attendance.

> *This is a daily reminder for her, restating what's most important*
> *every day, no matter what intervenes. It is the child—each and*
> *every one.*

"No Alyia today, she's sick," Mrs. Chambers announces. Bethany gives Corey a knowing look across the circle.

"Steven, you are first, can you put this into the pocket, please?" She hands Steven the class attendance card. He gets up and puts it in the pocket by the door.

> *It is so small a task it might go unnoticed. I recognize it as one*
> *of many opportunities Mrs. Chambers will create during the day*
> *to give children practice with real responsibility.*

As Steven is completing his task, Hector says, "We lost our line this morning."

"How did that happen?" Mrs. Chambers asks him. Hector tells her about a lot of running around outside before the bell. "How did you solve your problem?"

"We came in the second grade door. Some other Spanish kids came in the wrong door and got in trouble," Hector responds, both with their solution and a worry.

"We need to talk about this after morning meeting. I want you to know the right door to come in," Mrs. Chambers says, glancing at Hector and then smiling at Steven as he returns to his place on the rug.

> *The exchange with Hector has only taken as long as it's taken Steven to complete his task, less than a minute, but in these few seconds Mrs. Chambers has acknowledged a social need of an individual child. She makes a mental note of the way Hector said "some other Spanish kids got in trouble," wondering about broader cultural issues in the school community.*

TEACHERS, EXCUSE THE INTERRUPTION. PLEASE BE SURE TO GET YOUR SANTA PIC-TURE SLIPS TO THE OFFICE BY 9 O'CLOCK. THANK YOU.

Morning meeting continues with a greeting around the circle, each child bouncing a ball gently to another, followed by a respect-ful greeting. The greeting takes two minutes and is followed by five minutes of active dialogue. Several children share news: one printed cards on a computer at home, another visited an uncle who is sick, a third went to an older sister's basketball game. The sharer is in charge of the circle, sharing a few lines of news, calling on question-ers, and providing answers.

> *The teacher has deliberately taken a back seat, having taught the children through modeling and practice that they can be*

responsible for this exchange. Practice in language skills and social skills are woven together and Mrs. Chambers has already guided her children into the attitudes and structures she wants—polite listening, respectful questions and comments, thoughtful sharing—and which she will expect throughout the day, in reading groups and math and science lessons.

8:15–8:30

Morning meeting continues with a fun, vigorous activity involving rhythmic clapping, snapping and tapping, followed by Mrs. Chambers' review of the message chart which focuses on language skills: they look for **ing** endings and explore rhyming words with **day.** A boy leaves with the special needs teacher when he gets a bloody nose, but the class doesn't miss a beat.

> TEACHERS, PLEASE EXCUSE THE INTERRUP-TION. THERE IS A CAR IN THE PARKING LOT WITH ITS LIGHTS ON. LICENSE PLATE NUMBER XRP 4929.

Mrs. Chambers ignores the interruptions as easily as the children do and moves the class to the back of the room to check out the amaryllis plant mentioned in the morning message.

> *It is amazing to watch these 6- and 7-year-old bodies—all twenty-four of them—rearrange themselves so easily and with such care for each other in the crowded space at the back of the room. It is civilized behavior, quite a different picture from one I saw the previous evening in a department store where a dozen holiday shoppers jammed the space around a checkout counter.*

The children are bursting with intellectual curiosity and ideas. "Has the amaryllis grown taller than 3 inches? Let's see," says Mrs. Chambers.

Her questions and comments open the door to learning. There is no right answer or predetermined agenda lurking behind her words.

"You were right, Jonas. What do you think? Should we move it?" A chorus of NO'S!

"I don't know what will happen," says Mrs. Chambers. "I haven't watched one in a long time. My grandmother gave me one once."

The children look at their teacher in amazement. Mrs. Chambers has a grandmother!!?

Morning meeting is running overtime, (meaning it's taking longer than the recommended 20–30 minutes) but Mrs. Chambers doesn't mind because the children are happily engaged and she is in control of the time during this part of her teaching day. She takes the extra time because the children are doing well.

8:30–8:45

After the meeting and the Pledge of Allegiance, Mrs. Chambers knows some activity is needed. She begins a spirited dance and song with the record "Boogie-Woogie Rap" pulsating from the tape player. The intercom tries to interrupt for a sixth time.

TEACHERS . . . .

It is entirely unsuccessful. The room is hoppin'. It is nearly an hour since Mrs. Chambers picked up her young charges at the door.

The first hour of the day is an important time for learning because children are freshest when they first come to school, and many educators argue that this is the best time for language arts instruction or math lessons. Mrs. Chambers chooses to begin the day by building the social community of the classroom while teaching academics at the same time. She establishes her expectations for the rest of the day by providing vivid examples of them, first thing in the morning.

8:45–9:15

Mrs. Chambers begins a whole-class language arts lesson in which she is introducing a new series of books to the children called *Sounds of Language* by Bill Martin, Jr. The first book is called *Sounds of Home.* She will use a tape that leads the children through the first part of the book. But first she engages the children. "We're going to *look* at a new book today."

> *Her words are carefully chosen. Not all the children are "reading" yet.*

"Raise your hand and tell me what you notice," she instructs.

There is a sudden flurry of activity having nothing to do with reading. Another teacher appears at the door. "Can I borrow Marisol for one minute?" she says as she shepherds her quickly out the door. Marisol returns as quickly as she left. Then another teacher enters with a request to borrow some construction paper.

TEACHERS, PLEASE EXCUSE THE INTERRUPTION. THE STUDENT COUNCIL MEETING SCHEDULED FOR TODAY HAS BEEN POSTPONED UNTIL JANUARY FIFTH. THANK YOU.

> *I long for the intercom lady to begin next time with "Children and teachers, please excuse the interruption . . ."*

Somehow, Mrs. Chambers remains focused and undisturbed through it all. "Hmm—what do you think this could be about," Mrs. Chambers ponders out loud. "The title says *Sounds of Home.*"

The children's ideas explode from the page, from the idea of home, from the sounds of home, just the way Bill Martin, Jr. intended.

> *My mind drifts back to a public elementary school twenty years ago where I was principal. Bill Martin, Jr. is telling a group of teachers in a workshop, "the patterns of language have to go in before the reading comes out." Today, the patterns come out, the real sentences of real lives, popping out like popcorn all over the classroom.*

"I hear babies crying."

"Sometimes when there's traffic downtown."

"Our neighbors scream next door."

"The train by our house, the midnight train."

"When my dad saws to try to build a house in the basement."

"Start looking your books open!" Mrs. Chambers exclaims with a twinkle in her eye.

> *I realize that her words were not misspoken, but deliberately playful since many of the children are "looking" rather than "reading." The most important tools in the teacher's toolbox are the words out of her mouth, the tone and volume of her voice, and her facial expression. Mrs. Chambers' tools are precise and well-honed.*

"Is that doing OK, Daniel?" she asks with concern, examining the rash on Daniel's face as kids pore over their new books.

A child leaves for the bathroom, using the silent bathroom signal, a simple and practiced routine.

> *Responsibility is being taught in tiny steps. The patterns of behavior have to go in before the ethics come out, I think to myself. Mrs. Chambers develops these patterns carefully and deliberately during the first six weeks of school and reinforces*

them throughout the year. The time and energy used in many classrooms for repetitive interruptions, explanations and discipline can be filled, instead, with learning.

The children listen to the first story in the book as Bill Martin, Jr. reads to them from the tape recorder. They listen for the beep to turn pages. They are sprawled on the meeting rug. Some sit, some lie on their backs looking up at the words. Some follow words with their fingers. Others trace clouds. Still others are reading with the book upside down.

> *Teaching is never even and predictable and time for learning is never the same for any two children, yet we pretend that so many minutes of language arts each day will do the trick for all. Cumulatively perhaps, but certainly not daily or weekly.*
>
> *Today, Mrs. Chambers saw Erica focus on the colors of beetles and ladybugs as she listened to the story. Robert rolled the rhyming words around in his mouth:* fly, sky; pup, up. *Melissa read the whole story, word by word over and over again to whomever would listen. Today, Melissa learned to read: she made the connection between the patterns pouring in and the sounds coming out of her mouth.*

She knew something important was happening today. "Mrs. Chambers? Can I take this home and read it to my mom?"

> *The classroom is like a backyard in early spring. The crocuses nudge through the snow. The buds are appearing on the pussy willow. Leaves still blanket the tulip bed. Each flower in its own time, I once believed.*
>
> *Now I know that without the skill and the patience of the gardener, some flowers will never stand a chance. Nature has its grim side, too. Spring frost kills early blooms if they are not protected and covered at night. Skunks forage in the tulip bed.*

It is true that children develop at their own pace, that growth comes from the inside out. Pioneers like Arnold Gesell and Jean Piaget, Froebel, Pestalozzi, Steiner, and many others spent lifetimes and contemporary scholars continue to spend lifetimes studying the truths of maturation in children's physical and social growth, studying the importance of internal mental construction in intellectual growth. They know that without the bulb's natural internal time clock, the crocus would never appear.

It is also true that children develop from the outside in. Pioneers like Maria Montessori, Lev Vygotsky, and others spent their lives and their many colleagues and followers continue to spend lifetimes studying the construction of reality from the outside in, from social interaction with family, peers, teachers, and the environment. They know that without the sun's warmth and nourishment from the soil, the crocus would never bloom.

Nature or nurture? Both are critical. There is an essential symbiotic balance. Teachers must recognize the nature of students and provide the appropriate nurture for their growth. They need to protect and nurture the social world so as to allow optimal intellectual growth and learning. Quality education rests in the balance. In the early spring, there is much work in the garden. Mrs. Chambers is the gardener.

9:15–9:30

A major transition ensues. Children move quietly to their cubbies, carefully deposit their new books, retrieve their writing journals, and make their way to pre-known spaces at tables around the room. After the vice-principal tells her about a phone call from a concerned mom, Mrs. Chambers smiles and moves out into the classroom as children begin to write in their journals.

Mrs. Chambers has created a classroom in which there is clearly more than one teacher. Children converse and assist each other in their writing while she moves from one to another.

Enormous cognitive growth can emerge from the social inter-action of students throughout the school day: rich, textured, thoughtful teaching between learners who care about each other's ideas and are interested in bouncing their own off the nearest sounding board.

The more carefully a classroom is structured to allow for such productive social engagement, the more academic growth will emerge. Mrs. Chambers consistently encourages collaboration through careful arrangement of furniture, partner and small group activities, adequate time for project work, and even in her morn-ing message which read, "Good Morning, Teachers." *She monitors the social engagement to make sure it is productive and redirects when it is not. She is the gardener.*

"That's much better, Manny," says Lin. He points to six "M's" which have been erased and replaced with a neat "Manny" at the top, with Lin's direction and encouragement. Manny draws a picture of two boys playing catch with a baseball under his name and under the picture he writes a sentence. *We had gym.* Lin looks over. "We didn't do that, we played parachute first." Manny erases the baseball and draws a parachute over the two boys instead. He then begins to color his picture.

When Mrs. Chambers takes home these journals tonight and reviews them as part of her normal hour or two of preparation time each night, she will not be able to see all of the teaching and learning that went on between Lin and Manny, or many of the other students. She will see the completed work. She will see the erasures and revisions and know Manny is making progress, thinking about what he is doing enough to want to change it and make it better. She will try to remember to tell him that she noticed.

9:30–10:05

Children are busy with their writing. Mrs. Chambers slips out of the room and no one notices. There are two adults in the room—a parent volunteer and me.

> *A safe time for her own bathroom break. She must time these carefully when another teacher visits, the vice-principal is in, or the children are off at a special. These are her "break" times.*

In five minutes, Mrs. Chambers is back, but it has been just long enough for Steven to lose his self-control. Apparently *he* noticed she left the room. Children like Steven have built-in radar.

She sees what is happening immediately. Steven has left his writing, attracted like a magnet to the nearby shelf of math manipulatives. She quietly tells him to go to the "thinking chair." He continues to play with the colorful tower of cubes he has managed to construct in her absence, acting as if he has not heard her.

She moves her management skills into high gear. She turns away from the power struggle and whispers something to Tammy who is working on her picture of a giraffe. Tammy puts down the yellow crayon in her hand and leaves the room. Momentarily, she returns with another teacher who walks over to Mrs. Chambers.

"Steven needs to be in your room 'til I come for him," Mrs. Chambers says matter-of-factly.

"Steven, come with me," the other teacher says, motioning to Steven. He looks up, throws down his cubes and follows the teacher out of the room with a sour glance toward Mrs. Chambers, who is now busily engaged and smiling as she talks with Jordan about his tree-climbing story.

> *Having a "buddy teacher" has allowed Mrs. Chambers to go on teaching in those moments when children previously engaged her for lengthy periods with discipline issues, preventing her from teaching the children who followed the rules.*

At the end of writing time, she will retrieve Steven from her buddy teacher without comment, redirecting him to the next activity. Later in the day, when he is no longer angry, she will talk with Steven and help him to see why it is important to prac-tice his writing every day. She makes a mental note to consider whether tomorrow Steven should lose the privilege of using the cubes for a day, a logical consequence for his behavior.

She has learned that by not making a decision in the heat of the moment, her eventual action in this matter will be more reasoned and less emotional. Class learning is barely interrupted and her time with Steven later will be more productive for both of them.

10:05–10:25

Mrs. Chambers strikes a musical chime once. The children all stop talking and turn their eyes towards her, another moment of practiced routine.

"Mrs. D is here to take those children who are going to have their picture taken with Santa." A little over half the class move excitedly toward the door. The PTO sponsors a fund raising project this time each year. It is popular with those parents who can afford it. Angel looks at Corey and sticks out his tongue as Corey leaves with Mrs. D and the other children. Mrs. Chambers sounds the chime again and tells the rest of the class to gather at the rug.

"Raise your hand if you have gotten to see Santa." Half of the remaining children raise their hands. "I just want you to know you will all see Santa somewhere because Santa is for all girls and boys. Remember you can all see Santa sometime. I was lucky to see Santa in my town. He came on a fire truck. Terrance [Mrs. Chambers' grandson about whom the children have heard many times] told Santa, 'I want a Matchbox car and I want my Mimi to have a banjo.' I don't know where that came from. I guess I'll have to learn how to play if I get one," she laughs.

The children's attention is turning. As she quickly draws them into a song with clapping and movement, her mind is still fixed on Christmas and last night when she took her old artificial Christmas tree to Marisol's apartment along with a string of Christmas lights. "It isn't much," she had told Marisol's mom, "but it's a start toward Christmas."

Mrs. Chambers is like many other teachers I have seen, not only at holiday times, but throughout the year. They make special trips to the store, spending their own money on classroom supplies, visiting families, donating to special funds, and taking special care that part of the class is not left out of special events they can't afford. It demonstrates the reason so many go into teaching in the first place: they love children. Too often, this dedication goes unnoticed or is simply an unstated assumption of educational reformers.

10:25–10:32

The kids are happily engaged in a math song and dance when the other children return from their Santa photo-op with candy canes in their hands. Mrs. Chambers anticipated this potential problem and gives the remaining children a candy cane from a box she tucked in her desk when she arrived at school. She gets the children settled in their seats and assigns some of them to pass out a phonics worksheet. Again, the young teachers and students become immersed in collaboration.

10:32–10:40

The fire alarm goes off, a blaring, bleating, throbbing, fog horn crescendo, accompanied by a pulsing laser light show. This is more awesome and scary than anything on TV! The children jump up and move to the door as they have practiced. Some remember to cover their ears; all are wide-eyed. They move quickly and silently through the halls. They are without their coats and it is a cold and windy

December day. Outside, a distance from the door, they turn around and face the building.

PLEASE RETURN TO THE BUILDING

This time the intercom means something to the children. They do not hesitate.

10:40–11:10

Back in the room, Mrs. Chambers gathers the children on the rug. Phonics will have to wait. This is life. Yesterday, Melissa had shared in morning meeting about the fire in their apartment and how they are now living in a motel. Hector asks to go to the nurse for an asthma treatment, affected by the wind and the excitement.

"You did your job to get out of the building safely. I noticed some of you remembered to cover your ears. I noticed most of you were very serious going outside. When is it OK to have fun and be silly in school?" asks Mrs. Chambers.

"When we play outside," says Bethany.

"When we sing a song," says Erica.

"I feel dizzy," says Robert.

"Let's get back and finish our sheets while Mrs. Turner passes out the homework," says Mrs. Chambers.

It takes a while to get settled, the fire drill is still jangling inside these six- and seven-year-olds. "I need you to sit down in your seats," Mrs. Chambers says sternly. They are just about settled when the intercom interrupts and another Santa picture-helper appears to ask for children. Mrs. Chambers has to explain that they have already gone.

These are the everyday moments in the classroom the proponents of strict time standards need to see and understand. No matter how much they want children to use all their time in school on straight academic assignments, real-life learning just isn't like that.

"When you finish your worksheet you can put your homework in your backpack and get your snack," Mrs. Chambers directs, focusing the children back on their tasks. As workers finish, they weave their way to the comfort of the coatroom and the nourishment of their snacks. The room breathes a collective sigh of relief.

11:10–11:30

It is time for academic choice, where children choose their learning activity within the room, ranging from doing a math sheet to preparing a multi-part play. Mrs. Chambers observes, notices, assists, encourages, and redirects as necessary.

The room has a busy hum. This phrase is used frequently by experienced teachers as both a scientific and artistic descriptor. This "busy hum" is a special zone of learning, one Mrs. Chambers knows well, which teachers seek and revel in when it is constant and uninterrupted in their classrooms. This is teaching at its most rewarding.

I recorded fourteen individual engagements between Mrs. Chambers and her children during a span of twenty minutes as she moved about the humming room; meaningful, thoughtful, helpful encounters that embraced children's minds and stretched them academically and socially. Here are a few examples:

To Hector at the easel: "Be sure you get your name on that. There's soap in the jar, so you're all set." Both instructions deliver trust in Hector's ability to manage independently with paint, brushes, soap, water, smock, painting. What emerges are Hector's blue and white images of snow, one after the other, hung on the bulletin board behind the easel.

To Marisol at the art table who asks her, "What color are my eyes?" and she responds with no words while retrieving a mirror. Then, "Look here!" before moving on. Marisol gets the message of her teacher's unspoken confidence in her ability to look and make use of her research.

To the science table where she smiles and wipes off the magnifying stool as children prepare for their scientific observations.

To the drama area where children are wearing name tags identifying themselves as customers or cashier, "Let's see what you bought. Oh, it's your first time to be a customer?"

To herself out loud: "I can't believe no one chose blocks today!"

Back to the science area where some children are inspecting their plants under the grow light, "I'm really happy with these plantings."

To Corey, who is playing with the vortex bottle Mrs. C has made for them to experiment with, but who is perseverating on the small tornado he makes over and over, "Can you draw a picture of the vortex?" She gets him paper and stays with him until he is drawing.

To the computer where she looks over the shoulder of four engrossed children and says nothing.

To the art table: "I notice she has really long eye lashes," she remarks, getting back to Marisol and her eyes.

To Micki who asks, "How do you spell fish?" "Did we talk about 'ish' today?" she says, smiling.

> *Watching Mrs. Chambers is like keeping up with an Olympic skater; not like the speed skaters her class wrote about one morning, but a figure skater gliding across the ice without apparent effort, now turning, finding a new direction. Spectators can only keep up with her if they are ready for surprises and delighted by them.*
>
> *It's too bad that so many teachers feel more like speed skaters instead, driven by the clock, competing against it. What does it take to use time in such a disciplined, efficient, artistic, professional way?*
>
> *Mrs. Chambers is a skilled and experienced teacher with a loving heart. But she has also worked to create these opportunities for teachable moments, given herself time to teach, by using many of the strategies covered in Chapters 8 and 9. These help to set the tone and expectations for learning in her classroom and structure the time to allow periods when children follow their own keen learning interests.*

11:30–1:00

After a ten-minute calendar exercise which practices math skills, the children leave Mrs. Chambers for almost an hour and a quarter. After library they will go to lunch and then to recess.

> *This is Mrs. Chambers' one long break in the course of the week because her special happens to back up to lunch and recess today. Some days she will have recess duty, giving her a total of a half hour without the children. Today she has an hour and ten minutes. During this time she eats lunch with a colleague for the first twenty minutes, makes phone calls about getting Christmas presents to some of her needier families for fifteen minutes, runs off a holiday newsletter in the office for ten minutes, attends a special education meeting about one of her children for twenty minutes, and goes to the bathroom.*

1:00–1:15

Back in Room 18, Mrs. Chambers gathers her windblown flock around her on the rug.

"Tell me something that worked at recess," she says with a soft smile.

"We were pushing at basketball and the teacher lined us up," says Mark.

"I made a new friend!" Amelia exclaims.

"I didn't get pushed down, like yesterday," sighs Jordan.

"Tell me something that didn't work," Mrs. Chambers counters.

"I got pushed. I got my mouth locked," Hector says, frowning, searching for the word "whacked" in English.

"Could you solve it?" Mrs. Chambers asks.

"NO!" Hector shouts.

"Let's give Hector some help." She surveys her audience.

"You could tell on the person that pushed you down," Julio offers.

"I'd like to hear a different way."

"You could ask the teacher out there for help," Micki says.

"You are remembering some of the things we talked about," says Mrs. Chambers.

"Someone in this class tripped me by accident, but he helped me up," reports Bethany.

"It sure is good to know there are kids in our school who can do this," says Mrs. Chambers as she brings this recess reflection to a close. "It's time for afternoon work."

> Today, recess reflection took thirteen minutes of school time. If the teacher had not brought them together for this dialogue, they would already have been working on academic choices. It's a hard decision, one of hundreds Mrs. Chambers makes each day in the "all-at-once" pressure of a classroom in which so much is happening.
>
> After studying Japanese elementary schools for fourteen years, where reflection (hansei) is an honored part of the teaching and learning at the primary level, Catherine Lewis, director of formative research at the Developmental Studies Center in Oakland, California, concluded that "the heartfelt self-evaluation that often results [from hansei] is infinitely more powerful than the externally imposed tests, evaluations and incentives through which outsiders may attempt to produce educational excellence."[3]
>
> Today, Mrs. Chambers chooses to use these valuable minutes after recess to balance learning and reflecting on social skills with learning academic ones.

1:15–1:25

The reflection meeting in Mrs. Chambers' room took place after recess even before the children had their coats off. Now they move to hang them up and put away their lunch boxes in the friendly coat closet. But the transition is not a smooth one.

A Few Moments in the Mind of a Teacher

Mrs. Chambers is stretched to be there "all at once" during the next minutes, and after school we talk about what was she was thinking during this period. I have reconstructed her thinking along with the action of the classroom. It is one small example of what is required to make the "all at once" decisions which define good teaching.

Mrs. Chambers' thoughts are in italics and her words and others' words are not.

Uh-oh, there goes Steven, again, pushing and shoving, like a puppy. I should have had him wait with me until everyone else had their coat put away, but I thought, maybe today . . . well, Bethany, of course, really tried to help. I need to let her know without paying too much attention to her tears. She's strong and she knows I really am proud of the way she always helps in the room; plus now I've got to re-focus Steven quickly at the beginning of this period . . . a logical consequence for not handling himself well independently in the coats.

Bethany comes to Mrs. Chambers still clutching her lunch box with tears in her eyes. She gives Bethany a hug. *There, that was pretty direct and a little hug goes a long way.* She corrals Steven as he heads for the rug. "Steven, what's our first rule?"

"Be safe?" Steven shrugs.

Well, he can say the first rule, but he said it as a question. Does that mean he's not sure or he's just testing me, pushing me a little? Just be direct, Margaret.

"You need to help yourself remember how to be safe." Her tone is firm, kind, and insistent. *The rest of the children are sitting so patiently; I know they are dying to get to their choice activity.*

"You need to help yourself remember to be safe," she says, taking Steven by the hand. *There, hang on to my hand, no resistance, you really like being with me, don't you, Steven.* "Sit right next to me, Steven." *OK, let's see, who was working on ornaments yesterday? Melissa and Tony definitely need to be there today, so here you go Tony and Melissa, here are your clothes pins. Yup, look at 'em going right over to the art table. Oh, and good, Corey's going there too. I've been thinking Corey and Melissa would really make a connection one of these days; maybe today.*

OK, "Remember how many people can go to art. The ornaments are really popular." *Here you go, Amelia, Manny.* "When you are planting your seed, don't forget to put your name on the cup." *Sean, Wanda, Robert, Angel, Bethany, Brendan, Eduardo, Mark, Lin, Julio, Hector . . .ah, Hector . . .Jason, Jonas, Marisol. Oh, the loft. . . how am I going to figure out a way to have that be not so out of control? I've still got two clothes pins. Alyia's out, who am I missing? Oh right, Daniel went home sick. Now, Steven . .*

"What's something you could do to let Bethany know you're sorry about not listening to her and being mean to her in the coat closet?" *Apology of action . . . I wonder if he will get it . . . we keep practicing . . .*

"Say sorry?" Steven shrugs again.

. . . oops, nope, just a "say sorry" again . . . so we'll try some more practice, Steven. "Can you see where she is working in our room?"

The intercom blares out an announcement about an after-school activity. *Oh! @#$^^%&^% That darn intercom! I really don't want to know about the Christmas pageant rehearsal right now. I want to listen to Steven.*

"How many can work at pattern blocks?" she asks. Steven holds up two fingers.

Good, he knows. Everyone else seems to be settled in at their spots but I'm a little worried about the potting soil, even though it looks like they are being careful.

"Can you see where she is working in our room?"

Steven points to Bethany who is at the other side of the room with a bucket of pattern blocks on a table.

"I'd like you to go over and work there, too. Show Bethany you're sorry by following the rules and being friendly while you're working with her this afternoon." *Oh, that went over big! Look at that pout!*

"I want to go to blocks," Steven whines.

I know you want to go to blocks, but you are going to learn to think about someone else beside yourself before this year is over. "Today, Steven,

I have to make the choice for you. Tomorrow, you can make your own choice. I'll be watching," she smiles. Steven slowly heads for the other side of the room.

Big mama is watching you . . . I'll keep my fingers crossed . . . now where is my pencil? What room did the intercom say that committee meeting is in after school?

Oh, my goodness, will you look at that! Steven copied Bethany's pattern and she gives him a high five! What a sweetheart! Look at Steven beam. She's so incredibly generous; just think of what she's teaching him. I hope he can say something nice to her . . . well, maybe giving back the high five was his way of saying sorry. What a moment.

Mrs. Turner is sure doing a good job with them at the computer . . . I think I'll sneak out to the bathroom for a second.

Nothing seems to have fallen apart while I was gone . . . I wish I could let them work longer . . . look at those two in the blocks . . . they're still building structures to get into, that's awfully young behavior for first grade. How could I stimulate them to use the unit blocks more representationally? Maybe I should put in a challenge next week. I'll never get to introduce the fancy blocks if they don't start using the unit blocks differently . . . or maybe the fancy blocks will change everything . . . I could use the guided discovery of the fancy blocks to talk more about showing the world like a map or a model . . . hmmmm.

> *Mrs. Chambers and skilled teachers everywhere wear all the hats; they are nimble, acrobatic, inventive, flexible. They are instructors, gardeners, orchestra conductors, artists, healers, teachers.*

1:25–1:45

The school day concludes with the rest of the academic choice period and a short closing meeting where the children reflect on their afternoon work and what they are looking forward to tomorrow. Her last words to the class are "I want you to think about being safe getting your coats," punctuated with a smile at Steven. It is the end of the children's school day, but not Mrs. Chambers'.

1:45–2:45

Mrs. Chambers spends some time talking with me and Mrs. Turner, goes to a meeting, comes back and straightens up the room, writes her morning message for tomorrow, and heads home. Tonight, there will be phone calls to parents and lesson plans for tomorrow. On an average day, she works for at least an hour or two at school and often an equal amount of time at home. This is the profession of teaching.

The Structure and Use of Time

Mrs. Chambers' available "teaching time" was six hours, although her average work day includes an hour or two more. Using the same definition of core academics as in the previous chapters, the day in Mrs. Chambers' class looked like this:

CORE ACADEMICS *(homework checks, chart reading, morning meeting, language arts, academic choice, math, reflection and representing meetings)*	240 minutes = 4 hrs.
SPECIALS *(library, Santa pictures)*	40 minutes
TRANSITIONS *external (arrival, dismissal, lunch) and internal (moving from one subject/area to another, clean-up, etc.)*	30 minutes
PHYSICAL NEEDS *(snack, lunch, recess)*	50 minutes

As in the previous chapter, time on core academics was well shy of the Commission's recommended 5.5 hours. There were a total of seventeen transitions during the day, accounting for a total of almost

50 minutes, but many flowed easily into the next instructional period and could be judged as part of "time on task," bringing the total closer to 5 hours.

Mrs. Chambers had a total of 70 minutes away from the children for lunch, planning, a special needs meeting, and parent phone calls. She took two bathroom breaks for a total of eight minutes during the remainder of her instructional time.

In this heterogeneous class, the teacher maximized time for individual attention through the skilled use of "differentiated instruc-tion." She provided significant time in the "stretching place" or "zone of proximal development" where children learn in the company of and with the assistance of peers and adults. One way Mrs. Chambers accomplishes this is by establishing the social and behavioral expectations of the room early in the year and reinforcing them daily, and by organizing the day with different groupings which allow and encourage the social learning we know is central to educational growth. The day was balanced as follows:

FIXED TIME   90 minutes = 25%
lunch, recess, specials (over which
Mrs. C. had no control)

DIRECT WHOLE-GROUP
INSTRUCTION   105 minutes = 29%

SMALL GROUP   115 minutes = 32%
INSTRUCTION &
ACADEMIC CHOICE

WHOLE-GROUP   20 minutes = 6%
REFLECTION OR
REPRESENTING

TRANSITIONS   30 minutes = 8%

Assessing the Day

Mrs. Chambers is clearly a knowledgeable gardener who nurtures growth through a combination of sound professional strategies and personal skill. Yet in many instances, she has little choice about what happens during a school day and if judged solely by the standards of "time on task," she might be found lacking!

She fell short of the government commission's recommendation of 5.5 hours of "core academic" instructional time. The Commission identifies this gap in "time on learning" as the primary reason for the failure of America's schools to measure up to "world standards."[4]

Yet, how could Mrs. Chambers do more with her time? On this day before the winter holidays, she more than covered her language arts requirements, had a minimum math time, taught science through morning meeting and the planting choice in the back of the room, taught civics in morning meeting, during the fire drill, and in the reflective discussions the class had with each other about Santa and their work. History and geography were not on the map this day, but the arts were. Drawing and creative writing, ornament making and computer graphics abounded.

Where could she have added over an hour of instruction? The actual school day at Briarwood isn't long enough for her to do more and already she feels too rushed in her approach to the children.

Although she works in a school which provides considerable support for her dedication to meeting the individual developmental needs of children, she was clearly affected and limited by decisions over which she had no control:

- Twenty-four children assigned to her classroom, rather than eighteen or twenty
- Only a six-hour school day to encompass all learning activities including lunch, recess transitions, and "specials" such as physical education, library, Santa pictures, and fire drills

- A salary and teaching schedule which provide little or no paid time for cooperative planning, parent contacts, and professional improvement

- Thirteen intercom announcements, only one of which affected her or her students

The enormous weight that Mrs. Chambers and teachers around the country feel today about the lack of time to get their work done is a result of that work being defined by people outside the classroom—administrators, reformers, test-makers, politicians at all levels—not the skilled and dedicated educators who actually work with children.

Although they seldom say it directly, decision makers are defining education as a product and time as a unit of measurement under which the product is manufactured. This denigrates the product—a child's education—and the process—the unpredictable art of teaching and learning. Children are not expendable commodities and neither are teachers. Teachers need to be able to work in the time zones they have sculpted from the rough block of each day; they must be trusted to create with their own genius, utilizing the materials and approaches they know best.

We have watched Mrs. Chambers move from decision to decision, sometimes in milli-seconds, paying attention to twenty-four young learners. Sometimes she had them together as a group, sometimes in small groups where she concentrated on a few while never losing a sense of the whole, sometimes with an individual child when she had to focus intently.

In her management of time, she resembles a conductor before the orchestra, providing a mixture of response and direction, riding the wave of the moment to know it and guide the next. She thinks many thoughts as she tries to be there "all at once." And decisions are required in the time of an eighth note.

On good days, learning moments flow into one another like the measures of a symphony; they rise and fall with the energy of the children at different times of the day. The intercom, which was so glaring to me, was no more than a cough in the symphony audience, a sneeze, or a shuffle of feet to Mrs. Chambers. She connects with children as the conductor gains the attention of the woodwinds; she attends to the rough spots with profound understanding of the score, of how to silence a particular bit of nonsense with a glance and bring back laughter in the next measure.

This teaching artistry goes unnoticed and unappreciated by most of the public, but her real audience consists of hundreds of grateful parents whose children have played in her orchestra. They notice and appreciate what she has done, even if they have never completely understood the intricacies of her art.

It isn't right that a conductor can be told by the front office to make sure that the symphony is more staccato, that certain movements should be lengthened because they are more popular, or that during practice no one in the orchestra is to enjoy themselves. It is right that an orchestra's performance is rated and that the conductor takes a major portion of the responsibility for that performance. But the conductors and their peers, mentors, and colleagues know their craft and can help with improvements, not the politicians and front office managers far removed from the process.

Teachers should be held accountable, but the measure of their work can never be explained solely by statistical gatherings of bubble sheets, translated through computer analysis to compare the minds of children from class to class, school to school, city to city. To do so insults our humanity, and turns the glorious process of growth and education into a mere mechanical pursuit. If we succumb entirely to the quantifiable, analytical, production model of education, we will have no need for the loving gardener and inspired conductor because we will no longer value or utilize their skills or their creations.

And then, what will we have?

Section Three

TRANSFORMATIONS

CONSTANT CHANGE is the paradox of education. Learning requires students and teachers to change what they do moment by moment, lesson by lesson, day by day. The observation of change is part of the science of teaching and one of its greatest delights. At an evening presentation, I asked parents and teachers what they experience when they watch their children learn something new. They used words like "awe," "wonder," "a miracle," "relief," and "astonishment." Think of the children in Mrs. Chambers' class noting the change in their amaryllis plant day by day and the changes in Mark and Phoebe over the course of a year.

Without change there would be no learning. Too much change, too rapidly, however, creates confusion and sometimes chaos. Too much change all at once creates undue stress, anxiety, and even physical illness. Change in educational approaches, beliefs, and practices often come faster than teachers, parents and children can comprehend or assimilate them. New educational initiatives, curricula, and tests, piled one upon the other, leave little time for learning how to use them well. When new approaches are not successful immediately, they are often abandoned in favor of new ones before ever really being given a chance. For change to be effective, there needs to be time for changes to take root.

The strategies and techniques for educational reform vary widely. In the "Foundations" section we looked at the mixed blessings of the standards movement, the move towards increased testing as well as increased use of technology, the constantly expanding curriculum requirements, and mandates for more "time-on-task." There's more time being used on standardized tests to increase accountability. To raise achievement and test scores, elementary students are funneled into more solitary pursuits. Recess is reduced and time on the computer increased. Changes in content curriculum approaches, primarily in reading and math, are proposed as the key to educational improvement.

Who would disagree with the need for more accountability and the need for more focused attention on basic skills? But this need must be understood in a broader context: the social context of education. To ignore this is to ignore the reality of school. Many areas in education need change, but we must establish a hierarchy of these needs to make the changes effective and lasting.

Visit almost any school today and you will see that issues related to classroom management, social skills development, civility and public discourse, teacher and student morale, and, in some cases, basic safety are taking precedence over academic instruction. No matter how knowledgeable teachers are about content curriculum, instruction cannot be delivered in classrooms where children are unfocused, inattentive, and struggling with each other instead of helping each other.

Teachers must know how to create "trustworthy spaces" for learning before that learning can occur. This is not easy, quick, or formulaic, but it must be done. We must address the social context of school as we reform academic learning and performance. Without understanding and addressing the social context we are likely to simply keep changing the academic content over and over without seeing the desired results.

We want teachers to develop all students into capable learners. But requiring teachers to learn and implement several new textbook approaches at the same time, in a short time, and with minimal professional development doesn't help. I believe the current speed and volume of educational change does more harm than good.

Transformations in our schools and classrooms are essential, even urgent, in order for education to truly fulfill its public mission of teaching academic skills and modeling social standards. But urgency must not lead us to rush. The pace of change must be reasonable and related to the right pace for children's learning. Productive change has to be grounded in the practical experience of the teachers and administrators who live each day within our school communities. They need to speak more often and more strongly in the conversation of reform and their thoughts need to be heard and valued.

Politicians and theoreticians should and do influence educational change and act as watchdogs over the use of school time. But they need to spend more time in school and in conversation with teachers and administrators. By working together and understanding the primacy of the need for change in the social context of education, we can change the way we structure and use educational time. We can move our schools closer to the friendly and effective communities of learning we all desire.

In the chapters that follow I provide specific proposals for action. Chapter 7 provides suggestions and strategies for changing schools from the top down. By making changes at the administrative level, we can improve some of the conditions which limit and distract teachers like Mrs. Chambers at Briarwood and those at Longfellow Middle School.

Chapters 8 and 9 focus on how individual teachers can make significant changes in their teaching approaches and strategies so that the structures and uses of time in their classrooms better serve their students. Chapter 8 suggests and illustrates ways to change the structure of time in our classrooms and Chapter 9 looks at some of the ways we can use time once we change those structures.

Chapter 10 provides "3 Rs" to guide educational thought, design, and practice. It provides a vision of school in the future where time is structured to meet children's developmental needs and is used to facilitate the integration of social and academic learning which children need and want so desperately.

In an afterword, "Heroes in the Classroom," I honor those who teach in our schools and recognize their role in leading our nation—our children—into the future.

Chapter Seven

Changing School Time

CHANGES ARE NEEDED in how we structure and use educational time at every level—the political, administrative and instructional. Some changes require the action of school boards, or in some cases, state legislatures—changes such as lengthening the school year or creating year-round schools. Other changes can be initiated by principals at the school building level, such as restructuring the beginning of the school day.

This chapter covers changes at the political and administrative level. Some of these ideas require significant restructuring of available time and may seem difficult to imagine. Others are conservative, arguing strenuously for retaining time structures that have proven to make a difference in behavior and academic attention—such as recess! All of these proposals are designed to help us examine what we have traditionally taken for granted and thought of as immutable—the schedule of the classroom and the school.

The proposals in this chapter are presented in two sections. The first lists changes which require action by local school boards, state legislatures, or education departments. They are changes which require strong advocacy by professional educators and parents so that high-level officials hear the voices which are demanding quality education for all children.

The second section is addressed primarily to school principals and other administrators who are involved in children's daily lives at school and whose actions have a powerful effect on everyone in their immediate educational community: students, teachers, and staff.

Guidelines for Changes at the Political Level

- Lengthen the academic year and/or keep schools open longer each day to allow more time for academics and special interests.

- Support high-quality instruction by increasing teacher salaries so more highly qualified teachers can work a year-round professional schedule.

- Establish and enforce professional standards for teachers.

- Reduce school size.

- Reduce class size to under twenty so that teachers have more time with individual students, smaller instructional groups, and less time required for whole-group transitions and general management.

- Increase the quality of instructional time by eliminating formal tracking and supporting differentiated instruction within each classroom.

- Support "stand alone" social skills curricula and the teaching of social skills as an integrated part of the content curricula.

- Support the development of schools as "learning communities" at the school board and "bond issue" level.

Lengthen the academic year and/or day

There are many problems with the yearly school calendar. The vast majority of school districts still operate on an agrarian calendar left over from the time when children were needed in the fields in the summer and early fall for harvesting crops.

The average American school calendar requires approximately 180–190 days of school, or between 900–1000 hours. This is less than in most other countries but the curriculum is far wider. It requires "covering" more content than in other nations, in less time. It is no wonder, then, that teachers feel like they are on a "time train," as one teacher told me, with no way to get off.

If you divide the hours available by the time needed to cover the required curriculum, you end with a fraction, not a whole number. Any way the formula is constructed, teachers and students come out on the short end and teachers often feel personally responsible for what is actually a system failure. This morning, my Internet connection simply refused to operate. I immediately suspected that I was doing something wrong rather than considering that the problem was a failure of the system. When we look at the academic year and the curricular and social expectations, it is clear that we are victims of the very systems we helped create.

As covered in Chapter 3, the National Commission on Time and Learning did a good job identifying some of the problems associated with time use in education today.[1] Two of their eight recommendations follow:

Establish an academic day. The Commission suggested that anything outside the core academic day would be provided by adding time to the school day. Today, many children go directly from school to "after-school" care in their school buildings or community facilities. Why not reserve physical education, library, health, music, DARE, Santa Claus, and Valentine's Day for a 2–6 P.M. block with a different teaching staff? Activities related to these "special" areas could be more easily integrated into the "academic" day as well because children would be prepared with greater understanding, interest, and skills.

This makes sense but would require the implementation of their next recommendation as well.

Keep schools open longer to meet the needs of children and communities. The need for quality care of children outside the home, from early in the morning to early in the evening, is a fact of American life at the turn of the twenty-first century.

The National Commission proposes year-round schools which

are open earlier and later. They visited several schools and districts trying reform efforts using this recommendation and they were working well. However, most are funded by federal, state, or private grants, or a combination of grants and fees; few are being funded by local taxation. Long-range funding solutions are not immediately clear.

But at a national level, this is a wonderful recommendation because it truly speaks to the heart of the matter: making time in school more responsive to what we know about the quantity and quality of time children need at different ages and with different family needs, academic learning styles, and abilities.

If Mrs. Chambers' class had the library period later in the day, after the end of the traditional school day, she would have had more time for math or writing or science. If Phoebe had art after two o'clock, there would have been extended time for the math problems or her team "TV production."

Many schools have eliminated morning and afternoon recess as a way to find more time, leaving only a short lunch recess in the middle of the day. This does not meet children's physical needs for movement, play, and exercise (although regular classroom teachers can provide brief physical breaks throughout the instructional day in the classroom or outside). If regular physical education classes were scheduled for "School—Part II," more time would be available for core subjects in the first part of the day.

It would cost a great deal more to essentially hire two staffs at every school site, but the end results in academic achievement, behavior, health, and well-being for children and teachers alike would be enormous. It would also meet the need of the increasing number of families who must struggle to make some sort of arrangement for after-school care.

Envision the time teachers would have for planning after two P.M. Imagine the engagement in learning children would have until six P.M. given the right balance of activity, rest, nutrition, and care. Creative administrators would mix and match staffs from both parts of the day to maximize integration between the two programs and make budgets reasonable. Yes, it would cost more, but what price are we paying now in terms of school failure, poor or inadequate care for children before and after school, juvenile crime, and a host of other educational and social problems? Which is more expensive for the taxpayer and the parent? Is it better to spend money on teachers or jailers?

Increase teacher salaries

A legacy of the agrarian calendar is that it was only necessary to pay teachers for nine months of service. This continues today, leaving teachers grossly underpaid in contrast to teachers in other countries, often requiring them to have second jobs in the summer or to work second jobs during the school year. When professional educators work second jobs during the academic year, it severely diminishes their ability to devote necessary time to preparation or even to participate adequately with their colleagues. Few people are aware how common this is.

I remember sitting in a teacher's room in a Connecticut middle school (in the state with the highest paid teachers in America) and overhearing the idle conversation of teachers about their "other" jobs—in restaurants, selling insurance, real estate, coaching and refereeing sports. Many complained of lack of sleep and the difficulty of getting their papers graded in the little spare time they had between jobs. I worried about their classrooms (I was consulting in some of them) and about the time their families saw them at home.

Full-time, year-round teachers would be paid on a twelve-month contract with reasonable vacation time that could be taken at different times of the year and not just in the summer.[2] Some non-teaching time in the summer or during other student vacation times would be devoted to curriculum creation, assessment, and professional development. Teachers would be expected to work regular eight-hour days with six hours devoted to direct instruction and contact with students. This would be true for staff working on both sides of the core teaching day.

190 / CHAPTER SEVEN

These changes would require enormous study and cooperation between unions, school boards, and parents. Some schools have already taken this big step, others are planning to. These changes will not occur overnight. Nothing worthwhile ever does. But the reality of life for children in the twenty-first century in America demands that these ideas be considered seriously by the adults in charge.

Establish and enforce professional standards for teachers

Although most teachers in schools across the country are skilled, dedicated, and caring, there are bad teachers. Incompetent teachers and staff members exist in nearly every school and rarely is anything done about them. How many teachers do you know who have been fired for incompetence? In some states, testing teachers on academic content is now proposed or used to determine a teacher's suitability for the profession, when good teachers and administrators know that hiring and firing teachers on their ability to pass an objective test will not necessarily rid schools of bad teachers.

Bad teaching is a form of child abuse and should be treated as such. The screamers, demean-ers, hitters, and hurters should be cast out of the profession summarily and put under court order not to go near the children. This is education's dirty little secret: it is a profession without any serious enforcement of standards meant to protect the children from the weak, misplaced, and mean people who have found their way into schools. And some have been there a very long time.

Bad teaching wastes an enormous amount of school time and poisons the learning environment. Here is where real professional standards matter. But in many cases these standards don't exist, and if they do, they aren't enforced. As Jonathan Saphier has truthfully written, "Until we get the guts and the skills to dismiss incompetents and remediate unsatisfactory performers with clear procedures and do so consistently, we severely limit our chances of launching healthy collegial practices that will result in sustained teacher growth and become a permanent part of institutional life."[3]

The efforts to bring children up to an academic grade level standard are commendable, but will not make our schools or communities better places to live and learn by themselves. The true integration of academic and social standards must be implemented, beginning with enforced academic and social standards for teachers. Principals and superintendents must demand a high moral standard from all adults under their supervision. These grown-ups should be above reproach in their language, actions, and daily conduct with children.

When incompetent or cruel adults are allowed to continue working in schools and everyone knows, hears, and sees what they do, it sends a clear message to everyone in the school. The wrong message. It says that working hard, caring, and doing the right thing doesn't matter, because if you do the wrong thing, nothing happens anyway! If we want to "raise the bar," let's raise it so the adults can't get away with unacceptable behavior, day after day.

Principals and superintendents need to be held more accountable for better school management and more frequent, vigilant, and courageous supervision. Most teachers and school staff are observed by their direct supervisor once a year for thirty minutes. That is unacceptable.

If we gave more than lip service to the basic union contract and job description requirements for civil conduct in the workplace, the atmosphere in schools would change significantly and result in greater learning. We could feel the pleasant daily experience of being welcomed to work, reduce interpersonal tension and encourage genuine communication and sharing of responsibility.

Recently, I thought about the difference between the dedicated professionals in the classroom and the adults who do not belong there as I sat beside my 84-year-old mother in intensive care in the hospital following her emergency surgery. I watched as she struggled against the tubes and drugs so foreign to her experience. I also watched the reaction of the nursing staff who cared for her. When she became agitated and pulled the IV lines from her arm and tried to climb out of bed in her delirium, most of the nurses responded with a mixture of professional calm, patience, and caring; they kindly helped me lift her back into bed and reinserted the IVs. A few nurses were clearly annoyed that she was making more work for them.

I thought how like teachers they were, most of them dedicated, but some who should not have been there at all. As I sat by my mom's bed, I was reminded of a remark a strong principal made during a workshop discussion of discipline. He had told his teachers and school staff, "You can't dislike children on company time!" Now that's the kind of leadership and supervision we need in all our schools.

Reduce school size

In a school of 1,000 students it is nearly impossible for students to feel known and invested in their learning unless the school is divided into small learning communities, "families," or teams where eight to fifteen teachers work together to provide a "school-within-a-school" environment for about 200 students. In this structure, teachers have much more control over instructional time and are able to plan small community events, assemblies, and community service. They are also much better able to utilize their joint planning time, and plan parent conferences and professional development. Team leaders can serve on administrative teams with building principals to coordinate school-wide needs.

I remember being asked one summer to consult with a school that was just being constructed and readied for opening in the fall. The school would have 1,200 students and the principal proudly showed me the hallways and classrooms where workers were still installing light fixtures, computer stations, and chalkboards. She wanted suggestions about how to manage the size of the building, the number of students and staff. Unfortunately, a golden opportunity had passed at the architectural stage. Here was a first grade wing, there a sixth grade wing. A better arrangement for a school this size would be constructing four or five "pods" with classrooms for grades

K–6 in each pod; each complete with a teacher workspace, and each with its own assembly area.

Reduce class size

It is surprising that the most obvious variable for providing more time for instruction in our nation's schools was given only brief mention in the entire study of the National Commission on Time and Learning. In a final section of the final volume titled "The Unanswered Questions," only one out of thirty dealt with size: "What are the effects of *school size* on academic performance, retention, morale, vandalism, student behavior, parent involvement and efficient use of time?" [emphasis added]4 The Commission did not ask, "What are the effects of *class size* on time on learning, academic performance, retention, morale, vandalism, student behavior, parent involvement and efficient use of time?" In this critical study of time, *class size was not considered as a significant variable.*

In Chapter 3, the major focus of research questions addressed by the studies on class size we examined dealt with the relationship of class size to academic performance. In these studies, *time was not examined as a significant variable.*

The connection between time and class size has not been thoroughly considered or emphasized. I am puzzled by this because it is an issue which is obvious to every classroom teacher:

- Smaller class size changes the quality and use of time in the classroom.

As covered in Chapter 3, research has proven the following principle, on which teachers and serious educational researchers agree:

- Reducing class size below twenty students in the primary grades significantly improves the educational experience of all children.

Remove only five children from Mrs. Chambers' first grade roster and think about the changes in her teaching day. She would now have approximately 20 percent more time for the remaining children. This is time gained through less time for transitions, less time for students to wait for her individual attention, and small groups which are more easily managed and effectively taught.

To advocate for such an expensive change in your school or district is always difficult and politically unpopular in the face of tight budgets and questionable standardized test scores. But the best solution to raising test scores is to reduce class size which provides more time for learning. The impact would be immediate and long lasting.

Eliminate tracking

In Chapter 3 we explored the need to replace the practice of tracking students according to academic ability with the practice of differentiated instruction in heterogeneous classrooms. Extensive research supports this contention.[5]

We did not visit classrooms grouped by ability at either Longfellow Middle School or at Briarwood Elementary because, fortunately, neither school engages in the practice. I have visited many schools that do. In the "fast" track, students appear well-dressed, healthy, engaged, and excited to learn. They have many materials and options for learning and sit in well-equipped and attractive classrooms.

In the "slow" tracks, students present a different picture. Depending on their age, engagement in learning is clearly waning or has all but disappeared. I've observed second grade, low-achieving classrooms where the lights in the eyes of these young children have already gone out. This is a disgrace to the profession of teaching and a tragedy that none of these children need experience.

> Acknowledging that students learn at different speeds and that they differ widely in their ability to think abstractly or understand complex ideas is like acknowledging that students at any given age aren't all the same height. It is not a

statement of worth, but of reality. To accommodate this reality, teachers can create a 'user-friendly' environment, one in which they flexibly adapt pacing, approaches to learning, and channels for expressing learning in response to their students' differing needs.[6]

Teaching in this way requires knowledge of different approaches to instruction, knowledge of child development, excellent planning skills, and good assessment procedures—all skills we have a right to demand from everyone in the teaching profession today.

Learning in a heterogeneous elementary classroom or middle school team has all the advantages and challenges of living in a diverse society, something all of our students will experience as adults in the United States of the twenty-first century. Regardless of ability, students in Mrs. Chambers' class learned from each other throughout the day and were generally unconcerned with each other's skill levels. In Phoebe's seventh grade, students were acutely aware of skill level differences as well as differences of race, class, and social status, but they were still struggling with these differences instead of being tracked into the easy-answer groupings which might well be labeled "Success" and "Failure."

Well-managed, mixed-ability classrooms take time. Time blocks have to be longer to allow for more independent and small group work and to provide more time for the teacher to attend to individual needs. These longer blocks also allow for students to engage in varied types of project work, in addition to simply verbal and written expression as a way to show what they are learning in school. To make these time blocks effective, curricular expectations must be narrowed appropriately.

Support "stand alone" and integrated social skills curricula

Both "stand alone" social skills curricula and the teaching of social skills as an integrated part of content curricula can move schools forward in their important work in the social development of children.

There are several exemplary curricula that have demonstrated the usefulness of "stand alone" approaches to teaching specific social skills. Open Circle, Second Step, Resolving Conflict Creatively, and Social Decision Making and Problem Solving are four among many.[7] These have proven to be effective in changing classroom and school-wide behavior and in providing students with specific, life-long skills such as social problem solving, mediation techniques, and better listening skills.

An obvious potential difficulty of such programs is finding time to add one more content area to an already packed teaching schedule. Teachers who have successfully implemented programs such as these have usually built them into the beginning of their school day in some way or isolated them as a unit in their social studies or health curricula.

Approaches such as *The Responsive Classroom,* School Development Program, and the Child Development Project are examples of comprehensive, school-wide reform initiatives that provide teachers and administrators with tools to integrate the teaching and learning of social and academic skills throughout the school day. These approaches feature extensive professional development and on-site coaching over a number of years at both the classroom and school level.[8]

The Child Development Project includes a unique, graded literature curriculum that infuses social themes into reading units at each grade level. Other subject area textbooks are including more social themes and references to social problem-solving skills as well. In selecting and purchasing new books, districts should give consideration to how these life skills and issues are integrated into content material.[9]

To provide support for the integration of a social curriculum with the academic, school boards and administrations must give priority to professional development in this area, including supporting budget allocations that provide teachers release time for training. Teachers are given significantly more training in teaching content than they are in managing classrooms. This is true at both the pre-service and in-service level.

Helping a teacher shift her management approach with children is a lengthier and more involved process than training her to deliver new content material. But it is an investment of time and money which has important long-term implications: it will improve student behavior and performance.

Support schools as learning communities at school board and bond issue levels

Character education has been given considerable attention in schools over the last decade, but time devoted to building character has often been limited to "Honesty Month" or "Responsibility Week." Poster or essay contests about good character are not the avenue to good character. Regular, consistent practice is.

School districts that want to foster true character education should look first at school-wide approaches such as those advocated by Thomas Lickona and the Center for the Fourth and Fifth Rs at the State University of New York at Cortland.[10] His approach helped inform many of the school-wide reform initiatives mentioned above. Good character education is a part of good teaching that accentuates the integration of social and academic learning in every part of the school day. School boards or district administrations that want to support this approach can initiate a broad-based character education program in their community.[11]

Every year, new schools are built that pay little attention to how the physical configuration supports or discourages learning communities. In fact, most buildings continue to be designed and constructed on a factory model with the kindergarten wing at one end of the building and the sixth grade wing at the other. The teacher's room is located away from instructional areas as are the administrative offices. Places for the learning community to gather must double as cafeterias or gymnasiums. There is very little in the building itself that speaks of welcome and community.

Imagine that architects designed even large schools so that students spent the majority of their time in small learning communities.

Each wing would have six or seven rooms and a gathering space. Each wing would have a kindergarten room *and* a sixth grade room and every grade in between! There would be a teacher workspace and a gathering space in each learning community. At the center of the school would be the media center, the gymnasium/assembly space, and administrative offices. Students and parents would be able to enter their learning community through its own entrance.

Would these schools be more expensive to build? Perhaps. But meeting the community's goal of improved education and better citizenship would have a better chance of success in such a space than in the unfriendly and sometimes unhealthy atmosphere of current "learning factories." Small learning communities are the best option for fostering a healthy, lively learning environment.

Guidelines for Changes at the Administrative Level

- Allow time for in-depth learning, investigation, and contemplation by narrowing the scope of the curriculum and lengthening time blocks.

- Reduce the number of "specials" that pull children out of self-contained classrooms and send those special area teachers into the classroom wherever possible. Reduce transitions at the middle school level.

- Construct realistic daily schedules and adapt them to the needs and abilities of children at different grade levels. Support teachers working to meet the special needs of children whose behavior may classify them as ADHD/ADD.

- Adjust the middle of the school day to allow for a midday time of exercise, nutrition, and rest—in that order—to change the nature and productivity of the afternoon.

- Change the school schedule to allow more time for teachers, staff, administration, and parents to interact with each other.

- Attend to the physical and social environment of the school. Make school a comfortable and exciting place to learn and grow—physically, academically, and socially.

- Support the balanced integration of social and academic learning.

Narrow the curriculum and lengthen time blocks

Every teacher, whether in elementary or middle school, has a required amount of curriculum to cover each day. Getting to all of it is difficult, if not impossible. The answer to meeting curriculum expectations on a daily basis is again found in paradox. We must consider smaller topics for longer periods of time to accomplish more. This is clearly seen at the middle school level where recent research findings have made it evident that block scheduling, small classes, "advisory" periods, and other changes improve student behavior and academic performance.[12]

At the elementary level, teachers are mostly in "self-contained" classrooms. They generally have more flexibility in their daily schedules. But even so, the curriculum requirements are often overwhelming, especially when there seem to be more "special" activities every day which eat into precious time for curriculum content.

When students in well-managed, mixed-ability classrooms have more time in longer blocks to explore content in depth, they can learn research skills, write about content in depth, and revise and improve work over time. As covered in Chapter 3, research indicates that narrowing the curriculum is in the best interest of student achievement.

Working to align your school's curriculum with your state's standards is a good way to begin narrowing the curriculum. This, at first, may seem contradictory. There appears to be so much to cover at every grade level and in every subject area. But alignment is not the same thing as simply adopting a state curriculum. It means finding ways to combine and integrate content areas through themes or unit lessons that allow students (and teachers!) to work together to explore skills and subjects in great depth and in relational ways.

Taking the time to help students see the connections and applications of the skills and content they are learning deepens their reasoning and helps engender respect for the educational process in which they are engaged. This, in turn, allows them to see state tests designed to measure their academic growth as reasonable and, consequently, will produce better results on these assessments.

Good teachers know that a deeper and narrower curriculum sets higher standards of performance for teaching and learning. Administrators should encourage teachers to develop these approaches alongside more traditional scope and sequence designs. We need to have confidence that students will meet and surpass state standards if school schedules provide teachers with sufficient time to deepen their students' understanding of what they are learning, and sufficient time for the teachers' own planning as well.

A cooperative approach to narrowing the curriculum could not currently happen at Longfellow Middle School. But if the schedule were changed so that teachers worked in smaller teams and each teacher taught two subject areas (commonly English and social studies or math and science), then a narrower curriculum allowing for deeper learning would be possible.[13]

A narrower curriculum is already being taught in Mrs. Chambers' class. But for her to feel comfortable that she is meeting the state standards and readying her students for the state assessments they will take in years to come, she needs her administrators to make her part of a professional team of teachers (K–4) investigating curriculum alignment and the development of appropriate projects and units that integrate standard expectations across content areas.

Reduce the number of transitions at the middle school level

The reason to have special area teachers move instead of children (although painful for the adults) is compelling and important. The routine, structure, rules, and comfort of the regular classroom for students creates more time for learning. The less children are moved as whole classes from one space to another, the more time there is for learning.

Using this approach at the elementary level, special area teachers need to become included in the spirit, culture, and expectations of the home-base classroom, rather than having to create a separate set of expectations for their separate space. Under this plan, children are more easily able to internalize rules and follow directions from more than one adult. This creates more attention to content instruction, as in the art period in Mrs. Chambers' room in Chapter 6.

In the chapter on the Longfellow Middle School, I suggested one basic way for there to be less movement and fewer transitions for students. Having some subject area teachers move instead of the students, and reducing the size of teams and increasing blocks of time in the schedule creates more stability and regularity.

Special area teachers love having their own rooms and they should have them. But my belief is that these should be well-appointed offices or studios with space for tutorial lessons and an enormous supply room with a highly functional mobile supply vehicle (cart). If they had such a space, there would be less resistance to "art on a cart." These areas can be planned into new schools. In existing schools where special area teachers have their own classrooms, these can be transformed into the kind of space I'm suggesting (although teachers admittedly will be very reluctant to "give up" their space in this way). In existing schools where special area teachers have no space of their own, they should get an appropriate office and supply area so they can best prepare for moving into classrooms.

Construct realistic schedules

I am amazed at the number of school schedules that read something like this:

Homeroom	8:30–8:45
First period	8:45–9:07
Second period	9:07–9:49

This schedule makes it seem possible for students to "tesser" in time, as in the classic fiction of Madeline L'Engle where the fifth dimension is a "tesseract" in which, "you can travel in space without having to go the long way around."[14] In other words, students are due to begin second period at the exact moment first period ends, and this same expectation is repeated throughout the day. Quite a trick, if you can pull it off. This expected, fifth-dimensional time traveling is not a science fiction story, but a reality in too many schools. The illusion of such a schedule wreaks havoc on students and learning.

Students are made to feel late all the time and teachers must become enforcers of an impossible set of expectations. This is truly an "Alice in Wonderland" scenario and it is hard to imagine that it exists in real public institutions with well-meaning people trying to do the best for children. If you have a schedule like this, or one that provides insufficient time for transitions, change it so that the schedule matches the reality of time needed between periods.

If this makes it so that you no longer meet the "time on task" requirements of your state standards, then recommend a political solution. Propose to your superintendent and your school council the lengthening of the school day, the teacher contract, and the bus schedule in order to conform to state mandates for time on task. Don't allow yourself to bend or shrink the schedule and pretend you are meeting time requirements when you are actually making the time situation worse.

If the state is mandating time requirements, then focusing on a political solution lets your taxpayers and union members know it's a state issue, not your issue. If it's the law according to new state legislative guidelines for education, and there's only so much time in the day, then you are only recommending that your school conform to the new standards by creating realistic expectations about the use of time. The process will not be easy and, like most things worth doing, will take time, maybe years, to correct.

Remember that you can change school schedules, even if they have been in place for years, but avoid implementing major schedule changes until everyone has been involved in study and planning for these new approaches, and make changes at the beginning of a new year rather than in the middle.

For example, you can change your schedule to put recess before lunch. You can insert a period for morning meeting at the beginning of the day that allows special area teachers to attend and participate in regular classrooms. You can create a schedule that brings the whole school or sections of the school together once a week and you can create a schedule that encourages teachers to bring their students together for reflection at the end of the day. In middle school, the yearly schedule can also be enhanced by calendar breaks for mini-courses and other changes in the academic pace.

Keep bells and announcements to a minimum

Each day I observed Mrs. Chambers' class, the intercom interrupted at least seven times. In most cases, neither the teacher nor the students were able to listen or were interested in listening to what was said.

Every intercom interruption subtracts learning time from the class. Even with a polite, "Please pardon this interruption," learning *is* interrupted every time. Of course, emergency announcements are essential, but a daily staff bulletin in everyone's mailbox at the beginning of the day can eliminate the need for many public address system distractions. Two transitions are eliminated if there is no intercom to start the day—the one to stop the class to listen, the one to get them back attending to you.

I also am opposed to leading the flag salute and singing songs from the office at a fixed time, even when students are in charge. I know this is popular in many, many schools, but I believe it detracts from the creation of the small learning communities that improve learning, classroom by classroom. When this task is centralized, teachers must organize their time around a central schedule rather than their individual time needs on a given day. To me, it is obvious that this wastes learning time for individual teachers and classes. Opening exercises are best left to the individual classroom.

The beginning of the school day

How do students enter the building? Where do they go when they enter? How much time do they have before the first bell or the official beginning of school? If breakfast is served, how much time is allotted and what are the other students doing who are not having breakfast? In the Cortland, New York, elementary schools, students coming off the bus go to the cafeterias for breakfast or into the gym for "Morning Program." Morning Program begins with physical activity and music as the gym fills up with more and more bus arrivers and breakfast finishers.

Principals are in the gym, "directing traffic" and greeting students. A Morning Program Committee of upper-grade students readies a formal and set agenda. At a word from the principal over the sound system (the principal wears a lavaliere microphone), all students sit by classes or grade-level groups. The Morning Program Committee and the principal swing into action. Birthdays are celebrated, academic projects are shared by a class, special announcements are made, and occasional special guests lead an activity. Finally, everyone stands and salutes the flag, sings a song, and heads off to their own classroom and their own individual morning meetings.

What began as a response to problems when buses arrived and students had to wait on the playground has become a strong part of the learning community's culture. I have never seen a better example of character education at the school district level. It is a daily example of a school where respect, responsibility, and civility are central to an exciting learning process.

The first weeks of school

In *The Responsive Classroom* approach to the yearly school schedule, we teach that the "first six weeks of school" are a distinct and critically important time of year. Our recommendation is for a slow, thoughtful, and purposeful beginning. Teachers who come to believe in this approach talk about how hard it is to follow as they watch their colleagues zoom ahead in the curriculum, how much they worry they will never get their children to catch up.

But like the tortoise and the hare, slow but sure wins the race. During the first six weeks, teachers spend time on goal setting, rule generation, guided discoveries of new materials, equipment, and supplies. They explore the learning process as they introduce academic content. They take time to build that trustworthy space in the classroom which values taking a risk, having questions and ideas, and having a voice. When children enter such classrooms on the first day of school they are surprised by what they see (and so are parents, unless a pre-school conference has happened).

Bulletin boards are bare except for a neat border of color. Materials are not visible everywhere. Some bookcases are covered with signs that say, "Coming Attractions." On that first day, children will help the teacher make labels for shelves and put their own name tags by their coat hooks. As the days and weeks progress, the teacher will carefully introduce the social and academic expectations for the room through modeling, practice and role-playing. Eventually the bulletin boards are full of the students' own interesting writing and beautiful art, not the teacher's.

In the long run, time is gained and enriched for teachers and students alike. Discipline difficulties are fewer and less time-consuming than in other classrooms where the social expectations were not a clear focus. There is greater understanding of academic expectations and academic outcomes are improved.[15] Principals who understand, support, and recommend this approach to their staff help create a more consistent building climate earlier in the year.

In middle schools, the beginning of the school year ought to be radically different as well. In most middle schools there is inadequate orientation time before students are plunged into academics. There may be abbreviated schedules the first few days, with time given to learning locker combinations, explaining schedules, and passing out books, but concentrating on building a community of learners is seldom part of the lesson plans.

A week of homeroom, with getting-to-know-you activities, group initiatives, team-building activities, community service to the school (flower planting, bulletin board construction, sign making), and shared academic initiatives (learning homework expectations, practicing key study skills, taking academic assessments to determine strengths and weaknesses) would help create the kind of middle school spirit all desire. In middle school, the yearly schedule may also be enhanced by calendar breaks for mini-courses and other changes in the academic pace.

Other times of the year

Other times of the year require some special attention as well. Periods following vacations require reviewing social and academic expectations. Taking the time for this reexamination creates more time for learning (just as going slowly in the beginning of the year does). Many teachers ask students to create "New Year's Resolutions" and reflect on these revised goals for the academic year when they return from winter holidays. Using this as a school-wide theme can get things off and running smoothly at the beginning of the calendar year.

During "the last six weeks of school," it is also important and helpful for students to reflect on their learning for the year to see all that they have accomplished and to consider the coming academic year. During this period, it is important that more structure be in place, not less. The end of the year is not the time to relax and loosen expectations in the classroom or around the school.

Too often, we see June as the end when we should be seeing it as the culmination. This is a key time for exhibitions, performance assessments, science fairs, and parent nights. Despite the competition from spring sports, daylight savings time, and outdoor activity, the message should be that school is in session and what goes on during these last six weeks is as critically important as what happens in the first six weeks. Otherwise, an enormous amount of instructional time is lost at the end of the school year (which advocates of year-round school readily point out.)

Confront the realities of high-stakes testing

Standards are important, but we will continue to spend more time on more tests until we put testing in its proper perspective. If we saw the purpose of high-stakes testing as giving us the information we need to help students who are struggling, instead of comparing who's best and who's worst, student by student, school by school, we could change the inordinate amount of time we use to test children and, instead, have more time to teach.

Early childhood teachers are skilled at many informal assessment techniques and the individual developmental and learning queries which can identify which children need early intervention in Title I, Reading Recovery, and other extra help programs. Assessment testing in grade three and above, if taken in perspective and within reasonable time frames, is acceptable and useful for students, teachers, and parents.

But you can confidently advocate for the elimination of high-stakes testing before grade three (except for necessary Title I testing) because it is a grand waste of time and provides almost no returns for the children. Time for classroom instruction is much more important than formalized classroom assessment in kindergarten and the primary grades.

When high-stakes testing week in upper grades approaches, the very air is often charged with anxiety. Letters are sent home to parents urging them to make sure their children have a healthy breakfast and a good night's sleep. Does this mean that nutrition and rest are more important on test days for children than other school days? What message are we sending?

If enough practice time is encouraged prior to the actual tests, a different spirit about tests can emerge in the school. It won't guarantee higher performance, but it will put the value and importance of tests into some kind of perspective. At one school in Cincinnati, Ohio, the principal began testing week with a pep rally, bringing the school together to show solidarity and security about the strategies students had learned to "tackle" the test—a fitting analogy for a pep rally!

Re-order the middle of the day

This is one of the most important suggestions I can offer. In the middle of the day children need a break from the rigor of academics. It is important to remember, however, that even during this time there is much to learn. Teaching recess and lunch is just as important as teaching reading and math. In the schools where I have taught and been principal, we have always used a mid-day schedule which gives children recess, then lunch, then quiet time. I began this with the notion that eating and then going out was disruptive to both the educational system and the digestive system. Better to work up an appetite with exercise, come in to eat, settle down and take a rest.

Children, teachers, and parents report this structure for the middle of the day works. It especially helps children to be productive and engaged in the afternoon. The idea of a quiet time after lunch may be unimaginable to many teachers, given all they must fit in, but here, again, is a paradox of teaching and learning: quiet time away from academic demands increases learning.

During quiet time, the rule in most classrooms is that children must work completely alone in their own space and the room must be silent. This might be as little as fifteen minutes and as long as thirty. When you walk into the room, you will see children drawing, reading, writing, working on the computer, napping, doing an assignment. In the silence, they are often consolidating their learning, reflecting on their morning, "breathing out." In much of the rest of the world, "siesta" is a known necessity and cultural expectation. We Americans feel our minds and bodies dozing at mid-day but we push through, believing that we will accomplish more. Of course, we don't. It is the same with the children.

Make playground time a priority

Learning time is maximized in school environments where playgrounds are peaceful, friendly, and active. Principals can help in several ways. First, designate at least the first two weeks of school recess as "skillful play," when recess games, playground rules, and ways of playing together are modeled, practiced, and reinforced. Prior to the beginning of school, provide playground education for teachers, paraprofessionals, and others (including the school nurse) who will have important roles to play at and around recess.

Second, require that your physical education teachers teach playground games as their first academic unit at the beginning of the year. I recommend that physical education teachers, as part of their teaching duties, be given supervisory authority and be held accountable for the nature and quality of the playground/recess experience for children. This does not mean that they have "recess duty" every day. Instead, it means elevating their professional status to include being part of the administrative team of the school.

It may also mean eventually reducing the number of hours the head physical education teacher has with individual classes so her time can be devoted to training paraprofessionals and supervising the overall outdoor and indoor recess program. Where schools have taken this approach to heart, there are surveys indicating reduced playground referrals to the office and reduced injury reports from the nurse's office.[16] The result? More time for learning.

Allow more time for teachers, staff, administration, and parents to work together

Perhaps the best way to model your desire for more staff communication, engagement, and collaboration is to use some of your administrative time to "cover" a classroom for one teacher while she meets with another or observes in another room. You should then try to find a few minutes to meet with the two teachers so they can share what they're working on and so that you can share an observation from the classroom. Obviously, you can't do this every day, but even if you were able to do it once or twice a week, it would send a message that you value this way of using time to strengthen the adult community.

Creating schedules that allow time for grade level and team planning is also an important administrative function. Try not to create this time solely on the backs of special area teachers—that is, making planning periods for a grade-level team through simultaneous special area classes at a particular grade level. Some of this is necessary, of course, but special area teachers need to meet and plan with others as well. Otherwise, their jobs become highly isolating.

Schedule the first parent-teacher conference early

If it were possible, I would schedule the first conference before students entered the classroom! This conference would be for goal setting. Teachers would ask parents, "What would you like your child to learn in school this year?" By asking this question (a question seldom asked of parents as their children go through school), a partnership between home and school can be created before any problems or issues arise.

Teachers would share their goals for the classroom during this conference, learn as much as possible about the individual student, and explain such things as homework and discipline expectations. This would eliminate an enormous amount of time in missed or contentious communication. Teachers, then, might not hear the phrase "I would have done something about what you're telling me if I had known about it in September," so often in fall report card conferences.

Because of this initial, friendly contact, teachers and parents would be more likely to form a strong alliance in support of the education of a child. In schools where I have seen this done, real changes have been clear in the amount and quality of parent participation in the school. This ends up providing more time for the teacher to reach her students with more knowledge about their needs and more confidence in the support from home.

Care for the physical environment

The quality of time in school is improved significantly when the air quality is monitored, air ducts cleaned, and dusting accomplished regularly. Reduction in headaches and asthma means improved attention and attendance. A school where temperature is taken seriously has more time devoted to teaching and less time given over to complaints that it is too cold or too hot. These simple actions translate directly and tangibly into more time for learning.

I remember a year I spent working with a city school where the district painting crew was dispatched to paint the inside of the school, including each classroom, during the school year while children were present! Day by day, children and teachers were moved into the halls, rooms dismantled and "sealed off." Painters then spray-painted the walls and ceilings and moved on to the next room. Paint fumes permeated the building, children and teachers complained, but the painting went forward. "Get your school painted now, or not at all" was the message. Time to teach took a nosedive that year.

It is a national disgrace that we spend millions, if not billions of tax dollars annually to hermetically seal our historical treasures in temperature-controlled buildings with computer engineering stations, and ignore the daily health of children and teachers. You may not be able to have a museum-quality physical environment, but you can put air quality and temperature high on your priority list and that of your custodial staff. It is an issue which should be championed by teachers' unions.

You can also have a "museum mentality" when it comes to student display throughout the common areas of the school. For the same reasons that it's important for students to display their work in the classroom, you can reinforce and encourage the use of time for student curators to proudly exhibit work school-wide.

Facilitate a school-wide discipline policy and procedure

Consistent, fair, and well-understood discipline probably does more than any one thing to increase learning time in school. A review of your discipline policy and procedure will probably show you there are some holes. It's not a bad idea to spend a full year reviewing the situation with a school-wide committee or your site-based council.

In *The Responsive Classroom* approach, we recommend a process that creates a set of school rules from the hopes, dreams, and goals of parents, students, and teachers. This process moves from individuals to classes to school-wide ratification of a set of rules at a "constitutional convention." Once the rules are in place, practice and reinforcement of positive behavior precedes the implementation of logical consequences and a discipline procedure for when the rules are broken.

A discipline procedure with clear guidelines for its use is essential, especially for positive parent involvement and partnership with the school in relation to discipline. You will also need a clear chain of command in your building, so everyone knows who is ultimately in charge when the principal is away. I am surprised at the number of buildings I visit where only the principal and the next-in-command seem to know who is in charge in the principal's absence.

Make the rounds

Just like doctors in a hospital, good principals block out a portion of their own schedule to make rounds to classrooms each day. During this time, interruptions of your time should be kept to a minimum by your office staff. Let the school see that your time is being utilized to learn about how the school is working, how teachers are teaching, and how students are learning.

Plan your day

Just like teachers need daily lesson plans, you need to have a daily plan, too. If your daily schedule is carefully divided and apportioned, it will be harder for you to succumb to the routine of crisis management. Your model of organization—your calmness or anxiety—will be carefully noticed by your staff and students. Your example in how to use time will have a greater impact on teachers' and students' use of time than you think!

See yourself as the leader for the adult community

Just as teachers must view themselves as responsible for how students use time throughout the day, you must be responsible for how adults use time throughout the day. Only you can make common planning time possible. Only you can make faculty meetings socially and professionally respectful, fun, and enlightening. Others can help support you and work with you as a team, but you are the principal.

You can help improve a teacher's teaching by taking time for affirmative coaching. You can improve how paraprofessionals supervise children at lunch by taking time to observe the lunchroom yourself. It makes a difference if you notice time that is well-used and if you notice and address time that is poorly used. Supervision is, in the end, the most important use of your time and it requires brave action. But the good teachers are watching.

Support the integration of social and academic learning

We know how important the administrator's role is in establishing the climate of the learning community. Administrative expectations deeply influence the daily decisions of teachers and staff as well as their approach to more long-range planning.

Take, for instance, the beginning of the school year. If the principal is expecting that students are "hitting" the books the first day of school, then the entire pace of school is affected by that single message. If, instead, s/he expects that teachers will take their time to introduce students carefully to their academic routines, the care and use of materials and equipment, the purpose of textbooks and computers, and the social standards of the classroom, then a different message is sent. The pace and climate of the school will be quite different, as well as the learning.

Will the administrator send the message that learning is a process or a product? Will she encourage posting students' "work in progress" or only the "A" papers in the hallway? Will he ask students *how* they created their group projects or only ask what they learned? Will she acknowledge citizenship and scholarship? Will he help students and teachers see the connection between the two? Will she help parents see the connection?

In faculty meetings, will the principal give time to social interaction among adults and utilize cooperative learning and small dialogue group strategies to improve communication? Will the principal occasionally play on the playground and have lunch sitting down in the lunchroom? Will the principal read to kindergartners and help sixth-graders with homework in the media center once in a while? Proactive strategies implied by these questions teach—through modeling—a strong belief in the importance of integrating social and academic learning.

I remember years ago walking into a principal's office in Florida that had several desks and chairs and a chalkboard and bulletin board right in a corner of the office. There was no question in my mind what statement that principal was making!

Chapter Eight

Changing the Structure of Time in Classrooms

I don't know when we get to be with the children. When we're so busy with paperwork, the children are like mechanical creatures, so many faces. We have no time to be their teachers. We are too busy being their secretaries.

Connecticut teacher, *1998*

IT IS NOT EASY TO CHANGE the structure and use of time in the classroom, but it is essential to the well being of students and teachers alike. It's easy to believe that we have no power to influence how time is structured and used in schools. But with some concentrated work and advocacy, there are ways to begin changing school time at the administrative and political level.

The same is true at the classroom level. The quality of our teaching is what changes time in the classroom. As teachers, we have the power to control the clock, even if we often feel like the clock is controlling us. In Chapter 6, I compared Mrs. Chambers to a figure skater, her movements and actions graceful and smooth, effortless and unhurried. Often, however, she feels more like an Olympic speed skater, driven by the clock, competing against it. For many teachers, the exhausting drive of speed skating is the best description for most teaching days.

What does it take to structure and use time in the classroom so that we feel graceful rather than driven, calm rather than harried? The suggestions which follow can help every teacher, regardless of the institutional policies implemented by administrators and politicians.

They are divided into two chapters for ease of consideration. This chapter covers ways to change the structure of time in the classroom and the next details ways to change how we use time within those time structures. Again, these suggestions are part of a unified approach to classroom teaching founded on what we know about how children grow and learn, and the close relationship between structuring time appropriately and using it effectively.

Guidelines for Changing Time Structures at the Classroom Level

- Balance approaches to allow time for individual students, small instructional groups and whole-class lessons.

- Encourage the social context for learning through large and small learning groups and partner exercises.

- Reduce the number of transitions you have control over.

- Surprise your students with occasional long project blocks and short, unexpected breaks from the normal routine.

- Teach social and academic skills together through established practices such as morning meeting, guided discovery, cooperative learning, and other proven techniques.

- Adapt daily schedules to the needs and abilities of children at your grade level.

- Adjust the middle of your day to allow for a time of rest and quiet in your classroom.

Balance time with individuals, small groups, and whole-class lessons

The pace of the day and the amount and quality of learning is dependent upon the teacher's ability to provide a good mix of instructional formats and to know when to switch the format to improve learning. This is no easy task, but it has a profound impact on time in the classroom. As an example, consider a writing lesson I observed in Mrs. Chambers' room which began with a discussion of Olympic speed skating. After modeling an idea for a story—"I watched Olympic speed skating"—she demonstrates ways to elaborate it by writing sentences on a chart.

> I saw a nasty fall last night.
> The ice needed to be fixed.
> It took a long time to fix.

Several children work on sounding out the sentences she has written on the chart. They are hooked on the story now. Mrs. Chambers asks them why this story is getting interesting. The right time has come to send them back to their seats.

How does she know she's gotten the most she can out of them as a whole group? How does she know it is the right time for them to be working alone, but next to other children? For her, using a combination of knowledge and experience, it's second nature. They've been sitting for a while, they have some ideas and now they can go to work. Sort of.

Once the basic learning atmosphere is established, it is the fine tuning, the nuance, which matters most. Like the meter and tempo of orchestral music, each conductor must decide how fast or slow a particular piece will move, though the score may have a standard approach.

Had Mrs. Chambers sent the children back to their seats before her elaboration modeling, it would have been too soon for better writing to emerge individually, which was the intention of her modeling. If she had continued modeling, she would have lost their attention on the idea of elaboration. She is informed by what she knows about development as well as about writing process. A slightly older class, showing more seven-year-old behavior, might have attended a little longer. This class was ready to get going.

But, there's one more tricky piece—a necessary interlude. Her developmental knowledge of her students' concrete level of cognitive functioning requires her to make a point. "Remember, when you go back to your seats you don't have to write about the Olympics. What I want you to remember is that we can tell lots about one idea. Last time we did this, I saw people go on to more pages. You don't have to write about the Olympics," she reminds again, as she dismisses the children back to their seats a few at a time.

The children get out their writing journals. Mrs. Chambers passes by Corey's table. "Do we have to write about the Olympics?" he asks.

"No," Mrs. Chambers whispers and moves on. Six first-graders will write about the Olympics this morning, but many others will write more elaborate stories about their brothers, their sledding adventure, their birthday party. "We've got some ideas cookin'," she comments to the class as that satisfying hum permeates the room. By balancing whole group, small group, and individual instruction, she maximizes the time for learning—and makes it fun and lively!

Encourage the social context of learning

Academic productivity requires social productivity. It should be obvious I am not recommending social engagement in the classroom for its own sake. Our job as teachers is to maximize learning in the time we are given with the collection of children we happen to have each year. This requires some particular strategies.

Teach partner skills before group skills

In one-to-one relationships we learn to listen, appreciate, argue respectfully, compromise, and decide together what to do next. At all grade levels, students should have plenty of practice and instruction with partner work before they are thrown into large- or small-group activities. Cooperative learning in pairs should precede cooperative learning groups with chairpersons, timekeepers, encouragers, and checkers. Students should experience being class partners with everyone, not just with their best friends or those of the same gender.

Partners can be especially helpful in integrating a new student into the class after the beginning of the year. Brandy came to Mrs. Chambers' class in the middle of the year. A different child got to be Brandy's buddy every day until she had been buddies once with everyone. Her buddy did not spend the whole day with her, but perhaps walked with her to lunch, read a book with her, and answered any questions she might have about her new class or school. This time is important for Brandy and the other students.

Mrs. Chambers likes to tell the story of another first grade where she implemented her buddy system with a new student. At the end of twenty-eight days (she had a particularly large class that year), when Luis had been buddies with everyone once, he came to Mrs. Chambers and asked, "Could I please be buddies with Elizabeth one more time?" He had made a new friend: a girl and someone who did not live in his neighborhood. They had a wonderful time reading a story and drawing a picture together and Luis remembered. He wanted that same experience again. So did Elizabeth.

Too many children move into a new school and months pass before they are known or know others. This is a misuse of time because it keeps them away from learning and preoccupied with where they fit in the class. New students often posture, show-off, or fight with classmates to find a place or establish their territory or reputation. A buddy system saves time and children.

Make group work challenging

Students are formulating concepts as they engage in dialogue with you and each other about the great ideas of the world and in every trivial and magic moment of the day. This is the message of the developmental psychologists outlined in Chapter 3. Learning leads development. Learning is social first, internal second, then social again. "You learn from the company you keep," says Canadian reading expert and educator Frank Smith simply and eloquently in his synoptic new book, *The Book of Learning and Forgetting*.[1] Useful knowledge, knowledge that we are likely to hold onto for a lifetime, is acquired less from rote learning than from social learning.

If we believe this, then we must carefully plan the curriculum *for* social interaction when students are in groups. Teach students how to respectfully challenge another's ideas. Expect intensive work from each individual and teach students how to expect more from each other, how to elaborate their work, to revise it, to not settle for good enough. Teach students how to create museum-quality captions, matting, and mountings for their displays. Teach students how to rehearse presentations and how to coach each other on delivery. Teach students how to listen and respect all ideas about an assignment before leaping to a particular solution for their group. All of these skills will multiply the meaning of the time spent in social interaction.

Reduce the number of transitions

As I have pointed out repeatedly, moving teachers instead of children is the simplest way to reduce transitions. The more stable and trust-worthy we can make the spaces students work in throughout the school day, the more time they will be focused on their education.

Transitions can be reduced through simple schedule adjustments as well. One major transition is dramatically changed if you institute a quiet time in your classroom after lunch or recess because, after initial modeling has been done, you never have to give verbal instructions when students enter the room. They know to silently get what they need and go to work! If you have students bring their coats and lunch boxes to the rug at the end of the day for a dismissal meeting, there are no extra transitions when buses are called. As you examine your schedule with this mindset, you will find many ways to eliminate and change transitions in your room.

Surprise your students

When a standard schedule is rigidly enforced and mindlessly fol-lowed, it can prevent learning rather than encourage it. Everyone needs an occasional break from routines to heighten their interest and improve their attention.

When an activity or lesson isn't working, don't keep it going. Stop and do something else. Stop a busy lesson and move firmly to a quiet read-aloud. Stop a read-aloud when no one is paying attention and put on five minutes of dance music before beginning math. Changing the pace of learning provides students with different experiences with time, aids them in their diachronic thinking, and sharpens their ability to predict and remember!

Surprise delights children when it is unpredictable in a fun way, but don't surprise them with negatives or punishments. This kind of surprise always backfires.

Here is an example of a "pleasant surprise." Perhaps the children have been having a hard time during transitions and they have been taking a long time. You might say, "I've been noticing that it's taking us a long time to get ready for math every day, you seem to have so much to chat about. So, today, I'm going to give you a two-minute 'chat time' *before* you get ready for math. You can talk about whatever you want, but when Sandra rings the bell, you are to get your math book, ruler, and pencil and get to math in silence. OK, start talking!" This "silent transition" won't be something you use every day, but as an occasional surprise, it will be effective.

Use imagination

An occasional experience with guided imagery before a poetry lesson or before a math test can change how students experience time during the lesson or test. As we know, highly successful dancers, athletes, and actors have trained to be able to visualize themselves in successful action. Being playful with your imagination is one part of learning to do such concentrated visualization.

Shift the focus of attention

Constantly, we hear ourselves say in the classroom, "Give me your attention!" Once in a while try saying to yourself (if not to your class), "Let me give you my attention!"

Often when children are interrupting one of their classmates, I will say, "I'm listening to Mandy's idea right now." The message is "I'm giving her my full attention now and I expect others to do the same."

You can tell children how important it is to *you* to be able to give *them* your attention. "Let me hear what you think about that." "I'm really interested in your ideas." "Let me give you my full attention for a moment." By shifting and focusing your attention, you improve the time for learning in the classroom.

Teach social and academic skills together

If we were not social creatures, education would be a simple business. As mentioned in Chapter 1, children could be taught by computers and virtual teachers in their own rooms at home. That, of course, is not who we are. We have wisely placed children in the social institution of school because we understand at some somatic level that education is about survival of the social order, not just acquisition of academic content. We have always taught and reinforced in school the values, beliefs, and morality of the dominant culture.

Today we are a country that is learning that for one culture to dominate in a land of many cultures is to plan the destruction of our democracy. And so, as Dewey proposed, we really must educate for democracy if we expect democracy to survive. The best way to educate for democracy and to achieve academic excellence at the same time is to use school time intelligently and to fully integrate the teaching of social and academic skills at every grade level, in every subject area.

This approach must be based on professional knowledge of the social context of teaching and learning. It requires skillful teaching, including wise time management, to produce stellar academic and social results. It is not simple, but it can be done.

The Responsive Classroom

The Responsive Classroom is the professional development approach to teaching and learning I helped develop. (See Appendix B.) The thousands of classrooms currently using *The Responsive Classroom* approaches concentrate on a different sense and use of time. There is more time for relationships and for research. There is more time for inquiry and reflection. All children's ideas are valued, not just the best and the brightest.

These classrooms are not "tracked" classrooms and must work toward developing a new social and academic framework which provides "differentiated instruction" and which fully integrates social and academic learning. This is the teacher's first priority. To be successful, the social context of teaching and learning must be understood and valued, and character education must be seen as equally important as content education.

In classrooms and schools using this approach, curriculum tends to be more integrative between content areas and fewer subjects are studied, but in much greater depth, as recommended by the TIMSS report and other research.[2] Theme work, project work, unit work, and "academic choice" (covered later in this chapter) are cornerstones of these classrooms.

Morning Meeting

A teacher using *The Responsive Classroom* approach makes the social context of teaching and learning a part of her lesson plans each day. She plans her morning meeting to excite and motivate children for the academic day ahead and she makes her morning meeting a preview of that day. Many teachers start their day with some kind of morning meeting. Morning meeting follows a particular routine where children greet each other by name, share news from their lives or share academic work, participate in a class activity that engenders group cooperation and attend to announcements and academic "coming attractions" through the use of a daily written message.

Morning meeting is a time saver and a timekeeper. Teachers report that it creates the kind of trustworthy space in the classroom where every child's voice becomes important, where learning carries meaning for each child and where less time is taken up with trivial issues or disruptions.

In twenty to thirty minutes each morning, not only is the tone of the day set, but the scaffold for learning is put up beside the building of knowledge. Each morning children and their teachers say, "It is important to be here, there is much to do, each of us matters, and what we do together matters a great deal." Morning meeting makes time for more learning through the comfort of its daily routine, the academic encouragement and motivation that takes place within it, and the daily acknowledgement that in this class, students are known.

At the middle school level, I have named morning meeting the "Circle of Power and Respect" (or CPR for short). It is the centerpiece of homeroom in the middle schools using *The Responsive Classroom* approaches. It may not happen every morning (there are other events and activities that appropriately fill the homerooms of middle schoolers such as team projects, community service, test-taking practice, and homework help), but two or three mornings a week, adolescents will gather in the meeting circle to maintain a safe space for learning and belonging. This routine structure for the beginning of the day at the elementary and middle school level has changed time in school for thousands of teachers.

One small bit of advice for using time in morning meeting: don't "pass around" children's objects or pictures to share during morning meeting or a special report. When children are waiting for something to get to them or when they have it in hand, they are not usually listening to what the sharer has to say. Instead of passing it around, have the sharer determine where they might display their item during the day and whether they would like their classmates to be able to pick it up or just look at it. Giving this control to the student builds responsibility and increases the focus and attention of the other students.

Two books by colleagues—Ruth Charney's *Teaching Children to Care* and Roxann Kriete's *The Morning Meeting Book*—are useful resources for getting started with morning meeting.

Concentrate on classroom discipline

Another way to improve the quality of time in the classroom through the social context of teaching and learning is through your approach to classroom discipline. There are two sides to discipline. The proactive includes what we do to establish a caring community. The reactive is what we do to fix things when trust in that caring community is shaken. They are what we do before the rules are broken and what we do after.

As I work with teachers year after year, I notice the changes that take place in classrooms when more time is devoted to the proactive. First, because more time is given to thinking about and generating the rules of the classroom, children pay more attention to the rules. It sounds almost too simple to be true, but it is! When children see the context of rules, that rules help us to make our hopes and dreams come true, to accomplish the goals we set for ourselves and our class, then there is more time to accomplish these goals. More spelling is learned, more books read, more math problems solved, more friendships created and sustained, and more service rendered.

Gaining more time for learning by paying attention to the social context of learning does not occur simply by talking to children about rules or even talking *with* them about rules. Part of proactive discipline is allowing time for children to practice the rules you have established together. Modeling, role-playing, and practicing behavior at the beginning of the year is time well invested and utilized. It is guaranteed to help provide more learning time throughout the year.

Establish social expectations early in the year

The social context of teaching and learning is established in the classroom in the first few weeks of school. This time of the year is important because all the expectations for how time will be used are set during this period. Children need to understand the foundations for the classroom and practice the learning process, such as:

- Using the space of the classroom

- Caring for desks and cubbies

- Caring for and displaying work on bulletin boards and show shelves

- Moving in and about the room—"traffic patterns"

- Caring for and learning how different material, equipment and supplies can help them learn

- Caring for each other

- Caring for themselves

Teachers, who take the time to carefully introduce all of these things as they are introducing academic content in the first weeks of school end up with more learning time during the course of the year.

At the beginning of every year in Timmy Sheyda's fifth-sixth grade classroom at the Greenfield Center School, every student carefully designs, sketches, constructs, and paints a single baluster for a railing of the loft in his classroom. At the end of the year they come down and go home.

A new railing is constructed each year. This work is symbolic as well as concrete. It teaches the students many things at the beginning of the year: how to plan their work, how to take their time, how to work step by step, how to share tools, and how to make their own beautiful products while contributing to the safety and upkeep of the classroom. Students reflect on the project on the day it is finished. They sit back and consider what it took to accomplish such beautiful work. But the railing is there all year as a reminder of what they can do and what their teacher expects.

Of course, even a strategy as exquisite as this one is not foolproof. As the year continues, children will sometimes forget their lofty hopes and dreams, ignore the rules they helped establish, and disregard the physical environment they helped create and live in each day. But teachers who have taken the time early now have the ability to fall back on that previous experience, reminding children of their earlier agreements and understandings.

When even these admonitions fail, then reactive discipline can be applied through the use of logical consequences, which relate directly to the students' proactive experiences. Less time is spent on discipline because there is discipline in the structure of the classroom.

Provide a "talk-it-out" table or space

A "talk-it-out" table or space in the classroom provides students with time to try to resolve their own conflicts. This is especially useful for issues which you want them to resolve themselves (such as tattling as opposed to reporting) or when you are busy. Provide an egg- or sand-timer for their use so that there is a time limit for their attempt to make things better. Otherwise, these social problem-solving sessions can last a long time!

Use language carefully

To utilize time more effectively, teachers need specific tools. Teachers begin with some basic tools—their words, their tone of voice, body language, and facial expression. Everything else (the curriculum, child development knowledge, how well children are known individually and culturally) is communicated and implemented through language. In the social context of teaching and learning, language is the medium of exchange.

Because our primary tool is language, this tool needs sharpening from time to time. Paying attention to your use of language in the classroom accomplishes two things. First, it will slow you down. As you pay more attention to what you are saying, you will think more about what you are going to say. This will create more small spaces for your thinking and feeling, and slow the pace of your vocalizing. Second, as your language becomes more precise you will find that students understand you better and respond more quickly to what it is you are asking of them.

For example, in nearly every school I visit, I can almost guarantee I will hear a teacher say to a child or a class, "EXCUSE ME!" As you probably know, having heard this expression or used it yourself, (as I confess I did at one time in the classroom), these words are not said to convey a desire for the children to pardon the teacher for some impolite action. Rather, it is biting sarcasm, designed to rebuke, if not to humiliate. What the teacher really means to say is, "I need your attention" or "Listen" or "It's time for everyone to be quiet." But, instead what comes out is "EXCUSE ME!"

Students are sometimes cowed into submission by this remark, but more often than not it has a less desirable effect. It makes students more resistant, sullen, and less engaged. Young children, under the age of eight, when first hearing such remarks, have no idea what the teacher means. Irony and sarcasm are not well understood by children until about third grade, although tutoring by the Simpsons and Beavis and Butthead (two TV shows I hope will disappear from view someday) is exposing them to sarcasm at a younger age.[3]

Clear, respectful, precise language modeled by the teacher will be mirrored by the students. The more time and emphasis put on vocabulary development, whether in kindergarten or eighth grade, the deeper the intellectual discourse in the literature group or the block corner. The more attention given to language that elaborates—rather than elongates—a concept, the deeper the dialogue will be in science, the richer the discussion in mathematics. Precision language improves the quality of learning in the classroom.

Adapt daily schedules to your grade level

In *Yardsticks: Children in the Classroom, Ages 4–14,* I have detailed many of the classroom implications of the development of children at particular ages.[4] Time structures need to be adjusted appropriately. While every child responds differently to time, there are general or normative responses as well. Seven-year-olds want to finish things. Eight-year-olds are in a hurry. Middle schoolers need more sleep and should come to school later.[5] Within the daily schedule, the length of time for each period or lesson should vary according to what we know about children's behavior at each age. Trying to make every grade level adhere to exactly the same schedule guarantees anxiety, boredom, and meltdowns.

Talk to your students about time. What was the longest day of this school year in terms of daylight? What seemed like the longest day? Why? How long do you think this test will take by looking at the number of pages I have written on the board? How long did your homework take you last night? What part of our day feels most rushed? What can we do about it? What part of the day do you enjoy the most? Why?

Keeping longitudinal class records over the year increases your students' understanding and appreciation for how long things take to accomplish. In fifth grade, how long did it take for everyone in the class to learn their multiplication facts through 12? How many chapter books did we read this year? How many did you read?

Help children manage timed tests

One way to help children manage the stress involved in timed tests is to make them fun. You can de-mystify the power of time in an important test by giving students lots of practice in how to play with time in less important tests, quizzes, assignments, and games. For example, let your students construct test questions and take the test created by their combined efforts as practice. Give the practice test untimed first, then timed.

This helps them realize their power over the time provided during an achievement or basic skills examination. Their predictive abilities and ability to remember are enhanced by such activities. The key is to provide this practice long before you have to give *the* timed test that counts the most for your kids and you.

Also, during timed tests, don't interrupt concentration with time reminders. Announcing "five more minutes" while children are concentrating on their work breaks their concentration, heightens their anxiety and reduces performance. Instead, let them know well ahead of the test that they will need to manage their own time. If you've given them lots of practice with this on other tests and activities, they'll do better on the "big" test than if you remind them during the exam.

Provide rest and quiet in the middle of the day

There's nothing quite like quiet time, but few schools or classrooms have it. There's nothing like it for creating an atmosphere of calm, safety, reflection, and restoration. In my classrooms over the years, the rule for quiet time was simple. You could choose to do anything in the room *that I approved* as long as you did it by yourself and in silence. My approval was the key. Kids would check with me as they came back from lunch. They would then go off to read a book, work on a report, draw, write, work on the computer, do a science observation, sometimes sleep.

It is time which can meet children's needs for "breathing out" or "breathing in" depending on their mood and energy. It always restored me and gave me a time for a quiet, private conversation with one or two students, as well.

Chapter Nine

Changing the Use
of Time in Classrooms

HOW WE STRUCTURE TIME affects how we use time and vice versa. For example, if we use a balanced approach which includes small-group and partner exercises, we can allow more in-depth learning and contemplation and improve the pace of teaching during those times. And if we learn about the special needs of children with ADHD behaviors, we are better able to adapt our daily schedules to meet the needs of all our students.

The suggestions which follow are both practical and, I hope, inspirational. Teachers begin teaching because they enjoy children and being involved in their learning. By changing how we use time each day in the classroom, we can recapture some of the joy and deep satisfaction of teaching.

*Guidelines for Changing Time Use
at the Classroom Level*

- Change the pace of teaching to improve the pace of learning. More listening, open-ended questioning, and reflection by teachers gives students more time to think and to construct new knowledge.

- Allow time for in-depth learning, investigation, and contemplation by narrowing the number of lessons you teach in any given content area.

- Allow enough time for transitions and closure of

lessons. Use music, food and water, and exercise to refresh brains as well as bodies.

- Learn about the special needs of children who show behaviors which may classify them as ADHD/ADD. Work to make time expectations reasonable for them and to respond to their behaviors appropriately.

- Enliven the time used in everyday school routines by taking them seriously as valued parts of academic, social, and community learning.

- Open your room to parents and colleagues to model cooperative work, and utilize the strengths and ideas of other caring adults.

Change the pace of teaching

In all of my research and observation for this book, one of my strongest conclusions is that the pace of our culture is too fast for all of us and that the pace of most teaching is too fast for teachers and students.

As Richard DeGrandpre and others note, our current pace of life leaves millions of children unable to meet the demands on them for attention and behavior. I believe we have entered into an "Age of Tension and Anxiety" which threatens the health and welfare of our children and future generations.

The media often tells us that such worries, even hysteria, are the plight of every older generation. But it isn't simple nostalgia to look back and see that as children, we had more time than our students do today. My generation remembers hiding under our desks terrified of a nuclear strike. Anxiety, yes, but in quiet afternoons, we listened to chapters of *Wind in the Willows,* drew pictures of Toad Hall, and put our heads down on our desks to take a rest. After school, we had time to play in back lots or by small streams, inventing our own rules, and constructing boats to sail toward the open sea. There seemed "time for all the works and days of hands / that lift and drop a question on your plate," as the poet T.S. Eliot wrote.[1]

Perhaps most importantly, we were allowed our questions and the time to live with them for a while. "What makes the sea blue?" "Why can't we see the stars during the day?" "Who invented bubble gum?" "Where do babies come from?"

Today, children have the answers all too soon, especially to the last question. Our government insists we rush to get schools hooked up to the Internet so that questions can be answered instantaneously, factually, and in living color. The children can hear directly from scientists and writers. Factoids can fly at them with the speed of cyberspace.

We can't change everything about this Age of Tension and Anxiety. History and culture are not easily reversed. But we can change the pace of teaching and be rewarded as we watch children seize the time with thankful hands. We can give them the opportunity to learn fully and deeply, and come to the understanding that speed, in the wrong places and times, is much more dangerous to learning than reverie or contemplation.

Plan for observation time each day

The most effective way I know to change time in the classroom is to use more time watching and listening to individual children. If you examine the times when you feel most rushed in the classroom, I guarantee you it won't be when you are watching and listening to one child. It's more likely to be when you are speaking to the whole class and not getting the response you want, when clean-up isn't going well, when the physical education teacher is at the door and your kids are still writing at their desks, or when you have the PTO notice in your hand and they are calling the buses.

How can you find the time to watch and listen to individual children? Structure it into your lesson plans, into your teaching, into the core of your being. When I was teaching first grade, I made a sign on red construction paper. In big bold letters it said: **Observer.**

I laminated it, punched two holes in it, and attached it with yarn so I could wear it around my neck. I told my first-graders that when I had the sign on, they could not bother me unless it was an emergency. We had a bathroom procedure that everyone knew. We knew what to do if there was a fire drill. As much as they thought they needed me every minute of the day, and as much as I thought I was indispensable to them, I knew this time was important.

I believed then as I believe today: teachers must do constant, first-hand research and observation in the scientific discipline of child development. Just as doctors study the human body, teachers must study the human beings they teach. The way children grow and behave in the school setting is our food for thought, our inspiration, our guiding star.

It's important to read journals and books, take courses and workshops. But our direct observations are indispensable, making others' research come alive and guiding our understandings and techniques for each child and each class. I told the children in first grade, "It's part of the teacher's job to listen and watch how children learn!" As I watched and listened, I learned much about the children, but I learned many things about myself as a teacher, too.

I learned that I *wasn't* indispensable. In fact, when I was observing, the children were often doing just fine without me! They were helping each other, engaged as learners and teachers. I also noticed that when I was watching and listening, I was absorbed in what I was doing and time would stand still, if even for a few moments—a few magic moments. In those times, I realized I had peripheral vision in the classroom. I could be completely engaged and absorbed in the bubble of my observation, but still know if there was a problem in the room, or someone had come in the door.

You don't have to observe for long stretches. If you devise a structure that works for you, a few minutes a day can make a big difference. Start with one minute twice a day. Remember to explain to your students what you are doing and why you are doing it. Ask them why they think a teacher might spend time watching and listening to her students. Perhaps you'll jot a few notes on a note card, or enter a few words in a journal while you're observing, but the important idea is that you are deliberately and purposefully slowing time down at unexpected times of the day.

You will come to know your students better. You will see your interdependence rather than indispensability. You will be able to see how the children you observe are experiencing their learning time, just as we learned about Mark and Phoebe and their classmates though observations.

You will learn how well the child with ADHD behaviors can concentrate when deeply involved in his drawing and how unfocused he is when trying to complete a worksheet. You will hear the empathy your quietest child has for her neighbor with a toothache or heartache. You will remember the smell of crayons and clay and get lost in the blue shading of a colored pencil in a report illustration. And time will stand still. A minute later you will be back in the middle of the classroom soup, but you will feel refreshed, clear-headed, and appreciative of the importance of all that you do in the classroom, rather than resentful of all the things you have left to do.

Another product of observation is that children see you doing it. What you model during that time is focused attention, calm, and clarity of intention. You will see your students learn from what you do, and you will have learned from what you see them do. Observation, done well, is the best assessment tool we have. You can't write it all down, but if you do write about what you've actually seen, it will be the clearest and most objective record you'll ever be able to share with parents about their children.

Focus on the present

Learning to be alive in the present moment is also a way of slowing the passage of time, but it brings up a paradox because "time flies when you're having fun!" When you are fully involved and engrossed in the present moment, you are unaware of the passage of time or you feel you have all the time you need to accomplish the task at hand. After your concentration is broken, you become aware that more time may have elapsed than you thought. You are surprised. You wonder where the time has gone.

This is the world in which most of our students live. Most children between five and eleven are more aware of the present moment than the past or future (as covered in Ch. 2). This allows them to be absorbed and attentive to what they are doing, although this may not always be what we intend for them to be doing! Because the present moment is what they know and enjoy, the passage of time is relatively unimportant to them. When a bell rings or we ask for their attention, they, too, are often surprised by the time that has elapsed.

Remember that you, too, are allowed to get lost in the moment (while maintaining a peripheral sense of time, much like your peripheral vision). For example, think about a writer's conference you had with Janelle last week when she told you about the full moon she saw setting in the western sea at dawn, just as the birds started singing. She told you this while clusters of other children around the room were writing, getting up for paper, getting a drink, talking quietly with each other, sneaking a snack from their lunch-boxes, blowing their noses.

But you were on a beach somewhere in your imagination watching this small child watch the moon go down for the first time, her gray-haired grandmother beside her singing a gentle song. And after you had acknowledged the beauty of her words and how they could be kept forever in her story, you looked up at the clock and were surprised. But there was still time to say to the class, "It's time to put your writing away so we can hear a little about what people were working on before we go to lunch."

A seventh-grader in our lab school conducted an experiment for her science project to determine how children five to seven years old experienced time under different conditions. She told each of twenty-five children, on separate occasions, to tell her when a minute was up and then gave them an attractive object to play with. The next day she asked them to tell her when a minute was up and gave them nothing to play with. All but three of the children estimated a minute to be longer when they had the object than when they had nothing. They were surprised when told that more than a minute had gone by; it hadn't seemed to have been that long. When they had to wait without a focus for their attention, the time crawled and they were surprised to learn that a minute had not gone by. Everyone experiences the relativity of time and our seventh-grader demonstrated that in her simple, yet elegant experiment.[2]

For teachers, time flies pleasantly when attention is focused in the present. That focus may be on a single child or a group, on an activity or a discussion, on the room's productive hum or the pair that needs redirection. But remaining attentive, focused, and engaged frames the paradox of time: each moment is slow, rich and detailed, yet the moments pass quickly, one after the other, without notice.

Sing and dance with children

How can we have time for singing and dancing? The better question is "What is the cost if we don't make time for singing and dancing?" There must be time for joy. When you are singing and dancing, it is difficult to think or worry about something else—of what you didn't do last period or what you need to do next. You are singing or dancing; that is enough to think about at one time. At a workshop session I attended, we were asked by the facilitator, "What makes you feel most alive?" I answered, "Singing with children."

Read to children

I hope that read-aloud is a part of your teaching whether you are a second grade teacher or an eighth grade teacher. Students of all ages love being read to because it puts them in different time frames—the past or the future—and frees the flight of the imagination. I have always urged students to draw and color while I read but I insist that they draw and color about what they "saw" in relation to what I was reading! I quickly learned that the construction of two-page mazes by fifth-grade boys was not as enlightening for them as sketching the river they saw through Leslie's eyes in *Bridge To Terabithia*.[3]

Start every day with relaxing routines

Make sure children understand the morning routine. Perhaps you will have a morning message for students to read as they enter the room; perhaps music will be playing softly. Children will attend to the jobs of the morning; hanging up their coats, putting away their belongings, turning in their homework, taking attendance, doing lunch count, fixing a display, chatting with each other as they go about their chores. Even if you have a "special" first thing, there usually is some time before the children head off.

The key here is that there are expectations for what the *children* will be doing, not you. This leaves you with more freedom to speak with individual children about their needs. Someone had a hard time on the bus. Someone's dad has just moved away from home. Someone was up all night with a sick puppy. Someone didn't understand the math assignment. A morning meeting can follow these brief moments (as described in the observation chapters and the previous chapter). Such a routine helps create a safe and predictable beginning and reinforces the structure which children need to know is there each day. Math and reading and social studies and science will provide plenty of surprises later in the day.

Take time to get to know the children

Knowing your children involves more than remembering the things kids tell you about themselves. You need to let the kids know what you know about them. When children know that they are known in the classroom, they feel safer and are better able to use their time in school for learning.

A simple exercise created decades ago by writing expert Donald Graves can help you be more intentional about this process. Try writing down the names of the children in your class from memory, in whatever order they come into your head, then writing down an interest of the child's or something you know is happening in their life. Then, put a check by the child's name if you are sure you have communicated this to them—i.e., if the child knows *you know* what they are interested in or what is happening in their life. A check mark means that they know they are known.[4]

I have used this exercise for years in teacher workshops and it always helps teachers to see their children in a new light. It also helps teachers look at how they use their teaching time. The more time you use getting to know your children, the better teacher you will be.

Of course, you don't get to know children once and that's the end of that. The children in your class grow and change during the year and you do, too. When you know your students, you know how different they are at different points in the year. As Donald Graves notes, "The joy of teaching is contained in the mutual building of effective learning histories."[5]

A critical part of building effective learning histories is knowing your children, not only as individuals, but also as part of a cultural or ethnic group that may be quite different from yours or the majority of the students. Building a trustworthy space for all students means allowing time for sharing and understanding our cultural histories. All children can't afford Santa Claus pictures, as we saw in Mrs. Chambers' room, but in many classrooms today, Santa Claus insults the cultural reality of some children and their families. Our responsibilities in the new century need to focus on the new pluralism of which we are a part—a pluralism, we hope, which is based on understanding.

It also important to know your children developmentally. The science of child development is the most important academic discipline for teachers. It is a foundation for what we see when we observe and listen to our children. Without it, we have only partial sight and hearing. When the third grade children start showing more and more anxiety about homework in the spring, we need to understand that the typical anxiousness of nine-year-olds is beginning to gain the upper hand and that less homework may alleviate the situation. Growth and learning is up and down, not just up and up.

Give yourself a break—in silence

Find five minutes in each school day to be alone with your own thoughts. I know this is not an easy assignment, especially in elementary school, but try! A walk around the school grounds or around the block during your lunch break (I know it's not a lunch hour!) may be the difference between a clear-headed afternoon and a headache. Fresh air helps too.

Allow silence after someone speaks

Try not to let one student trample on the heels of another student's ideas and try not to let your words interrupt or talk over the words of a student. After a student speaks, allow silence, then an acknowledgment before a response. Often a simple "thank you" is most powerful of all.

"I saw the skating," offers Amelia in Mrs. Chambers' class during writing time, but when she begins to elaborate, she is quickly contradicted by other children with what they saw.

"This is Amelia's idea," Mrs. Chambers reminds them, "and she can think a little clearer if our hands are down."

Amelia adds a sentence. "The speed skating is very exciting!"

Mrs. Chambers adds this sentence to the story she is writing on the chart and smiles at Amelia. "Thank you," she says.

Creating small silences helps slow the pace of teaching while increasing the amount of learning.

Organize and keep your classroom simple

When all the walls are covered with displays and several mobiles hang from the ceiling, the room decorations can be over-stimulating, confusing, and demand too much attention. Simplicity reduces the time it takes to "read" the room. Keep the clutter down. Make displays meaningful by working with children to choose what to put out and up in the classroom. Remember, your goal is to create a trustworthy space where students feel safe and significant and where they are part of an important learning community. Such a space need not resemble a party store!

When you don't know what to do, stop and think

Good decisions usually require some thought. If you're not sure about what to do, a few moments to think will often bring the situation into focus.

Montangero wrote about the struggle to gain a "knowledge perspective," where "it is necessary to comprehend the current data of a situation in order to produce an appropriate behavioral response."[6] A good example of this is a practice employed by the British Navy described by Mark Link: "When a British ship encounters an unexpected disaster at sea, the 'STILL' is sounded. The signal means pause! Check your situation! Determine the wise thing to do. When the STILL first sounds, few crew members know the wise thing to do. But during the pause enforced by the signal, they discover it."[7]

In the classroom, you might say, "Everyone go back to your desks and take out your independent reading books. I need a minute to think about how we can make things a little quieter and more friendly in our class today."

I watch skilled teachers use the eye gesture of looking up at the ceiling to let their students know they are thinking of what to say or need a moment before making a decision. I watch children in these classes raise their heads and look heavenward when searching for a test answer or a synonym.

Allow time for in-depth learning

Ask more of your students and they will give you more in return. Go deeper into the curriculum, cover less of it and teach children more knowledge and more skills. This is the message of the TIMSS report issued by some of the most respected and conservative educational standard bearers in our country and a central part of the message of this book. Spending more time on a particular unit or subject or concept, such as the solar system in third grade or American history in the seventh, doesn't automatically mean having students read more books or do more research. Instead, it means taking time to insure that students understand the important concepts deeply and personally and that they are directly involved in creating this learning.

Using an inquiry or Socratic approach to teaching adds depth and exploration to the learning process. But it doesn't mean asking rhetorical questions to which we already have the answer in the teacher's guide. Real questions, to which we do not already have the answers, require us to really listen to what our students have to say.

Bob Strachota, a teacher at our laboratory school, Greenfield Center School, and a deep thinker about children, puts it this way in his stimulating book, *On Their Side: Helping Children Take Care of Their Learning:*

> I've come to define a real question as one which engages the teacher and the learner in exploring the mysteries of the universe, rather than one which engages the learner in exploring the mysteries of what the teacher wants her to know or do.[8]

Give students choices

We ask more from our students and gain more time from and for them when we give them more choice in their learning. One way to structure this is through "academic choice," an approach which is a central part of *The Responsive Classroom* techniques.

Whole time blocks devoted to digging into questions students have identified as important to them create periods of intense learning. Teachers have found many ways to structure academic choice in their classrooms. In general, they begin by asking students what they know about a subject they are going to study. Using "K–W–L charts" generates excitement for both teachers and students:

- K—What we already know about a subject. This respects the fact that we are never starting from scratch about any curriculum content.

- W—What we want to know about a subject. This opens the social and intellectual pathways in a class-room for unusual and dynamic social and cognitive connections.

- L—What we have learned about a subject. This honors reflection, assessment, and the learning process.

The K-W-L approach is now common in elementary teaching, found in many teachers' guides, and utilized routinely in reading, social studies, and science. It can also become badly banal and conventional when we lead students through the exercise in order to push them toward the curriculum standards required in a particular unit of study, rather than letting the students' questions lead where they will. But when we let the questions lead, covering the standards follows naturally, and the learning is deeper.

In the work that students do together to research their own questions, collect their facts, ask more questions, talk to outside experts, search the Internet, and read books about particular aspects of the subject under study, something quite critical is being developed—a point of interest.[9] Sometimes this "point of interest" is pre-established by the teacher to help focus the work of a student or a whole class. For instance, she might set the expectation that each student in a fifth grade would understand the importance of rivers in the class's study of the westward expansion of the United States.

Other times, a point of interest can be a focus that a student zeroes in on about a particular subject area. If a student is researching cheetahs for the animal unit, the point of interest may be speed. If it's Gettysburg in the unit on the Civil War, the specific point of interest may be field hospitals. A point of interest can heighten student motivation and deepen the learning process when others respond to student reports or project presentations. Imagine this fourth grade class discussion at the end of a unit about endangered species:

> *Student One:* "I studied fish for my project. I found out that there are many species of fish that used to be plentiful, but now are endangered. The reason for this is that fishing boats are so huge and they have big nets and stuff that drag the bottom of the ocean and catch all the fish, not just the ones the fishermen might want. And this dragging destroys the bottom of the ocean for miles so the fish don't want to go back there. I'm ready for questions and comments," says the student, having shared the essence of her research.
>
> *Student Two:* "That's bad! Was the dragging your point of interest?"
>
> *Student One:* "Actually, I got fascinated with how fish have babies and how long it takes a fish to grow, 'cause I figured one of the reasons there might be less fish is cause they're catching more of them faster and it might take a long time for them to grow, 'cause you know how a fish has to be so long to keep it if you go fishing?"
>
> *Student Two:* "What did you find out?"
>
> *Student One:* "Well, actually . . ."

The point of interest helps students "to organize the work," a central tenet of Montessori education, from which the concept of "point of interest" grew.[10] It sparks academic interest and motivation, and provides focus for the researchers, classmates, and teacher, keeping them from straying all over the map in their work. Researchers, peers, and teachers can also do on-the-spot evaluation and gauge the depth of understanding on the subject. Using a "point of interest" approach provides an exciting starting point for academic research, deepens the dialogue about it, and ultimately makes learning more meaningful.

Use technology sparingly and wisely

I always ask myself this question when I plan or help teachers plan for the use of technology in the classroom: "What is the student *not* doing while they are on the computer (or tape, CD, or video deck)?" If my answer is "She is not engaged in meaningful dialogue about important ideas or questions," then I may question if "plugging in" is the best use of school time right then. (Children may also *not* be engaged in meaningful dialogue while the teacher is talking or while they are doing a written assignment.)

There are definitely appropriate times and uses for technology. The Internet is a marvelous research tool and a potential dialogue link to other students and teachers globally. But the primary purpose of having children spend their days in large learning groups called classrooms and schools is to provide *social engagement* and a community of learners to explore the great ideas of the world.

Our romance with the computer is fascinating when we consider that we have not chosen to bring the technology of the telephone into the classroom for children. Is it because computer skills are currently needed and promoted as tools for business while the academic and communication aspects are perhaps only the means to that end?

For every type of lesson, it's important to ask two basic questions: What is it that we are trying teach the children? And what technology is best suited to do that?

Plan and implement schedules

Lesson planning is important and time planning is part of lesson planning. Although we are bound by certain pre-set schedules, it is our job to plan and implement the schedule for the time which we control. It's essential to sketch this out before each day begins. If teachers try to rely on their intuitive knowledge to get them through daily time frames, I guarantee that they won't fully utilize the time they have.

Planning also helps teachers avoid the recurring difficulty of not having enough time to finish. I believe this is as much a function of our own poor time planning as it is of having too much to do. Estimate time for each assignment, activity, and period. Write it beside your

250 / CHAPTER NINE

plan or period schedule. Evaluate how good your estimates are and get better at them.

Help children be "on time"

Harness time as a friend of children. "Hurry up" is a phrase that contradicts the nature of childhood. When children are not ready for the next activity, class, recess or lunch, it is our teaching which needs adjusting, not the pace of the children. To make time a friend of children, we cannot constantly give them the experience of being late.

Our job is to structure available time wisely. If you stop your fourth grade math class five minutes before the official math period is over, you can allow children to gather their materials, tell you what is coming next in their school day, hear you recite a silly math poem, and review a single idea you've discussed in class. This helps children experience the routine of being on time and experiencing time as well-filled, not frantic. The comforting, controlled experience of a daily routine in math class affects their attitude toward math. It provides them routine experience with feelings of calm and readiness.

This is as important for students in kindergarten as in seventh grade. The key idea is that you can't teach up to the last minute of the class period, no matter how pressured you feel to cover the curriculum and get everything in. It is counterproductive for you and the children if you do. It's hard at first to stop before the bell rings, but you'll soon see the difference in your classroom and your kids. Harnessing time means not letting time be in charge of you.

Make time for closure

The end of the day is often frantic. Teachers teach right up to the last bell, trying to cram more in. As with other periods, it works better to stop sooner. Ten minutes before dismissal, schedule a final five-minute clean up. Expect children to be on the rug in a circle with all their things to go home, five minutes before dismissal. (Of course, clean-up might have to start earlier with young children and for older students on days with messy projects.) Once on the rug, engage in some reflection about the day with questions like these:

- What did we do well as a class today?

- What might we do better tomorrow?

- What was something that surprised you today?

- What was something that disappointed you?

- What are you looking forward to tomorrow?

- What is something you need to remember about your homework?

- Who is going to sit next to someone new on the bus today?

- Who will bring in some empty boxes for dioramas tomorrow?

Children will go to the bus more settled, and you will go to the faculty meeting more settled. You need this time as much as the children do. It is a part of your breathing out so that you can breathe in again. It needs to be part of the rhythm of the day.

Simplify bathroom procedures

Don't make children ask you if they can go to the bathroom and don't wait until a specified time and take all the children at once. Even if the bathroom is out of the room, a simple system of tags hung by the door (one or two for each gender) eliminates much wasted time. Of course, you will need to model this system with the children, discussing potential "what ifs" and you will still have bathroom issues to discuss during the year, but more of your time will be available for teaching rather than toileting.

An exception is in old buildings where the bathrooms are in the basement, sometime three floors away from the classroom. In such cases, the whole class has to go together for safety's sake. When I observed teachers in New England before teaching there, it took me a while to figure out why all the kids kept asking their teachers to "go to the basement."

Make transitions predictable and pleasant

Let children know how long a transition will be. Give them a verbal preview of the transition: "In five minutes we will stop math. You'll have a three minute break before science."

Soothing music helps calm a room in transition. It can be a classroom job for a student to put the music on. In middle school, music can play on the school-wide system during some transitions.

A "clean-up tape" really helps students sweep the room, pick up papers, rearrange furniture, and be ready for the next lesson efficiently. Talk about the clean-up tape: it goes for three minutes and when it is over you expect them to be finished cleaning up and in a circle on the rug. Whether in kindergarten or fifth grade, this technique is respectful of children's growing ability to predict how long something will take them to do. In kindergarten, it helps stretch children in their diachronic understanding of time.

Use clear signals for attention

Raising your hand may mean Stop, Look, and Listen: "When you see my hand up, stop what you are doing, put down what is in your hand, look at me, and then I'll know you're ready to listen." Have two signals, a visual signal such as a raised hand for most occasions, and an auditory signal for those times when the class is so busy no one is going to see you raise your hand. Practice the signal with your students often. Make it a game. Time how quickly they can respond. Do not speak over the signal. Wait until everyone has given you his or her attention before you speak.

Signals are perhaps the simplest and generally the most poorly utilized time managers available to teachers. One day I watched a teacher ring the clapper right out of her bell! She rang it once, but the class did not respond. She rang it again, no response. She rang it again and again until—boing! Out came the clapper! Then she was stuck, no auditory signal and no attention! Ring the bell once and wait. What may seem like a long wait at first generally improves with repetition.

Use a stopwatch

Every teacher should own one and use it often and in many different ways. For your own information, time how long certain things take: transitions, getting class attention, circling up on the playground. Challenge your kids with the stopwatch to see how long it takes to get the chairs in a circle for morning meeting and to get them back to the desks at the end. Keep track of class "bests" at certain tasks, games, or races.

Create a self-regulating snack procedure

Children don't all need to eat at the same time because they don't all become hungry at the same time. Model and practice the procedures for getting snack out, eating, and clean-up. Individual responsibility for this quick energy boost provides a short break for students while others may be busy around them.

Go outside with your children

Time changes when we move from the artificial environment of the classroom to the natural environment outdoors. Where there is room to run, we move faster. Our hearts beat faster. Oxygen replenishes our brains. Then, we can move back indoors and bring our brains to attention because we gave attention to our bodies. So don't just go outside with your children, play with them too!

On a city playground, I watched a teacher play a game of Red Rover with a large group of children at one end of the playground.

She showed them how to be safe when they were "busting through." She was vigilant *and* having fun. The air felt good and the children were all laughing and running, following the rules of their bodies and spirits, letting their minds recess. To me it is a crime, a form of child abuse, that schools across the country are reducing or eliminating recess in the mistaken belief that by increasing the so-called "time on task," children will learn more basic academic skills. The research paints quite a different picture.[11]

Make time expectations and responses appropriate for children's special needs

In Chapters 1 and 2, I suggested that many children experience temporal trauma in their school day and that some exhibit behaviors which classify them as ADHD. Without identifying a definitive cause or even a group of causal factors, research does show that the most severely affected children live in a different world than others, one in which time runs together in a constant rush of the present.

As teachers, we need to work to understand these children and their behaviors so that we can help them learn and grow in school. Before looking at suggestions for specific changes in our approaches and responses to children with attentional disorders, consider the following graphic representations from The Self-Control Classroom by Levin and Shanken-Kaye.[12]

The first "Concept Map" provides a linear picture which begins with Barkley's theory that children classified as ADHD are "insensitive" to time (unable to retain past events or predict the future) and details the consequences of this insensitivity which result in understandable behaviors.

The second represents the internal clock of an ADHD child. The time is always "Now" and inattention, impassivity, and hyperactivity create a constellation of emotional and behavioral problems.[13]

Concept Map

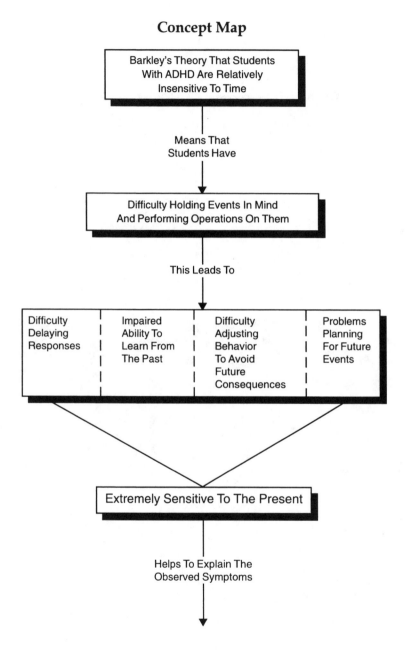

From The Self-Control Classroom, *by James Levin and John Shanken-Kaye. Copyright © by Kendall/Hunt Publishing Company. Used with permission.*

Concept Map

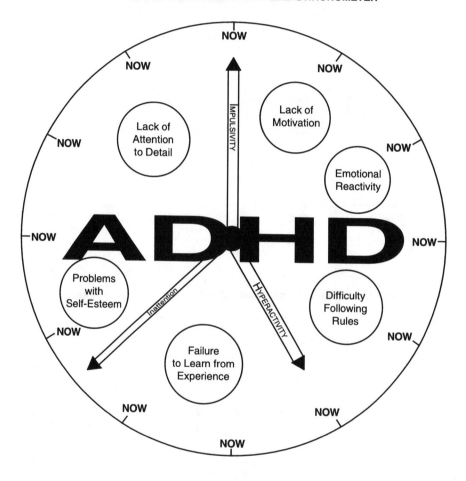

From The Self-Control Classroom, *by James Levin and John Shanken-Kaye. Copyright © by Kendall/Hunt Publishing Company. Used with permission.*

Teachers can be enormously helpful to children with attentional disorders if they adjust how they structure time and how they respond to the ADHD behaviors which can be so disruptive to a learning environment and exhausting for the teacher. These children need a clearer sense of the passage of time and it is the teacher's job to structure time in school for *all* children so that it is predictable. For ADHD children, the more predictable the better. Providing activities which are directly related to their interests and abilities helps them learn more and function better within a "normal" classroom.

Consistent schedules

Having a clear beginning, middle, and end of the day, as previously suggested (with comforting and predictable morning routines, a break in the middle of the day, and closure at the end) has a positive impact on children with ADHD behaviors. But these children will benefit from an even more detailed schedule, taped to their desk or in their notebook. To be able to use this schedule to their benefit, children with attention issues need to learn at least two things about time.

First, they need to learn to tell time. Step one in this process is knowing what time it is. Having their own watch is a good idea and having it match the classroom clock (sweep hand or digital readout) is also a good idea, so that they are reading the same time in the same way on their wrist and on the wall. Their schedule should also graphically *show* the time in the same way they read it on the wall and on their wrist. "Consistency in all things" is an important phrase to remember in working or living with children with attentional struggles.

Second, the child needs to know his/her job for each period of time. "It's 9:30, it's time for math." For this to be true for the child, the classroom schedule must be as consistent and predictable as possible. If it's 9:30, but we don't have math today because there's a special assembly and the rest of the day will be changed because of it, the child with attentional issues is bound to have more difficulty, both in the assembly and throughout the rest of the day. This does not excuse his/her behavior, but it does explain it.

On a day like that, (and we have far too many of them in school!), the best a teacher can do is try to get the class back on its regular schedule as soon as possible in the day. Better to get back on the regular schedule, skipping part of math that day, than to try to cram it all in.

Stimulating lessons

The student who knows what time it is and what his/her job is will still have trouble if the task at hand is boring or lacks stimulation. "Time flies when you're having fun" is doubly true for children with attention issues. Tactile or colored materials, manipulatives, and headphones have all been shown to help such students do better in class. Short assignments within specific time frames, with reinforcement as soon as possible after each completion, will also increase success.

Rewarding success

Success is an important word for students with challenging behaviors. Many have experienced only failure in school, both academically and socially. I believe in the concept of "incremental success"—providing these children with bite-sized experiences with success which accumulate hour by hour, day by day, throughout the school year. It is far better for these children to complete four homework problems correctly and turn them in to you on time, than to take home the same twenty problems as the rest of the class and arrive with four done, or be unable to find their paper.

The time we spend asking for homework from these students could be better spent congratulating them for four wonderfully completed problems. Tomorrow the student may want to reach for five or six! Success builds success. Failure builds defeat.

Organizing and managing the classroom

The physical organization and management of the classroom has an effect on the passage of time for all children, but especially for children with attention issues. These children often need special seats away from group tables during times of the day when intensely focused concentration is important.

Noise is also a consideration. Having a headset on while working may help while the noisy activities of peers could prove distracting. When the room becomes confusing for the child, time becomes confusing as well. It becomes harder to know what time it is or what the task for this time is.

These are the times we see children "off task." It's important to remember that it is not their fault that they are off task. It is more the fault of the present environment and it is your job to do something about it. A change in the situation for the child may be what's needed (a walk down the hall and back for a drink of water) or you may see that the whole class needs redirection and a better sense of what time it is and what the task is before them.

Transitions

Transitions can be especially difficult for children with attentional issues because, during these times, external structures often disappear. Children are milling around, doing a variety of things: getting a drink of water, going to the bathroom, throwing something away, talking to a friend, fooling around, trying to finish some work. Sometimes it is useful for children struggling with transitions to have a job to do during the transition.

Perhaps it is their job to start the transition by ringing the bell and announcing that it is time for snack or to get ready to go to music. Perhaps it is their job to collect the papers at the beginning of the transition. Perhaps they are responsible for keeping a stopwatch, timing how long the transition took and reporting this to the class at the beginning of the next period. Perhaps it is their job to bring the group back to attention at the end of the transition by ringing a bell or going around the room telling classmates it's time for reading. The point is not to control the child every minute of the transition, but to give the transition some predictability and to give the child a sense of responsibility during the transition.

Physical activity

Physical activity is very important to the way children with ADHD behaviors navigate time. I believe it is important to all children. Growing bodies need exercise to grow properly and to keep time with their natural rhythms of activity and rest, wake and sleep, breathing in and breathing out. A short physical break between assignments within a predictable time period can help the child who is losing focus. For instance, during language arts, which is typically an hour-long period in elementary school, children with attention issues might take a break for "jumping jacks" in the hall between doing their spelling list and going to their reading group. Not all children will need this break.

When the other children ask why Charles gets to jump in the hall and they don't, they are asking an important question about fairness. They are not just whining and complaining, although sometimes it can feel like that. I like to remember a quote by Melvin Konner I used in my book, *Yardsticks*. Konner writes, "In order to be treated fairly and equally, children have to be treated differently."[14] This is important to convey to all the children as you build the trustworthy space of your classroom together. Differentiated time structures for different children are an expression of treating them fairly by treating them differently and other children will understand and accept this if they believe that their own special needs will be met as well.

Further information

As we all know, these children, and our inability to always know what to do with them in certain situations, can wreak havoc with time in the classroom. Out-of-control behavior not only disrupts the time schedule of the day; it disrupts the emotional climate of the room as well. This changes everyone's sense of time. When the world is not a safe place, time moves neither slowly or quickly. It becomes unpredictable and uneven and often unhappy. These times are particularly unproductive for learning.

There are three sources I especially recommend for more detailed strategies for working with children who present challenging behaviors. Russell Barkley's book, *Taking Charge of ADHD*,[15] *The Self-Control Classroom* by James Levin and John Shanken-Kaye,[16] and the work of Ross Green in *The Explosive Child*[17] provide a wealth of sound ideas for day-to-day classroom practice. While I do not agree with every practice in any of these approaches, I find them among the soundest and most useful for teachers.

For example, while Barkley's book is addressed primarily to parents, his list of ten guiding principles for raising a child with ADHD behaviors is just as important for teachers. Barkley recommends the following list be taped to the refrigerator door at home. I recommend it be taped on the teacher's desk at school.

1. Give your child more immediate feedback and consequences

2. Give your child more frequent feedback

3. Use larger and more powerful consequences

4. Use incentives before punishment

5. Strive for consistency

6. Act, don't yak!

7. Plan ahead for problem situations

8. Keep a disability perspective

9. Don't personalize your child's problems or disorder

10. Practice forgiveness[18]

We know that children experience time differently as they grow and develop. We know that some children continue to struggle with their diachronic understanding of time throughout their childhood. A time disability is just as real and potentially devastating as a hearing or visual disability and can contribute to reading and math disabilities as well as to behavioral problems. Some children need more help than others in managing time. It is our job to provide this help just as we do for children who need more help learning to read or spell.

"Get real" with routines

Throughout my teaching career I have always thought we waste an enormous amount of time on repetitive routines that hold little meaning for our students. These routines should and can be important to children, but we tend to treat them more as time to be endured rather than enjoyed or explored. These routines may include:

- daily attendance and lunch count
- morning announcements over the loud speaker
- the Pledge of Allegiance
- the moment of silence observed in some schools
- the daily calendar

A better way of using the time available to us in the classroom is to "get real" with the routine. For example, think about "The Pledge of Allegiance." We are all amused by the misunderstandings of young children as they struggle with the complicated vocabulary of the pledge such as " . . . and to the republic for widget stands." But how many teachers actually spend time teaching the meaning of this pledge at any grade level? Where did this pledge come from and what does it mean? Why do we say it every morning and why should it be important to us? What does pledging allegiance mean? What are we pledging allegiance to? To the flag? Or to something deeper and harder to understand? What is a republic? What is a nation? How can it be under God? How is God related to our nation? What does it mean when it says "indivisible"? What is the difference between liberty and justice? What does it mean when it says "for all"?

Each of these questions is important to every United States citizen, young and old. Yet classrooms in American schools seldom examine them in depth, except perhaps by an inspired civics or social studies teacher. To make this routine meaningful and real, the great lessons of the pledge need to be taught. These lessons can be explored in morning meeting or in social studies; in a reading class or a civics class. When they are given meaning and significance, then the daily pledge takes on cognitive value in the hearts and minds of the students who say it daily. Students think about what they are saying when they understand what it is they are saying.

This is part of our goal as teachers: to use our time so wisely that teaching is a part of every moment we have available in school. The Pledge of Allegiance can carry us further in our work together as a learning community. Are there other things we should be pledging allegiance to? Could we write a pledge of allegiance for our class? For our school? What would we put in such a pledge and why? How would it help us and how could it hurt us? How could we find out more about different kinds of pledges and how they have helped or hurt groups of people? If we are working with kindergarten students, we may translate the pledge into something more understandable like:

> The work of my hands
> And the words of my heart
> I give to my flag

Then the class can talk about what that means in the simplest of terms.

If we are teaching middle school students, we might make the pledge a unit of study in social studies, perhaps in eighth grade, conceivably involving the reading of challenging texts such as *The Giver*[19] or *The Children's Story*[20] as young adolescents explore the meaning of authority and what it really means to be a responsible citizen.

When the routine is simply mindless, it is more dangerous and debilitating than when we take it seriously and make it part of the curriculum for our students. The Pledge of Allegiance consists of thirty-one words that take about fifteen seconds each morning to say. But it matters what teachers are doing during these fifteen seconds. Children learn what is important by watching our actions.

I have seen middle school classrooms where the pledge comes over the loud speaker and is ignored by teachers and students alike. I have been in elementary classrooms where the children are doing the pledge and the teacher is talking with her assistant or working at her desk. I have been in teacher's rooms where the pledge is totally ignored. And I have also been in teacher's rooms where teachers rise and salute the flag and recite the pledge.

The issue is not patriotism, but rather what we are communicating about our values through our actions and whether we value each moment of educational time. These can be fifteen seconds filled with meaning and thinking or fifteen seconds that are mindless at best, dismissive or derisive at worst. All our time together in school makes a difference, one way or the other.

We can take any of the routines and make them real, even the ones we might not like. Some day, when the announcements come over the PA, surprise your students by telling them there will be a pop quiz at the end. We can make a fun nutrition quiz out of the menu, a vocabulary quiz out of the faculty meeting announcement, a math quiz out of the game scores.

We can make the routine real when we stop doing the calendar with the children in first grade and make it a job for varying pairs of students to report the calendar to the class. They will *do* the calendar as a job when they come in first thing in the morning and announce their work at morning meeting or at the beginning of math. This responsibility makes the routine more important for everyone.

A moment of silence at the beginning of the day or before a meal is a moment to bring the divine into the routine. Nothing needs to be taught about divinity in this moment except that we are showing respect for each person's right to silence and reflection in all its forms: a prayer, a dream, a hope, or a wish. Sharing this stillness speaks of our respect for each other and for our learning community.

Open your room to parents and other adults

Parents at the doorway are never an interruption. (Well, almost never!) Sometimes it's hard to think like that when you are in the middle of so many things, but if you can see your classroom door as always open, especially to parents, their time and your time in the classroom will improve.

An open door requires some planning and action. Appoint a class host each week as one of your classroom's jobs. They can greet parents when you are busy, show them around the room and give them a place to sit while they wait for you to finish with a lesson or speak with a student. Invite parents to morning meeting or other special times of the day. Invite parents to share their stories and talents during morning meeting. Let your students see how much you value their parents through your actions, not just your words. Learning increases when the cooperation between school and home improves.

Fellow teachers, paraprofessionals, older and younger students, and volunteers can all help the learning process by expanding the social context of the classroom. For example, when buddy classes get together and your twenty-five fifth-graders are reading to twenty-five second-graders, the learning community is in full swing.

In preparation, you and the second grade teacher have matched partners carefully, modeled how to help the second-graders pick appropriate books, brainstormed good questions for fifth-graders to ask second-graders, and practiced the general process in both classes. This type of thoughtfulness, thoroughness, and adult cooperation models the collaborative process necessary in a highly social world and provides learning opportunities unavailable in a class with one adult teacher rather than many of varying ages. Because you've taken the time to arrange and plan this, you have created an extraordinarily valuable time for learning.

Chapter Ten

Time to Teach

IN THIS BOOK, we have reviewed the research on time, growth, and learning and followed one teacher and two students through a full day of school. My suggestions for changing today's schools and classrooms are detailed in several chapters.

We have learned from the past and observed and analyzed the present. Now it's time to teach and look to the future.

The 3 Rs

The vision I hold for our collective well being—for students, teachers, schools, and our society—and a new sense of time in school is rooted in the social context of education. The widening spiral of learning includes social action between learners, the solitude of thinkers, the social interaction of learners, and the solitude of thinkers again. This book emphasizes the social context of education and the power it holds for more engaged learning between teachers and students, and among the students themselves.

I envision "3 Rs" for schools of the next generation: Rigor, Recreation, and Reflection. These are based on the root meaning for the word school, from the Greek word *scoleri,* leisure. They would not replace Reading, 'Riting and 'Rithmetic, but absorb them into a richer concept—the concept of leisure time.

Rigor

To enrich and improve students' basic skills and raise general academic standards in the future, rigorous techniques and expectations must be applied. As we saw in the TIMMS research, students who spend time on fewer ideas and concepts, but study them in greater depth, show significantly higher achievement than those who cover a broad spectrum of knowledge superficially. We also saw that tracking students has an inverse effect on student achievement from what is desired and expected. This research reinforces what we know about the cognitive benefits of social interaction.

But social interaction, by itself, will not guarantee results. Rigorously structured social interaction is required. By rigor, I do not mean inflexibility, but rather "scrupulous accuracy; precision" in classroom practice (as in one of Webster's definitions). The kind of rigor I am referring to will be seen in those classrooms where the morning meeting gathering of students is a rich blend of friendliness and academic challenge. Students may greet each other in foreign languages or solve math equations to determine whom they will greet. They will share news from their lives and reports from their science class. They will ask thoughtful, respectful, and difficult questions of each other. They will engage in activities that require cognitive cooperation.

Their literature groups, math groups, science classes, and spelling lessons will demand no less than their morning meetings. Rich dialogue, probing questions, estimations, risk taking, demanding assignments at a level just slightly above their current one, but not out of reach of every student—that is the kind of rigor I am talking about.

To create such classrooms, teachers need to be rigorous in their preparations and in their instruction. They will need to rehearse and elevate their use of language in the classroom. They will need to be rigorous in scheduling the available learning time so that it feels leisurely and productive. They will need to be rigorous in their knowledge of the content of their subjects. The strategies listed in Chapters 8 and 9 require this type of rigorous application of teaching skill.

There will be rigorous tests and assessments of student work, but students will not be overwhelmed with anxiety by them because teachers will have regularly used testing practice and taught test-taking strategies. Time will seem to pass quickly, but will feel leisurely because students and teachers will be so deeply engaged in their learning together.

Rigor will be reinforced for teachers through peer coaching, frequent supervision, and observation in other classrooms. This will become the norm rather than the exception. Teachers will be given professional days to visit in their own school. Teachers will be paid a year-round salary and be expected to engage in professional development activity when they are not teaching or on a well-earned vacation.

Recreation

I use the word "recreation" as my second "R" quite deliberately, with an emphasis on its root meaning as well as our more common usage. As I understand the developmental process, academic and social cognition occurs and grows through constant re-creation. We are who we are because we are constantly changing. Our interaction with the environment and with others continually reshapes who we are and how we perceive and understand the world around us. Our awareness of this generative process, and our ability to use it for the greatest academic and social benefit is dependent on our psychological and spiritual state of being.

If our life is overly full of busyness, deadlines, pressure, and anxiety, we are less likely to look deeply, think complexly, produce creatively, complete work accurately, or be receptive to other's ideas and feelings. When we engage in what we typically call recreation, we try to reclaim the ability to live a more balanced and fruitful life. We all know what it feels like to be in the middle of a real vacation, when all the cares and responsibilities of work have been shed and we have not yet started to think about what will be there when we return. This is the feeling of recreation.

This re-creative energy is what is needed in school to create the best learning environment and outcomes for children and teachers. To promote and support this energy, the school schedule needs to have breathing room. Sylvia Ashton-Warner taught us that room to breathe in and breathe out keeps the learner balanced and ready to learn.

Recreation in the school day, then, is much more than recess, although recess is essential recreation. Recreation also includes the quiet time in the middle of the day, and the singing and dancing. It includes poetry and precise patterns in parquet. It includes chess and chapter books. In the schools I envision, no one need feel guilty about time spent in these pursuits. Results will show that achievement in mathematics, science, reading, and writing are directly tied to an integration of rigor and recreation in the school day—and to a third "R."

Reflection

Taking time to remember, consider, reconsider, sift, and tell others about our experiences is part of the development of diachronic thinking. Recently, I was interviewed by four third-graders about stories from my growing-up years. Their questions asked me to relate stories about "getting in trouble," "showing off," and "having a favorite sport"—all issues important to them in their current stage of growth. By hearing about my past, they were able to understand their present experience in new ways and understand, at some level, that some day they too will have their own past. I could tell this was true from the smiles of recognition, especially during the "getting in trouble" story!

Time for reflection allows re-creation. Children tend to go from one thing to the next without much conscious reflection because they live predominantly in the present. School seldom helps the situation. When children and teachers are rushed from one subject to another, one bell to the next, one place to another, several things happen. Not only are we limited to thinking about the present moment, but we are also much more likely to limit ourselves to only thinking about ourselves and our own needs. It's all there is time for!

"Where am *I* supposed to be? What do *I* need for this next class? What is *my* assignment? When will *I* have time to go to the bathroom?"

Empathy requires perspective. Some distance in time and space allows us to reflect and recognize what it is someone else needs. It's hard to put yourself in someone else's shoes when your shoes are always on the run.

Another thing that happens when we are "pressed for time" is that we cannot see our mistakes. The ability to recognize mistakes is not only important for test-taking, it is essential for revision of writing, spelling, math problems, and maps. Time for reflection in the school schedule and in teaching approaches and strategies is necessary for social and academic excellence.

In American schools of the next generation, I would like to see reflection become as important as it is in Japanese primary schools, although in slightly different ways. I would establish Reflection as a period in the schedule fifteen minutes before leaving the building in the afternoon, and I would encourage the process throughout the day. Teachers who couldn't fit this period in would see their paychecks docked because it would be considered so important to achievement and to a civil school.

Rigor, recreation, reflection—these can be the cornerstones of the schools of the next generation.

A Vision: A Day in School

I have a vision of a day in the future where time is structured to meet children's learning needs and is used to offer the opportunities for growth which are central to healthy individuals, schools, communities, and our larger society.

8:00–8:45

It's Monday morning and children are streaming into the classroom like sunlight. An electronic message chart by the door announces the new day in primary-print-sized letters on the LED screen. The second-grade children excitedly hang up their backpacks and coats, get their PC pens and write their answers to the teacher's question on the message screen. Their teacher, Ms. Alvarez, has asked them how many *different* kinds of leaves they collected over the weekend. The answers range from one to fifteen.

At morning meeting, children greet each other using tree names as adjectives. "Good morning, Maple Martha." "Good morning, Sycamore Sam." "Good morning, Elmie Emma." "Good morning, Aspen Alysha." For sharing, four children each have a single leaf carefully displayed in a clear plastic frame. When it is their turn, they hold the frame up and say, "I'm ready for your conjectures" (a new BIG word they have just learned).

"Is it a sugar maple?" Penny asks.

"What's your evidence?" the sharer responds.

"It's the biggest, like on our chart," says Penny.

"Right!" says the sharer. "Your turn, Melissa," she continues, smiling to the girl next to her who holds up her leaf frame.

For an activity, the class plays "tree challenge." Children who choose to challenge themselves come to the center of the circle and try to name as many different kinds of trees as they can before the "tree toad"—a small stuffed animal—gets passed around the meeting circle. Chandra names twelve trees and the class applauds enthusiastically. Brian names four and the class applauds enthusiastically again.

At the end of the twenty-five-minute meeting, the teacher draws their attention to the electronic message board and asks them to estimate the average number of leaves collected by each classmate over the weekend. A lively math dialogue ensues as second-graders exchange their different ideas about what an average is. The teacher brings out their class chart showing how long it takes to get quiet when the bell rings. "What do you think our average might be for this activity?" she questions, with a twinkle in her eye. She then dismisses the class back to their worktables, well spaced about the bright and airy classroom.

8:30–9:00

Some children retrieve their snack and then their writing journals. Others go straight for their journals. It's whole-class writing time. The teacher puts on a CD. Peaceful piano music quietly surrounds the classroom. As children write, the teacher circulates, asking them about their stories, their sketches, their lives. Some children are working on rough drafts of poems. Others are revising short stories. Still others are illustrating final drafts with the "publishing markers" reserved for such occasions. Max and Maurice are having a writing conference, listening to each other's stories, asking for suggestions about making their endings more surprising. Carrie and Paulo are fooling around at the art table where they are supposed to be making covers for their published work. With a look, the teacher sends them back to their worktables. They get out their writing journals. No cover making today.

9:00–9:30

The teacher turns off the CD and sounds a chime. Everyone puts their work down and looks at the teacher. When the room is still, she speaks. "Put your writing stuff away and come to the rug. Lisa and Charise will be in the author's chair today." Within a minute everyone is gathered respectfully on the meeting rug, Charise is in the author's chair, and there is an air of expectancy in the room. When Charise finishes reading the beginning of her story, she asks for questions and suggestions.

"I didn't quite get when the dragon came out of the cave," Phillip says. "Was the girl beside the rock right by the cave or further away?" Charise makes a note on her story and thanks Phillip for his question. "I'm not sure. I guess I better fix that," she says.

At 9:15, after the brief author's circle, the class lines up and goes outside. Today they are lining up by height, shortest to tallest. It's fun and doesn't take long, except for Michael S. and Michael P., who are the same height and have the same name. They think that's neat and keep changing places in line. Nobody seems to mind. Soon everyone is outside and running in every direction—for the climbing structure, the play forest, the jump ropes in the teacher's hand. After fifteen minutes of play, the teacher gathers the jump ropes and moves to the school door. The other children see the line forming and run to the building. "Presto change-o!" says the teacher and suddenly there is a scramble to line up tallest to shortest.

9:30–10:15

Inside, children disperse to math groups of five at each worktable. Some children get their snacks now. Each group has the same math assignments as every other group for the next forty-five minutes. Each group will decide together what to tackle first and how to work together. The math consists of "easies" (daily practice and drill on facts), "meadies" (medium difficult challenges dealing with averages this particular day), and "hardies"(estimation problems dealing with GIANT numbers).

Everyone stays engaged for the full period except for a few children whom the teachers asks to "take a break" when they get out of hand. No one seems to notice. The workflow of the room is not interrupted and the disengaged children soon return to their groups. As math time draws to a close, each group records their answers to problems in the group log, turns in their individual assignments, and takes five minutes to reflect on how they worked as a group today.

"It would have been better if we'd tried Sadie's idea sooner," says Joyce. "I jumped in and my idea didn't work. Sorry, Sadie."

"That's OK," Sadie responds. "Jonesy had a good idea about how to measure the tree."

Throughout the morning, as children have needed to go to the bathroom, they have unobtrusively taken one of the bathroom tags off the hooks by the door and headed to the facilities that are just down the hall. When George took a little too much time out of the room during math, his partners got on him about it when he returned.

10:15–10:45

The physical education teacher is at the door. "What's your line up scheme today?" she asks, "let me guess ..." as children line up shortest to tallest. Down in the gym, second-graders exercise for ten minutes and learn a new playground game for fifteen before returning to class. The classroom teacher has had a half-hour break for a cup of coffee, a phone call, some conversation with a colleague, and the bathroom.

10:45–11:30

The room is alive with the sounds of language. Another teacher's fifth grade has arrived for partner reading. Children are paired up and fifth-graders are reading the picture storybooks they have written and illustrated in their classrooms to the younger children. They are proud of their work, which has taken nearly the first two months of school to accomplish. The second-graders are delighted with the work of their partners and have many questions and compliments for them. The fifth-graders will come weekly during the next few weeks and each time they will have a new second grade partner to listen to their stories.

It's 11:15 and the teacher directs the children to get out their independent reading books and read quietly for fifteen minutes. While the class is reading, the teacher conferences quietly with several students individually.

11:30–12:00

It's time for recess. A family team—a cluster of grades 2–5—is out together with their teachers. This is a time for "skillful play," not the spontaneous play of earlier in the morning or the structured play of physical education. There are several mixed-age group games going which are led by teachers or in which teachers are playing. Some second-graders are playing in the "Capture the Jewels" game—a new version of Capture the Flag. Others are part of the Continuous Kickball game and some have joined soccer.

12:00–1:00

The mid-day teacher, Mrs. Daley, lines up the second-graders while Ms. Alvarez heads for the teacher workspace for an hour of relaxation and team work with her mixed-grade "family" colleagues. The mid-day teacher takes the second grade to lunch and then brings them back to the room for quiet time when they are finished. Since lunch only took them twenty minutes today, they will have a forty-minute quiet time.

Twenty minutes will be spent on silent, individual academic choices: reading, writing, science observations, computer tasks, and worksheets. Afterwards, the mid-day teacher will read the chapter book *Walk When the Moon Is Full,* a book Ms. Alvarez will be using this afternoon to begin her science unit on the cycles of the moon. At the next full moon, she and Mrs. Daley are planning a family night for second-grade families to share some learning about science and the experience of being out in the night together. They plan the night to end with singing, cider, and donuts. While Mrs. Daley reads, some children look at the beautiful illustrations by Robert Katona. Others follow along silently in their own classroom copies of the book. Still others choose to draw their own sketches of what they see as Mrs. Daley reads.

1:00–1:30

Mrs. Daley gathers the class on the rug just as Ms. Alvarez enters the room. "They really love the book," she tells Ms. Alvarez. Privately, she says, "Francine needs to know that I told you she had a hard time with her friends at lunch today. Can we take a moment?"

Ms. Alvarez speaks to the class. "So, how does the moon get 'full'? What do you think? Talk with your science partner about this question for five minutes and then Mrs. Daley and I have something exciting to tell you." She takes Francine aside and says, "Mrs. Daley and I have something to speak with you about."

While science partners exchange hypotheses on the rug (and

Francine's partner waits for her), there is a brief discussion at the round table about lunch and then Francine goes back to her partner. Mrs. Daley and Ms. Alvarez talk together while the science partners are finishing up. Mrs. Daley is paid to be with this class until 1:30, allowing for a smooth transition and adult partnering in the class.

Now Ms. Alvarez asks for some science partner ideas and Mrs. Daley writes them down on the electronic message board. "Well," says Mrs. Daley, "how would you like to go out in the night at the next full moon with your family and the whole class so we can find out more?" Now everyone is really excited and full of questions. "Ms. Alvarez will tell you more during science and I'll read the next chapter of the book with you tomorrow," says Mrs. Daley as she takes her leave of the classroom for the day.

1:30–2:45

Ms. Alvarez directs the children back to their worktables and gives each of them a worksheet with the phases of the moon on it. She teaches them how to label the phases and teaches fractions at the same time. She gives them homework: try to find the moon in the sky tonight, draw a circle around the phase they think it is, and write why they think that on the back of the sheet. She tells them they should have a family member help them and that if it is cloudy and they can't see the moon, to see if they can find out from the newspaper or TV. At 1:45 she asks everyone to stand up, puts on a CD and does a quick movement activity. She then directs the children to forty-five minutes of academic choice.

Some children go back to their writing, some to the computer, some to the easel. Some children copy down the spelling list from the chalkboard, something that every student had to find five minutes to do at some time during the day. Some children are playing cribbage, an approved second grade card/math game. Some children are reading independently. Others are off to the library to do some research on the moon.

At 2:30, Ms. Alvarez asks for five students to say what they did during academic choice this afternoon. Then it's time for clean-up. Ms. Alvarez puts on "clean-up jazz," the CD the kids know will take exactly six minutes. As the time winds down to the end of the jazz piece, children hustle to complete their clean-up chores, get their back-packs and coats and gather at the meeting rug.

2:45–3:05

It's "Reflections" time school-wide. The PA system, which has not been on all day, chimes twice. It means the principal has something to say. The class is quiet. "I'd like to thank family teams during the second recess for picking up the paper left on our playground over the weekend. Mr. Duncan thanks you too. Have you seen the new salamander display in Family East? It's worth a class visit. Please spend a portion of Reflections today talking about the buses. Thank you."

Ms. Alvarez asks, "What's the best thing about riding the bus?" In the discussion that ensues she also asks, "What would your family think, or have to do if you lost the privilege of riding the bus for a day?" and "What can you do to make sure your bus ride today is fun and safe?"

When the issue of fifth grade behavior on the bus comes up, she tells the class she'll invite members from that fifth grade class down for a class meeting later in the week even though they're not in their family team. She then asks the class what the best part of their day was. Many enjoyed physical education today and speak about how much fun it was to learn a new playground game. Some talk about the moon project and Ms. Alvarez takes the opportunity to remind them of their science homework.

At 3:05 bus tones begin to sound and children leave the room quietly, moving toward the exits like falling leaves.

3:10–4:30

By 3:20 Ms. Alvarez has written her message into the electronic

message board for tomorrow. It asks the children to pin their homework on the bulletin board. She has a song about the moon for
morning meeting tomorrow. She makes a note to herself and also
jots down a reminder to talk with Mrs. Daley about new lunch partners for the following week and what the next chapter book might be.

At 3:30, her Family Team meets in the library to share some ideas
about their part in the school fall festival at the end of the month.
They sit in a circle; they listen intently to each other's ideas. There
are no interruptions and everyone's ideas are acknowledged. There
is disagreement about which activity they want their Family Team to
sponsor, but no one is disagreeable.

At 4:00, the current team leader asks for any personal concerns
anyone on the team wants to share. Ms. Alvarez tells the team she is
going to visit her grandmother in the hospital this evening. There are
questions and expressions of support and concern. The team leader
reminds Ms. Alvarez that she is team leader next week, but lets her
know that she will keep the role if Ms. Alvarez' grandmother is still
ailing. The meeting ends at 4:15 and Ms. Alvarez heads home after
gathering her papers and plan book. Her union contract extends
from 8:00–4:30 with an hour break in the middle of the day and four
half-hour breaks elsewhere during the week.

The Structure and Use of Time

This day is obviously a vision rather than a real observation. It is a
day which meets children's myriad developmental and educational
needs and requires the teacher to work an intense, challenging, but
reasonable day in a time frame very close to what we currently work.

The school size was relatively large but the "families" of about
200 created manageable and cohesive learning communities. Ms.
Alvarez taught a class of eighteen with a wide range of abilities and
included children who showed ADHD behaviors and other special
needs. Her time structures and balanced formats (whole class, small
groups, pairs, individual students, mixed-age grouping) allowed her

to vary the expectations to meet individual student's needs.

Instruction in social skills and academic skills were seamlessly interwoven, through scheduled, structured meetings and consistent expectations and reinforcement throughout the day. Learning activities were rich and varied, supporting in-depth investigation and contemplation, student direction and choice in selecting subjects, and social interaction which stretched and motivated individual and group learning. There were a minimal number of well-managed transitions, and children's needs for food, exercise, elimination, and closure were respected and met throughout the day.

Teachers collaborated to expand the learning opportunities for their classes and were provided time for planning. The physical and social atmosphere of the school helped create an atmosphere which was both comfortable and challenging. Although no parents or other adults visited or participated during this particular day, communication with parents is consistent and clear, and parents regularly visit the classroom to observe and assist in the learning process.[1]

It's a Matter of Time

Beyond all the positive outcomes we can identify when time is structured and used constructively to meet children's needs, there is a magical quality to a day filled with learning. These children were allowed to have questions and to wrestle with them. They were offered what is today a rare luxury—time for reverie, contemplation, and investigation; time to breathe out and breathe in; time to experience time as a child, involved in the moment but gaining a sense of past and future. It was filled with Rigor, Recreation, and Reflection.

This pace helped the children stretch and grow, and allowed Ms. Alvarez, Mrs. Daley, and the other adults in the learning community to use their skills in an atmosphere of respect and spirited collaboration. They were the loving gardeners, the intense orchestra conductors, the graceful ice skaters. They used their knowledge and skills to practice the art and science of teaching.

Heroes in the Classroom

Teaching and learning are critical to our individual and collective survival and to the quality of our lives. The pace of change has us snarled in complexities, confusions, and conflicts that will diminish us, or do us in, if we do not enlarge our capacity to teach and to learn.

Parker J. Palmer, *The Courage to Teach*[1]

IN AN ADDRESS TO A NATIONAL CONFERENCE, Parker Palmer named public school teachers "the cultural heroes of the late twentieth century"[2] and I believe he would say the early twenty-first as well.

I agree. Educational policy makers and politicians constantly attack the state of American public education, blaming teachers for poor student performance and behavior. In truth, teachers are holding the fabric of the future together with their determination, perseverance, and extraordinary skill. Not all teachers, but most.

Mrs. Chambers uses a portion of her time after school talking to mothers whose children are having a hard time in her class. She gives them tips on things they can do at home to help their children learn to read and to mind. She knows where they can get extra food without being embarrassed, where they can get a winter coat for their first-grader. She regularly attends professional workshops to get better at what she does and to figure out how to deal with children's behavior that gets more difficult to understand and manage each year. She has been teaching for over twenty years and continues to care deeply for her students and their families. I have seen her in tears at the end of the day.

Mr. Fielder, in the middle school we visited, is always doing something extra. He has his eye out for his school wherever he goes and brings resources to it in the form of guest speakers, magazine articles, new books, and ideas. He is constantly thinking about the teachers on his team, what would help lighten their load, and improve their work together. He leaves school right at the bell and before the buses two days a week in order to make it to his graduate courses across town.

I have known such teachers in Washington, D.C. and Baltimore, Tacoma and Chicago, rural Vermont and suburban Cincinnati. They are professionals who give of themselves in the same way as dedicated doctors, nurses, and police. They are extraordinarily aware of what it takes to make a difference in the life of a child today. They care enough to keep learning the skills to do it right. They care about each child they teach. They teach them how to read. They teach them how to get along. They teach them before and after school, and they teach them in their dreams.

These teachers really do know how to reach the children each morning, but they are repeatedly handed different time structures and expectations and told to use that time differently as well. When they know it's right to listen, they're told to drill. When they know the story is more important than the worksheets, they feel pressured to spend more time on the worksheets. When they know the test results are only part of the story, they are told they are the most important part of the story.

One of the issues in modern education which bothers me the most is that decision makers seldom draw on the knowledge and skill of real classroom teachers. No one asks their opinions, and if the teachers do speak up, their opinions are generally discounted or patronized with knowing glances and smiles of understanding by the powerful politicians and bureaucrats.

If this sounds overdrawn or melodramatic, run down the list of any national committee examining school reform, check out the standards people, the test makers, the curriculum bakers, the textbook shakers, the budget passers. Search for the teachers and you will find their participation and power rare.

At the same time, teachers work in conditions which are sub-standard, at best, because there isn't enough funding for maintenance or custodial services. Playgrounds are littered with glass and worse. At a recent workshop for teachers on skillful play, the leader reminded teachers not to let their children reach into piles of leaves gathered along the fence for fear they might be stabbed by a discarded hypo-dermic needle used to inject drugs. Basic health standards are not met in schools where air ducts are clogged and which recycle bad air in a closed environment. It's like teaching in an airplane with poorly recycled air, six hours a day.

Loyally, most teachers keep on going without seeing conditions improve and agree to try new initiatives, new teaching practices, new solutions to problems that seem intractable. They are the medics who stay at their posts while the generals bark orders and move on. New principals and superintendents bring new policies and practices to school as often as every two or three years. Families move so fre-quently that the make-up of teachers' classes often changes by as much as fifty percent within a school year, and even more in some communities. Constant change is the only constant in many schools. But the teachers stay at their posts. They are heroes, meeting the challenge at the schoolhouse door each morning, giving children their hearts, their minds, their souls.

Leading the Country

There is no question that the quality of the adult community in a school determines the quality of the school culture for children and adults. At a workshop I was leading, a teacher asked, "Does the cul-ture of our country lead the school or does the school need to lead the country?" It's a question we've all asked at some point in our teaching careers. It gets to the heart of the purpose of education. Is education about maintaining the status quo or making life better? Is education designed to teach children how to fit into the past or step into the future? It is an either/or question, but most schools have never behaved that way. Instead, they have answered "Yes!" and tried to do both.

I answered the question that day more unequivocally than I might have earlier in my career. I believe we have no choice but to lead the country. Every day children and grown-ups are brought together by law so that the children can learn from the grown-ups. In a concentrated time and space, for over 180 days each year, the message is clear: it is important to learn to read. It is important to learn math and science, to spell and write. For this to happen, it is also necessary and important to have rules, to follow the rules, to treat each other with kindness and compassion. Every day we lead the nation into the future with our words and actions simply because we are teaching the future of our nation. "Children are living messages we send to a time we will not see," says an anonymous quotation which leapt out at me from the wall of a teacher's room.

Each day I am in school, I look carefully at the faces of the children and try to see the adult faces that will emerge in a few short years. I think about all the potential for good and all the potential for evil. Parker Palmer is right. "Teaching and learning are critical to our individual and collective survival." We must "enlarge our capacity to teach and to learn."3 We must lead the country.

Appendix A
Standards

DURING A SUMMER INSTITUTE I was leading on standards in a neighboring state, I engaged teachers in an exercise where I asked them to write down a list of their own teaching standards. As I sat and watched these teachers bent over their notebooks on a hot August morning, I felt an enormous respect for the integrity and commitment of these professionals. Few outside the workshop would ever know the professional struggle each was occupied with that morning or what impact that struggle would have on their teaching in September.

As I watched, I thought back to all the days I had spent in their classrooms as a consulting teacher over a period of eight years—a few days each year—and watched their personal teaching standards grow and expand. I found myself asking, "What about me? What standards mean the most to me? What mattered most in my classrooms all those years?" I stopped watching and joined the teachers around me—as a writer. The room disappeared around me and I was lost in a sea of remembered children.

When some of the teachers shared their lists of personal teaching standards at the end of the exercise, I did something I seldom do as a facilitator: I shared my list too. I list my standards here, not because they are definitive, but because they are deeply held and guide my suggestions for change.

I urge you to write down your own list before you read mine, as I asked the teachers to do that summer morning. Ask yourself, "What are the standards I hold most important in my teaching?" Whether your list is short or long, whether it bears any resemblance to my list or not, it is an important list.

The standards movement is also important. Good teachers need the reinforcement this movement can offer to good teaching. Inadequate teachers need the concerted pressure from peers, superiors and the public to get better at what they do or get out of the profession.

Perhaps the most important outcomes of the standards movement at the state and federal level will be not only the actual manuals of standards created and distributed, tested and assessed, but also the opportunities provided for teachers and administrators to honestly examine the standards they hold essential to teaching. By comparing your own teaching and learning standards with state requirements, you can help define what is most important for the children, for you and for your time together in school.

Here is my list, just as I jotted it down that humid morning, with fans whirring and teachers around me lost in the memories of their own classrooms, their best moments of teaching.

My Standards in the Classroom

1. Learning is inside the student, not the teacher.

2. Teacher knowledge facilitates student knowledge when I uphold the standards of:

    - Valuing every question

    - Not answering every question myself

    - Providing resources to answer most questions

    - Helping students to help each other

3. Honor "draft" work and "museum" work.

    - Draft work includes work that describes a process, includes sketches and schematics of the students' unfolding ideas.

    - Museum work includes correct spelling, beautiful handwriting, clear labels, careful mounting of displays, names of workers proudly shown.

4. Daily vocabulary enhancement for every child, with a standard that each child learns at least one new word a day.

5. Daily drill in intellectually appropriate math facts with a partner.

6. Daily drawing, especially observational drawing.

7. Every day needs a silent time for personal reflection and journaling—for me and the students.

8. Every day I will provide a group reflection time so we can see how we are doing as a class.

9. Students will hear stories, poems, and math problems read aloud each day.

10. Use writing process that stretches students to use the next available skill (analogies, similes, and alliteration, whatever is next possible) every day. My standard is to know what their personal best is—and stretch them.

11. Homework, if I've assigned it, will be honored by spending time on it the next day in my teaching.

12. All students will contribute vigorously to the physical beauty and order of our learning space.

13. All students will contribute to the social safety of the classroom and will demonstrate a growing ability to solve problems.

14. Play is necessary to achieve cognitive standards. All my students are expected to play—safe, hard, fairly. I will play alongside my students.

15. Every student's voice is as important as any other's voice. My standard is that every voice is known and heard equally over the course of the year.

Appendix B

The Responsive Classroom®

SINCE 1981 I HAVE WORKED with a group of teachers dedicated
to increasing the use of developmental and social learning theory in
our nation's schools. During this time, we established and continue
to run a small K–8 grade laboratory school in Greenfield,
Massachusetts, home of our parent organization, Northeast
Foundation for Children. NEFC publishes books, newsletters, and
other educational material and provides nationwide teacher education programs under the banner of *The Responsive Classroom.*
Thousands of teachers annually attend weeklong summer institutes
and inservice programs in their school districts to learn effective
strategies for maximizing the balanced integration of social and academic learning for their students.

Through my work with *The Responsive Classroom,* I have had the
privilege to be in an extended conversation with many excellent
teachers. These are educators who have chosen to work on educational reform in the classroom and we have chosen to join them
there. *The Responsive Classroom* is one of a handful of national reform
efforts initiated and promulgated by practicing teachers. There is a
difference between riding on a bus full of children on a field trip and
debating educational standards on a hotel shuttle on the way to
a national conference. Reflective, dedicated, hard-working, and
conscientious teachers have the knowledge we need to make schools
different now. There are ways to balance and integrate social and
academic learning, meet or surpass state standards, and restore our
schools to places of civility and decency.

I have codified seven basic principles in *The Responsive Classroom* that serve as a foundation for its practice. These are based on developmental theory, and informed by years of educational experience. These ideas are meant to bring a meaningful and balanced integration of approaches, not extremes, to our schools and classrooms. Balanced approaches and good timing can make our schools sites for success for all children as well as the grown-ups who support them.

1. **The social curriculum is as important as the academic curriculum.** The balanced integration of the two is essential to social and academic growth. This requires teachers who are skilled and knowledgeable and who are given support for their attention to the complementary sides of learning.

2. **How children learn is as important as what they learn.** The key is in the balance between content and process. Knowledge cannot be attained if the instructional process is too laissez-faire or too constrictive. Teacher-directed learning and student-initiated learning are both important. Inquiry-based learning needs to be balanced with more didactic approaches.

3. **The greatest cognitive growth occurs through social interaction.** Social interaction does not provide the only cognitive growth because children are learning when they are reading a book, taking a test, or completing a worksheet on their own. But children are learning the most when they are engaged with each other. It is important, therefore, to know just what they are doing and talking about in order to facilitate cooperative learning most productively.

4. **There is a specific set of social skills that children need in order to be successful academically and socially.** They can be remembered by the simple acronym CARES. These skills are: cooperation, assertion, responsibility, empathy, and self-control.[1]

5. **Knowing the children we teach is as important as knowing the content we teach.** The better we know the children individually, culturally, and developmentally, the more they will learn. The scientific and academic discipline of the teaching profession is child development.

6. **Knowing the parents of the children we teach is as important as knowing the children.** Parent involvement is essential to children's education. I dream that at a parent conference before the first day of school each year, every teacher in America might ask, "What would you like your child to learn in school this year?" and that every parent could relate their hopes and dreams for their children.

7. **How the grown-ups at school work together to accomplish our mission is more important than our individual competence.** Meaningful and lasting change for the better in our schools requires good working relationships. Children are always watching.

Notes

Introduction

1   Ruth Charney, Marlynn Clayton, Marion Finer, Jay Lord and Chip Wood, *A Notebook for Teachers: Making Changes in the Elementary Curriculum* (Greenfield, MA: Northeast Foundation for Children, 1985), p. 3.

2   Ruth Charney, et al., *A Notebook for Teachers: Making Changes in the Elementary Curriculum.*

3   Ruth Charney, *Teaching Children to Care: Management in the Responsive Classroom* (Greenfield, MA: Northeast Foundation for Children, 1991).

4   Thomas Merton, *Conjectures of a Guilty Bystander* (Garden City, NY: Doubleday, 1966), p. 73.

Chapter One / Time to Learn

1   Elliot Eisner, keynote address at the Conference on Developmental Education sponsored by Gesell Institute (Oakland, CA, March 23, 1988).

2   Barbara Rogoff, *Apprenticeship in Thinking* (NY: Oxford University Press, 1990), p. 6.

3   Karl V. Hertz, "What if we had the highest test scores?" *Education Week* (May 13, 1998), p. 44.

4   Dirk Johnson, "Many Schools Putting an End to Child's Play," *The New York Times* (April 7, 1998), A1.

5   Dirk Johnson.

6   Al Gore, "Should Schools Be Wired to the Internet? Yes—It's Essential to the Way Kids Learn," *Time* (May 25, 1998), p. 54.

7   Mary Pipher, *The Shelter of Each Other* (NY: G.P. Putnam's Sons, 1996), p. 76.

8   Teresa Thomas, "Carnegie Mellon Study Reveals Negative Potential of Heavy Internet Use on Emotional Well Being," press release (Aug. 30, 1998), Carnegie Mellon University. Full study in *American Psychologist,* a publication of American Psychologist Association.

9   Catherine E. Snow, Susan M. Burns, Peg Griffin, editors, *Preventing Reading Difficulties in Young Children* (Washington, DC: National Academy Press, 1998), pp. 1–16.

10   The behavior referred to here was called hyperactivity in the medical profession prior to 1989. Between 1989 and 1994 it was referred to as ADD. Currently it is defined as ADHD in the *Diagnostic and Statistical Manual of Mental Disorders* as documented in Richard DeGrandpre's *Ritalin Nation,* p. 38.

11   Russell A. Barkley, *Taking Charge of ADHD* (NY: The Guilford Press, 1995), pp. 3, 80.

12   Richard DeGrandpre, *Ritalin Nation: Rapid-Fire Culture and the Transformation of Human Consciousness* (NY: W.W. Norton & Company, 1999), p. 18.

13   Russell A. Barkley, p. 47.

14   Barbara Vobejda, "Study finds children reducing time spent at TV, eating," *Washington Post* (Dec. 2, 1998).

15   Snow, et. al., *Preventing Reading Difficulties in Young Children.*

16   Marianne Jennings, "Kitchen Table," NPR Commentary, January 7, 1998. © NPR, 1997. Used with permission of NPR.

17   David W. Johnson and Roger T. Johnson, *Reducing School Violence* (Alexandria, VA: Association for Supervision and Curriculum Development, 1995), p. 2.

Chapter Two / Time, Growth, and Learning

1   National Education Commission on Time and Learning, *Prisoners of Time: What we know and what we need to know* (September, 1994).

2   Dylan Thomas, "Fern Hill," *The Collected Poems of Dylan Thomas* (NY: New Directions, 1957), p. 179.

3   Jean Piaget, *The Child's Conception of Time* (NY: Basic Books, 1927).

4   Jean Piaget, p. 259.

5   Jacques Montangero, *Understanding Changes in Time* (Bristol, PA: Taylor and Francis, 1996), p. 80.

6   Jacques Montangero, p. 180.

7   Jacques Montangero, p. 181.

8   E.D. Hirsch, Jr., *The Core Knowledge Sequence* (Charlottesville, VA: Core Knowledge Foundation, 1993).

9   E.D. Hirsch, Jr., *What Your Second-Grader Needs to Know* (NY: Dell Publishing, 1993).

10   Lucy Sprague Mitchell knew this in the 1930s, and in her pioneering work, *Young Geographers,* created a cognitive map for helping us to know how children understand the world differently at different ages.

11 E.D. Hirsch, Jr., *Cultural Literacy* (NY: Vintage Books, 1988).

12 Susan Ohanian, *Standards, Plain English, and the Ugly Duckling* (Bloomington, IN: Phi Delta Kappa Educational Foundation, 1998), p. 38.

13 Paul Fraise, "The Adaptation of the Child to Time" in William J. Friedman, ed. *The Developmental Psychology of Time* (NY: Academic Press, 1982), p. 115.

14 Sylvia Ashton-Warner, *Teacher* (NY: Simon & Schuster, 1963).

15 Sylvia Ashton-Warner, pp. 89–91.

16 Sylvia Ashton-Warner, p. 91.

17 Chip Wood, *Yardsticks: Children in the Classroom, Ages 4–14* (Greenfield, MA: Northeast Foundation for Children, 1997).

18 Eric Jensen, *Teaching with the Brain in Mind* (Alexandria, VA: Association for Supervision and Curriculum Development, 1998), p. 45.

19 DeGrandpre, p. 206.

20 DeGrandpre, p. 56.

21 Russell A. Barkley, pp. 43–54.

22 Alan Lightman, *Einstein's Dreams* (NY: Warner Books, 1993), pp. 130–131.

Chapter Three / Using Time Wisely

1 Daniel Goleman, *Emotional Intelligence: Why it can matter more than IQ* (NY: Bantam Books, 1995), pp. 33–36.

2 Glen E. Robinson and James H. Wittebols, *Class Size Research: A Related Cluster Analysis for Decision Making* (Arlington, VA: Educational Research Service, Inc., 1986).

3 Glen E. Robinson and James H. Wittebols. See Glass and Smith studies in this volume for more detail, p. 19.

4 Frederick Mosteller, Richard Light, Jason Sachs, "Sustained Inquiry in Education: Lessons from Skill Grouping and Class Size," *Harvard Educational Review* (Vol. 66, No. 4, Winter 1996), pp. 797–828.

5 E. Word, et. al., Student/Teacher Achievement Ratio (STAR), Tennessee's K–3 class size study: final summary report, 1985–1990 (Nashville, TN: Tennessee State Department of Education, 1990) and The State of Tennessee's Student/Teacher Achievement Ratio (STAR) project: technical report, 1985–1990 (Nashville, TN: Tennessee State Department of Education, 1994).

6 Frederick Mosteller, et. al., p. 821.

7 U.S. Department of Education, Office of Policy and Planning, *Trying to Beat The Clock: Use of Teacher Professional Time in Three Countries* (Washington, DC: 1988), p. 83.

8   Lev S. Vygotsky, *Mind In Society,* Harvard University Press, (Cambridge, MA: 1978), p. 57.

9   Among the more important contemporary scholars are: James Wertsch, Alex Kozulin, Barbara Rogoff, Martin Packer, Roland Tharp, Ronald Gallimore, to name just a few. This is a major and significant theoretical construct of teaching and learning, known at the university level but not yet accepted by the mainstream educational establishment serving children in our public school systems.

10 Ellice A. Forman, Norris Minick, C. Addison Stone, editors, *Contexts for Learning* (NY: Oxford University Press, 1993), p. 11.

11 Barbara Rogoff, *Apprenticeship in Thinking: Cognitive Development in Social Context* (NY: Oxford University Press, 1990) and Ruth Charney, Marlynn Clayton, Chip Wood, *The Responsive Classroom Guidelines* (Greenfield, MA: Northeast Foundation for Children, 1997).

12 Mazamo Mangaliso, "Toward an Affirmation of African Philosophical Thought in Management Discourse," *Entrepreneurship, Innovation and Change* (Vol. 4, No. 3, 1995), pp. 249–250.

13 Mazamo Mangaliso.

14 U.S. Department of Education, p. 83.

15 U.S. Department of Education.

16 Catherine C. Lewis, *Educating Hearts and Minds* (NY: Cambridge University Press, 1995), p. 208.

17 Catherine C. Lewis, p. 91.

18 Catherine C. Lewis, p. 98.

19 Catherine C. Lewis, p. 208.

20 See such books as Dewey's *Democracy and Education,* Noddings' *Caring,* Meier's *The Power of Their Ideas* and Berman's *Children's Social Consciousness and the Development of Social Responsibility.*

21 TIMSS U.S. National Research Center, Report No. 8 (Michigan State University, April, 1988), p. 4. Schmidt is Dr. William H. Schmidt, Professor, Michigan State University and National Research Coordinator for U.S. TIMSS and Executive Director of the U.S. National Research Center. The National Steering Committee for these reports is a blue ribbon panel of leading national figures working for higher standards in education.

22 U.S. National Research Center.

23 Susan Ohanian, p. 35.

Chapter Four / Floating on the Surface
in Seventh Grade

1   Langston Hughes, *Collected Poems* (NY: Knopf, 1994). Reprinted by permission of Alfred A. Knopf, Inc.

2   Chip Wood, *Yardsticks: Children in the Classroom, Ages 4–14* (Greenfield, MA: Northeast Foundation for Children, 1997), p. 165.

3   Richard DeGrandpre, p. 22.

4   Barbara Rogoff, p. 6.

5   Mary Pipher, *Reviving Ophelia* (NY: Ballantine Books, 1994).

6   Mary Pipher, *Reviving Ophelia,* p. 290.

7   Nancy E. Adelman, Karen Panton Walking Eagle, Andy Hargreaves, editors, *Racing with the Clock* (NY: Teachers College Press, 1997).

8   Alan Lightman, p. 47.

9   See, for instance, *Turning Points: Preparing American Youth for the Twenty-first Century* (Carnegie Council on Adolescent Development, 1989); *The Impact of School Reform for the Middle Years* (Phi Delta Kappan, March 1997) and other related articles in this issue; *Teaching Ten- to Fourteen-Year-Olds* by Chris Stevenson (Longman, 1992).

Chapter Five / On Your Mark, Get Set ...
Seven Years Old in First Grade

1   American Psychiatric Association, *Diagnostic and Statistical Manual of Mental Disorders* (Fourth Edition, 1995).

2   Eleanor Duckworth, *"The Having of Wonderful Ideas" and Other Essays on Teaching and Learning,* Second Edition (NY: Teachers College Press, 1996).

3   Sylvia Ashton-Warner, p. 101.

4   Richard DeGrandpre, pp. 92–93.

5   As atypical middle schools have demonstrated, young adolescents are fully capable of more sustained and thorough work over longer periods of time when their developmental needs for food, exercise and conversation are met as part of their daily schedule (see Chapter 4, footnote 9). This has also been the clear experience for the past eighteen years in the 5–8 grade program at Greenfield Center School, *The Responsive Classroom* laboratory school of Northeast Foundation for Children.

Chapter Six / Working to Be "All There at Once"

1   Sylvia Ashton-Warner, p. 9.

2   John Goodlad, *A Place Called School* (NY: McGraw-Hill, 1984), p. 102.

3   Catherine Lewis, p. 208.

4   National Education Commission on Time and Learning, *Prisoners of Time* (Washington, DC: April 1994), pp. 23–24.

Chapter Seven / Changing School Time

1   National Education Commission on Time and Learning, *Prisoners of Time: What we know and what we need to know* (Washington, DC: September, 1994).

2   This is true in the growing number of schools with year-round calendars. Contact the National Association for Year-Round Education for more information at P.O. Box 711386, San Diego, CA 92171-1386.

3   Jonathan Saphier, *How to Make Supervision and Evaluation Really Work* (Carlisle, MA: Research for Better Teaching, 1993), p. 11.

4   National Education Commission on Time and Learning, p. 51.

5   In addition to the sources in Chapter 3, see *Constructing School Success: The Consequences of Untracking Low-Achieving Students* by Hugh Mehan (ed.) (Cambridge, MA: Cambridge University Press, 1996) and *Alternatives to Tracking and Ability Grouping* by Anne Wheelock (American Association of School Administrators, 1994).

6   Carol Ann Tomlinson, *How to Differentiate Instruction in Mixed-Ability Classrooms* (Alexandria, VA: Association for Supervision and Curriculum Development, 1995), p. 2.

7   *Open Circle Curriculum,* Reach Out To Schools: Social Competency Program, The Stone Center, Wellesley College, Wellesley, MA; *Second Step Violence Prevention Curriculum,* The Committee for Children, Seattle, WA; *Resolving Conflict Creatively Program,* New York, NY; *Social Decision Making and Problem Solving,* Rutgers University, New Brunswick, NJ. For a more complete listing of programs, consult: *Promoting Social and Emotional Learning: Guidelines for Educators,* Elias, et. al. (Alexandria, VA: Association for Supervision and Curriculum Development, 1997).

8   *The Responsive Classroom,* Northeast Foundation for Children, Greenfield, MA; *School Development Program,* Yale Child Study Center, New Haven, CT; *Child Development Project,* Developmental Studies Center, Oakland, CA.

9   One excellent guide is *Friends and Relations: Using Literature with Social Themes K–2* by Carol Otis Hurst and Rebecca Otis (Greenfield, MA: Northeast Foundation for Children, 1999).

10 See *Educating for Character: How Our Schools Can Teach Respect and Responsibility* by Thomas Lickona, Ph.D. (NY: Bantam Books, 1991).

11 For more information contact the Center for the Fourth and Fifth Rs, Education Department, SUNY Cortland, Cortland, NY or the Character Education Partnership, 918 16th Street, N.W., Wash., DC, 20006.

12 Robert D. Selner, et. al., "The Impact of School Reform for the Middle Years" (*Phi Delta Kappan,* March, 1997), pp. 528–550.

13 For a more in-depth exploration of these possibilities at the middle school level see Chris Stevenson's *Teaching Ten- to Fourteen-Year-Olds* (White Plains, NY: Longman, 1992).

14 Madeline L'Engle, *A Wrinkle in Time* (NY: Farrar, Straus and Giroux, 1962).

15 Stephen N. Elliott, "Does a classroom promoting social skill development enable higher academic functioning among its students over time?" Executive Summary of Year One of a Three Year Study 1996–1997.

16 Jay Lord, "Evidence of improved social skills and academics as a result of the implementation of *The Responsive Classroom* in elementary schools" (Greenfield, MA: Northeast Foundation for Children, 1999).

Chapter Eight / Changing the Structure of Time in Classrooms

1 Frank Smith, *The Book of Learning and Forgetting* (NY: Teachers College Press, 1998), p. 9.

2 TIMSS U.S. National Research Center, Report No. 8.

3 See a brilliant discussion of irony in Ellen Winner's *The Point of Words: Children's Understanding of Metaphor and Irony* (Cambridge, MA: Harvard University Press, 1997).

4 Chip Wood, *Yardsticks: Children in the Classroom Ages 4–14.*

5 A special section of the January 1999 issue of *Kappan* magazine is devoted to "Adolescent Sleep Needs and School Starting Times" (*Phi Delta Kappan,* 1/99, Volume 80, No. 5), pp. 344–372.

Chapter Nine / Changing the Use
of Time in Classrooms

1   T.S. Eliot, "The Love Song of J. Alfred Prufrock" from *The Complete Poems and Plays 1909–1950* (NY: Harcourt Brace and Company, 1958).

2   Aubry Nelson Koehler, "Time Flies when You're Having Fun!" seventh grade science report, (Greenfield, MA: Greenfield Center School, 1998).

3   Katherine Paterson, *Bridge to Terabithia* (NY: Avon, 1977).

4   For a recent and full explanation of this exercise see Donald Graves' *A Fresh Look at Writing* (Portsmouth, NH: Heinemann, 1994), pp. 25–30.

5   Donald Graves, p. 27.

6   Jacques Montangero, p. 164.

7   Mark Link, *Breakaway: Twenty-Eight Steps to a More Reflective Life* (Allen, TX: Argus, 1980), p. 10.

8   Bob Strachota, *On Their Side: Helping Children Take Charge of Their Learning* (Greenfield, MA: Northeast Foundation for Children, 1996), p. 8.

9   Thanks to my colleague, Linda Crawford, for exploring with me this key aspect of academic choice.

10 See *Dr. Montessori's Own Handbook* (NY: Schocken Press edition, 1965).

11 Anthony D. Pellegrini and David F. Bjorkland, "The Role of Recess in Children's Cognitive Performance" (*Educational Psychologist*, 32, 1997), pp. 35–40.

12 James Levin and John Shanken-Kaye, *The Self-Control Classroom: Understanding and Managing the Disruptive Behavior of all Students Including Students with ADHD* (Dubuque, IA: Kendall/Hunt Publishing Company, 1996).

13 From *The Self-Control Classroom,* by James Levin and John Shanken-Kaye. Copyright © 1996 by Kendall/Hunt Publishing Company. Used with permission.

14 Melvin Konner, *Childhood: A Multicultural View* (Boston, MA: Little, Brown and Co., 1991), p. 405.

15 Russell A. Barkley.

16 James Levin and John Shanken-Kaye.

17 Ross W. Green, *The Explosive Child: A New Approach for Understanding and Parenting Easily Frustrated, "Chronically Inflexible" Children* (NY: HarperCollins Publishers, 1998).

18 Ross W. Green, p. 136.

19 Lois Lowry, *The Giver* (Boston, MA: Houghton Mifflin Company, 1993).

20 James Clavell, *The Children's Story....but not just for children* (NY: Dell Publishing, 1963).

Chapter Ten / Time to Teach

1   A similar scenario for middle school has been described eloquently by Chris
    Stevenson, a leading middle school reformer at the University of Vermont. In
    two volumes, *Teaching Ten- to Fourteen-Year-Olds* and *Teacher Teaming Handbook,*
    Dr. Stevenson has provided guidelines for effective middle school classrooms,
    including ways to change the time, space and structure of the middle school
    day. He proposes that time can be structured in ways that are sympathetic to
    the young adolescent and to his/her teachers.

Afterword: Heroes in the Classroom

1   Parker J. Palmer, *The Courage To Teach* (San Francisco, CA: Jossey-Bass, 1998),
    p. 3.

2   Parker J. Palmer, Opening remarks, *Education as Transformation* (Education as
    Transformation National Conference, Wellesley College, September 27, 1998).

3   Parker J. Palmer, *The Courage To Teach,* p. 3.

Appendix B: The Responsive Classroom®

1   These skills were identified by researchers Stephen N. Elliott and Frank
    Gresham in their groundbreaking standardization and norming of the Social
    Skills Rating System (American Guidance, Circle Pines, MN: 1990).

References

Adelman, Nancy E., Karen Panton Walking Eagle, Andy Hargreaves, ed. *Racing with the Clock: Making Time for Teaching and Learning in School Reform*. The Series on School Reform. NY: Teachers College Press, 1997.

American Psychiatric Association. *Diagnostic and Statistical Manual of Mental Disorders*. Fourth Edition. 1995.

Arnold, John and Chris Stevenson. *Teachers' Teaming Handbook: A Middle Level Planning Guide*. Fort Worth, TX: Harcourt Brace College Publishers, 1998.

Ashton-Warner, Sylvia. *Teacher*. NY: Simon & Schuster, 1963.

Barkley, Russell A. *Taking Charge of ADHD*. NY: The Guilford Press, 1995.

Carnegie Council on Adolescent Development. *Turning Points: Preparing American Youth for the Twenty-first Century,* 1989.

Charney, Ruth. *Teaching Children to Care: Management in the Responsive Classroom*. Greenfield, MA: Northeast Foundation for Children, 1991.

Charney, Ruth, Marlynn Clayton, Marion Finer, Jay Lord and Chip Wood. *A Notebook for Teachers: Making Changes in the Elementary Curriculum*. Greenfield, MA: Northeast Foundation for Children, 1985.

Clavell, James. *The Children's Story....but not just for children*. NY: Dell Publishing, 1963.

DeGrandpre, Richard. *Ritalin Nation: Rapid-Fire Culture and the Transformation of Human Consciousness*. NY: W.W. Norton & Company, 1999.

Duckworth, Eleanor. *"The Having of Wonderful Ideas" and Other Essays on Teaching and Learning*. Second Edition. NY: Teachers College Press, 1996.

Eisner, Elliot. Speech entitled "The Role of the Senses in the Creation of Mind." Oakland, CA, 23 March 1988.

Elias, Maurice, et. al. *Promoting Social and Emotional Learning: Guidelines for Educators.* Alexandria, VA: Association for Supervision and Curriculum Development, 1997.

Elliot, Stephen. "Does a classroom promoting social skill development enable higher academic functioning among its students over time?" Executive Summary of Year One of a Three Year Study 1996–1997. Greenfield, MA: Northeast Foundation for Children, 1997.

Farnham-Diggory, Silvia. *Schooling.* The Developing Child Series. ed. Jerome Bruner, Michael Cole, Barbara Lloyd. Cambridge, MA: Harvard University Press, 1990.

Felner, Robert D., Anthony W. Jackson, Deborah Kasak, Peter Mulhall, Steven Brand, Nancy Flowers. "The Impact of School Reform For the Middle Years: Longitudinal Study of a Network Engaged in Turning Points-Based Comprehensive School Transformation." *Phi Delta Kappan* (March 1997).

Forman, Ellice A., Norris Minick, C. Addison Stone, editors. *Contexts for Learning.* NY: Oxford University Press, 1993.

Fraise, Paul. "The Adaptation of the Child to Time" in William J. Friedman, ed. *The Developmental Psychology of Time.* NY: Academic Press, 1982.

Goleman, Daniel. *Emotional Inteligence: Why it can matter more than IQ.* NY: Bantam Books, 1995.

Goodlad, John. *A Place Called School.* NY: McGraw-Hill, 1984.

Gore, Al, "Should Schools Be Wired to the Internet? Yes—It's Essential to the Way Kids Learn." *Time* (May 25, 1998).

Graves, Donald H. *A Fresh Look at Writing.* Portsmouth, NH: Heinemann, 1994.

Greene, Ross W. *The Explosive Child: A New Approach for Understanding and Parenting Easily Frustrated, "Chronically Inflexible" Children.* NY: HarperCollins Publishers, 1998.

Hamerstrom, Frances. *Walk When the Moon is Full.* Freedom, CA: The Crossing Press, 1975.

Hertz, Karl V. "What If We Had The Highest Test Scores?" *Education Week* (May 13, 1998).

Hirsch, E.D. *The Core Knowledge Sequence.* Charlottesville, VA: Core Knowledge Foundation, 1998.

Hirsch, E.D. *Cultural Literacy*. NY: Vintage Books, 1988.

Hirsch, E.D. *What Your Second-Grader Needs to Know*. NY: Dell Publishing, 1993.

Hughes, Langston. *Collected Poems of Langston Hughes*. NY: Knopf, 1994.

Hurst, Carol Otis and Rebecca Otis. *Friends and Relations: Using Literature with Social Themes K–2*. Greenfield, MA: Northeast Foundation for Children, 1999.

Jennings, Marianne. "Kitchen Table." NPR Commentary (January 7, 1998).

Jensen, Eric. *Teaching with the Brain in Mind*. Alexandria, VA: Association for Supervision and Curriculum Development, 1998.

Johnson, David W. and Roger T. Johnson. *Reducing School Violence*. Alexandria, VA: Association for Supervision and Curriculum Development, 1995.

Johnson, Dirk. "Many Schools Are Putting an End to Child's Play." *The New York Times* (April 7, 1998).

Koehler, Aubry Nelson. "Time Flies when You're Having Fun!" seventh grade science report. Greenfield, MA: Greenfield Center School, 1998.

Konner, Melvin. *Childhood: A Multicultural View*. Boston, MA: Little, Brown and Co., 1991.

Kriete, Roxann. *The Morning Meeting Book*. Greenfield, MA: Northeast Foundation for Children, 1999.

Levin, James and John Shanken-Kaye. *The Self-Control Classroom: Understanding and Managing the Disruptive Behavior of all Students Including Students with ADHD*. Dubuque, IA: Kendall/Hunt Publishing Company, 1996.

Lewis, Catherine C. *Educating Hearts and Minds*. Cambridge, UK: Cambridge University Press, 1995.

Lickona, Thomas. *Educating for Character: How Our Schools Can Teach Respect and Responsibility*. NY: Bantam Books, 1991.

Lightman, Alan. *Einstein's Dreams*. NY: Warner Books, 1993.

Link, Mark. *Breakaway: Twenty-eight Steps to a More Reflective Life*. Allen, TX: Argus, 1980.

Lord, Jay. "Evidence of improved social skills and academics as a result of the implementation of *The Responsive Classroom* in elementary schools." Greenfield, MA: Northeast Foundation for Children, 1999.

Lowry, Lois. *The Giver*. Boston, MA: Houghton Mifflin Company, 1993.

Mangaliso, Mazamo. "Toward an Affirmation of African Philosophical Thought in Management Discourse." *Entrepreneurship, Innovation and Change*. Vol. 4, No. 3, 1995.

Mehan, Hugh, ed. *Constructing School Success: The Consequences of Untracking Low-Achieving Students*. Cambridge, MA: Cambridge University Press, 1996.

Merton, Thomas. *Conjectures of A Guilty Bystander*. Garden City, NY: Doubleday, 1966.

Mitchell, Lucy Sprague. *Young Geographer*. NY: Bank Street College of Education, 1991.

Montangero, Jacques. *Understanding Changes in Time*. Bristol, PA: Taylor and Francis, 1996.

Montessori, Maria. *Dr. Montessori's Own Handbook*. NY: Schocken Press edition, 1965.

Mosteller, Frederick, Richard Light, Jason Sachs. "Sustained Inquiry in Education: Lessons from Skill Grouping and Class Size." *Harvard Educational Review*. Vol. 66, No. 4, Winter 1996.

National Education Commission on Time and Learning. *Prisoners of Time*. Washington, DC: April 1994.

National Education Commission on Time and Learning. *Prisoners of Time Research: What we know and what we need to know*. Washington, DC: September 1994.

National Research Council. *Preventing Reading Difficulties in Young Children*, ed. Catherine E. Snow, M. Susan Burns, Peg Griffin. Washington, DC: National Academy Press, 1998.

Ohanian, Susan. *Standards, Plain English, and the Ugly Duckling*. Bloomington, IN: Phi Delta Kappa Educational Foundation, 1998.

Palmer, Parker J. *The Courage to Teach: Exploring the Inner Landscape of a Teacher's Life*. San Francisco, CA: Jossey-Bass Publishers, 1998.

Palmer, Parker J. Opening remarks. *Education as Transformation.* Education as Transformation National Conference. Wellesley College. September 27, 1998.

Pellegrini, Anthony D. and David F. Bjorkland. "The Role of Recess in Children's Cognitive Performance." *Educational Psychologist,* 32, 1997.

Phi Delta Kappan. "The Impact of School Reform for the Middle Years." *Kappan,* March 1997.

Piaget, Jean. *The Child's Conception of Time.* NY: Basic Books, 1927.

Pipher, Mary. *The Shelter of Each Other.* NY: G.P. Putnam's Sons, 1996.

Robinson, Glen E. and James H. Wittebols. *Class Size Research: A Related Cluster Analysis for Decision Making.* Arlington, VA: Educational Research Service, Inc., 1986.

Rogoff, Barbara. *Apprenticeship in Thinking.* NY: Oxford University Press, 1990.

Saphier, Jon. *How to Make Supervision and Evaluation Really Work: Supervision and Evaluation in the Context of Strengthening School Culture.* Carlisle, MA: Research for Better Teaching, Inc., 1993.

Selner, Robert D., et. al. "The Impact of School Reform for the Middle Years." *Phi Delta Kappan.* March, 1997.

Smith, Barbara Herrnstein. "Cult-Lit: Hirsch, Literacy, and 'The National Culture.'" *Opening the American Mind: Race, Ethnicity and Gender in Higher Education,* ed. Geoffrey M. Sill, Miriam T. Chaplin, Jean Ritzke and David Wilson. Newark, DE: University of Delaware Press, 1993.

Smith, Frank. *The Book of Learning and Forgetting.* NY: Teachers College Press, 1998.

Snow, Catherine E., Susan M. Burns, Peg Griffin, ed. *Preventing Reading Difficulties in Young Children.* Washington, DC: National Academy Press, 1998.

Stevenson, Chris and John Arnold. *Teacher Teaming Handbook: A Middle Level Planning Guide.* Fort Worth, TX: Harcourt Brace College Publishers, 1998.

Stevenson, Chris. *Teaching Ten- to Fourteen-Year-Olds.* White Plains, NY: Longman, 1998.

Strachota, Bob. *On Their Side: Helping Children Take Charge of Their Learning.* Greenfield, MA: Northeast Foundation for Children, 1996.

TIMSS U.S. National Research Center, Report No. 8. East Lansing, MI: Michigan State University, April 1998.

Tappan, Mark B. "Sociocultural Psychology and Caring Pedagogy: Exploring Vygotsky's 'Hidden Curriculum.'" *Educational Psychologist,* 33(1), 1998.

Thomas, Dylan. *The Collected Poems of Dylan Thomas.* NY: New Directions Books, 1957.

Thomas, Teresa. "Carnegie Mellon Study Reveals Negative Potential of Heavy Internet Use on Emotional Well Being." Press Release. Carnegie Mellon University, 30 Aug. 1998. Full study in *American Psychologist,* a publication of American Psychologist Association.

Tomlinson, Carol Ann. *How to Differentiate Instruction in Mixed-Ability Classrooms.* Alexandria, VA: Association for Supervision and Curriculum Development, 1995.

U.S. Department of Education. *Trying to Beat the Clock: Uses of Teacher Professional Time in Three Countries.* Washington, DC, 1998.

Vobejda, Barbara. "Study finds children reducing time spent at TV, eating." *Washington Post,* Dec. 2, 1998.

Vygotsky, Lev S. *Mind in Society: The Development of Higher Psychological Processes,* ed. Michael Cole, Vera John-Steiner, Sylvia Scribner, Ellen Souberman. Cambridge, MA: Harvard University Press, 1978.

Wheelock, Anne. *Alternatives to Tracking and Ability Grouping.* Arlington, VA: American Association of School Administrators, 1994.

Wood, Chip. *Yardsticks, Children in the Classroom, Ages 4–14.* Greenfield, MA: Northeast Foundation for Children, 1997.

Word, E., et. al. Student/Teacher Achievement Ratio (STAR), Tennessee's K–3 class size study: Final summary report, 1985–1990. Nashville, TN: Tennessee State Department of Education, 1990 and The State of Tennessee's Student/Teacher Achievement Ratio (STAR) project: technical report, 1985–1990. Nashville, TN: Tennessee State Department of Education, 1994.

Acknowledgments

MANY PEOPLE GAVE TIME AND TALENT to the creation of this book. They did so generously and provided me constant encouragement over a two-year period.

The solo time I needed to create the original manuscript was provided through the thoughtful planning, care, and vision of Roxann Kriete, publishing director of Northeast Foundation for Children, whose persistence and skillful shepherding of every stage of the book was an act of artistry. Roxann was both a friend to and a critical reader of the text and provided a keen editorial eye at various points along the way.

My primary editor, Allen Woods, cared for what Maria Montessori called "the organization of the work" with a constructivist approach that would have made Dr. Montessori proud. He rebuilt the structure of the book and helped me work diligently on chapter after chapter to fill in the holes, provide more clarity, pare the unnecessary and say what I meant. He is a master craftsman whose work strengthened every aspect of the book.

Gretchen Bukowick was responsible for an enormous amount of research in the early stages of the manuscript. Her enthusiasm and clear thinking greatly aided my initial writing. Laurie Euvrard painstakingly provided copy editing and source checking in the final stages.

Several diligent readers of draft manuscripts provided ideas and insights that sharpened my thinking and helped shape my words. Very special thanks to Linda Crawford, June Kuzmeskus, Jennifer Jacobson, Parker Palmer and Celeste McPartland. Thanks also to Ruth Charney, Richard DeGrandpre, Jennifer Fichtel, Kathy Brady, Melissa Correa-Connolly, and Reenie Wood who also provided specific key ideas.

Thanks to the students and teachers at all of the schools I visited that created the composite pictures of Longfellow and Briarwood, especially, of course, Mrs. Chambers, Mark and Phoebe and their families.

Without the daily support and commitment of many people at Northeast Foundation for Children, I would never have found the time I needed to write this book. Thanks to Penny Ricketts and Tracy Wilkinson of the Consulting Teachers Division, Mary Beth Forton and Jean Truckey of the Publishing Division, as well as Beth Watrous and all the teachers and staff of Greenfield Center School. My colleagues "on the road" with *The Responsive Classroom*—Nancy Richard, Melissa Correa-Connolly, Pam Porter, Susan Roser, Carol Davis and Eileen Mariani kept making it clear to me, through their stories from the schools, how important this book was to write. Marlynn Clayton, my teaching companion through nearly thirty years of professional collaboration in classrooms and schools, helped shoulder the load of my work with NEFC while I wrote. I also especially want to thank my friend and colleague, Jay Lord, for his wisdom, kindness and attention to this project during an extraordinarily difficult period in his life.

Finally, thanks for the fun of family egging me on, asking me how the book was going, giving me the love I needed to keep going. Thanks Reenie, Jon, Heather, Joel, Claudia, Woody, Emily, Whitney, Ricky, Jean, and Mom.

Index

About the Author

CHIP WOOD is a teacher and teacher educator with 30 years of experience in K–8 education. He is a co-founder and served as the first director of the Northeast Foundation for Children and Greenfield Center School, Greenfield, MA. Chip taught in elementary classrooms in both public schools and in the Foundation's laboratory school for a total of 19 years. He was teaching principal of a Massachusetts public school for nine of those years. He has also taught child development and education courses at the high school and college level and is on the adjunct faculty at Fitchburg State College.

Currently, the primary focus of Chip's work is teacher education. He spends the majority of his time speaking and providing classroom consultation and program design for public school systems as a teacher of *The Responsive Classroom®* approach, which he co-created. He is also a facilitator for *The Courage to Teach Program* based on the work of Parker Palmer.

In addition to *Time to Teach, Time to Learn,* Chip is author of *Yardsticks: Children in the Classroom Ages 4–14* (1997), a book for teachers and parents, and co-author of *A Notebook for Teachers: Making Changes in the Elementary Curriculum,* (1985). He contributes regularly to educational books and magazines. He is a speaker at local, state, and national conferences on curriculum, character education, developmental education and social and emotional learning.

Chip received a B.A. degree from Rockford College and a M.S.W. degree with a specialization in community organization from Howard University, where he was awarded a Carnegie Fellowship. He has done doctoral level work at the University of Massachusetts and extensive training in child development with the Gesell Institute of Human Development. He lives in Greenfield, MA.

Responsive Classroom®

Northeast Foundation for Children (NEFC) is a private, non-profit educational foundation working to improve elementary schools by helping educators integrate the teaching of social and academic skills.

In addition to its publications, NEFC shares the *Responsive Classroom®* approach with educators through workshops and long-term collaborations. To find out more, contact us at

Northeast Foundation for Children
85 Avenue A, Suite 204
PO Box 718
Turners Falls, MA 01376-0718
Phone: 800-360-6332 Fax: 877-206-3952
www.responsiveclassroom.org